D0984847

Henry Hotze, Confederate Propagandist

Henry Hotze, Confederate Propagandist

Selected Writings on Revolution, Recognition, and Race

LONNIE A. BURNETT

THE UNIVERSITY OF ALABAMA PRESS

Tuscaloosa

Library of Congress Cataloging-in-Publication Data

Hotze, Henry, 1833–1887.
[Selections. 2008]
Henry Hotze, Confederate propagandist : selected writings on revolution, recognition,
and race / [edited by] Lonnie A. Burnett.
p.   cm.
Includes bibliographical references and index.
ISBN 978-0-8173-1620-4 (cloth : alk. paper) — ISBN 978-0-8173-8111-0 (electronic)
1. Confederate States of America—Politics and government. 2. Propaganda, Confed-
erate. 3. Secession—Southern States. 4. Southern States—Race relations—History—
19th century. 5. Gobineau, Arthur, comte de, 1816–1882—Political and social views.
6. Racism—Philosophy. 7. Hotze, Henry, 1833–1887. 8. Journalists—Southern
States—Biography. 9. Soldiers—Alabama—Biography. 10. United States—History—
Civil War, 1861–1865—Personal narratives, Confederate. I. Burnett, Lonnie A.
(Lonnie Alexander), 1958– II. Title.
E487.H83 2008
973.7′82—dc22

2007046799

Contents

Preface

Henry Hotze began his translation of Gobineau's *Essai* by reminding us that "A good book seldom requires, and a bad one never deserves, a long preface." While certainly endorsing this sage advice, a few points regarding the purpose, sources, and style of this present work must be offered. Over the years, Hotze has undergone several investigations. The earliest accounts came from his contemporaries. Paul Pecquet Du Bellet, in his *Diplomacy of the Confederate Cabinet of Richmond and Its Agents Abroad*, as well as Edwin De Leon, in his *Secret History of Confederacy Diplomacy Abroad*, both briefly discussed Hotze's work.[1] Additionally, with the release of the *Official Records* of the Civil War, as well as memoirs produced by many of the key players on the Confederate diplomatic stage, Hotze's career received added scrutiny. In many of the early secondary diplomatic studies, such as those done by Samuel F. Bemis, James M. Callahan, and Frank L. Owsley, Hotze received at least passing mention. In the second half of the twentieth century, Hotze's personal writing's began to receive more attention. In 1952, Richard Barksdale Harwell gave us an edited version of Hotze's "Three Month's in the Confederate Army." William S. Hoole would later edit a collection of letters Hotze contributed, under the name CADET, to the *Mobile Register*. Perhaps the most complete treatment of Hotze came in Charles P. Cullop's *Confederate Propaganda in Europe, 1861–1865* (1969). Charles L. Dufour included a chapter on Hotze in *Nine Men in Gray* (1993). Over the years, several journal articles have appeared, again primarily treating Hotze as a peripheral topic. Stephen B. Oates did a feature on Hotze entitled "Henry Hotze: Confederate Agent Abroad" for *Historian* in 1965, and, most recently (2006), Robert E. Bonner wrote "Slavery, Confederate Diplomacy, and the Racialist Mission of Henry Hotze" for *Civil War History*.

What becomes clear when reading the above-mentioned works is that, in nearly every case, the authors tend to compartmentalize their subject. Hotze is seen as the likable aristocratic soldier (as in Harwell and Hoole), the clever, tireless editor/diplomat (as in Cullop), or as a dangerous racial propagandist (as in Bonner). What I hope to accomplish in this highly selective collection of Hotze's writings is to show the common thread that bound his brief public career. I was particularly impressed with Robert E. Bonner's scholarly discussion of the transformation of Hotze's guiding philosophy from one being guided by slavery to one guided by race. My biographical essay and supporting documents will show how this transformation shaped every part of his career, including his military service. In so doing, we can place Hotze in the context of overall nineteenth-century Southern thought and, more importantly, the place of Southern thought in the international context. The transformation of Hotze can thus be seen as a picture of the overall change seen in the South as state-sponsored slavery gave way to state-sponsored racism.

A word about my primary source material is also in order. I am indebted to the staff of the British Library in London for helping me acquire complete microfilm runs of the *Index*. The transcriptions for "Three Months in the Confederate Army" come from these reels. The CADET letters were reproduced from copies of the *Mobile Register* at the Mobile Public Library in Mobile, Alabama. The MODERATOR letters are transcribed from microfilmed copies of the *Morning Post* also acquired from the British Library. The best source of Hotze's writing is in his own *Index*. However, since Hotze employed many writers to contribute unsigned pieces to his journal, I have used material only when I could independently verify Hotze himself as the writer. In addition to the *Index,* the material in Part 2 comes from the Henry Hotze Papers in the Library of Congress, Manuscript Division, Washington, D.C. The racial "leaders" of Part 3 all come from the *Index*. The excerpt from the "Analytical Introduction and Copious Historical Notes" as well as "The position and treatment of women" were transcribed from the 1856 edition of *Moral and Intellectual Diversity of Races*. The "Letters to Gobineau" were copied from the 1910 edition of Ludwig Schemann's *Gobineau's Rassenwerk*. In nearly every case I have let the original language and spelling stand and tried to avoid the tiresome use of [*sic*].

No work of this sort can be adequately presented to the public without a humble acknowledgment of debts. I have already mentioned the excellent service of the British Library. To this I must add my sincere appreciation to the always courteous and professional people at the Library of Congress and the National Archives in Washington, D.C. I also received expert advice and help at the New York City Public Library Manuscript Division and at The Woodruff Library, Manuscript Division, at Emory University in Atlanta, Georgia. In my own state, I never cease to be impressed with the level of commitment shown by the staffs at the Hoole Special Collection Library at the University of Alabama, the Alabama Department of Archives and History, the University of South Alabama Archives, the Historic Mobile Preservation Society, the Mobile Public Library Local History Division, the Delaney Historical Reference Collection at the University of Mobile, the Museum of Mobile, the Mobile Municipal Archives, the Mobile Medical Museum, and the Mobile Probate Court. The good people at The University of Alabama Press have, as always, been extremely helpful. I especially appreciate the thoughtful comments and suggestions offered by the press-assigned anonymous readers. Any shortcomings in this work are mine alone.

Henry Hotze,
Confederate Propagandist

Henry Hotze, ca. 1861. (Courtesy of The Museum of Mobile)

INTRODUCTION
Henry Hotze,
Confederate Propagandist

Lonnie A. Burnett

In late summer of 1855, a youthful Henry Hotze was en route to Philadelphia to hand deliver his completed manuscript of an English translation of Count Arthur de Gobineau's *Essai sur L'inégalité des Races Humaines.* Hotze carried with him a letter of introduction from his friend and mentor, Dr. Josiah C. Nott. In this correspondence, Nott referred to Hotze as "the greatest intellectual prodigy you ever met." Nott, himself of no small reputation among the scientific world, continued to brag on the not-yet naturalized citizen, noting that he "though but twenty-one knows everything."[1] In these brief remarks, Dr. Nott highlighted two unique features of Hotze's public career—his impressive intellectual prowess and his youth. Hotze would live only fifty-three years. Forty of these years (the first and last twenty) are shrouded in mystery. However, for one eventful decade, from 1855 to 1865, the "literary soldier of fortune" compiled a notable record of service to his adopted homeland and left a wealth of written material for us to ponder. During this ten-year period, Hotze translated and edited a major work on scientific racism, served in various Mobile, Alabama, municipal positions, was appointed secretary to a foreign diplomatic legation, worked as an associate editor for a major Southern newspaper, spent a brief time in the Confederate army, was named to an important Confederate diplomatic post, and edited a London-based newspaper. A sometimes overlooked figure from the American Civil War, Hotze was perhaps the most effective propaganda agent of the Confederacy.[2]

Henry Hotze was born in Zurich, Switzerland, on September 2, 1834.[3] Almost nothing is known about his childhood. His father, Rudolph Hotze, was a captain in the French Royal Service; his mother was Sophie Esslinger. Hotze apparently received a very strong Jesuit education. From his youth, he was absorbed in the study of science, ethnology, and particularly, history. Of the latter subject, he would later note, "History has been my mistress from the earliest period of my self-thinking existence and in my acceptation of the term, its study comprises all that is worth knowing." Hotze combined his love for history and his interest in the emerging field of anthropology into a personal quest to examine the origins of man and, more important, the origins of what he clearly believed to be the diversity of the races. It is somewhat odd that Hotze concerned himself with such matters as, at this time, racial theory was primarily the domain of naturalists and physicians. Around 1850, the Swiss teenager came to the United States where he ended up in Mobile, Alabama. It was in this Southern city that on June 27, 1856, he became a naturalized U.S. citizen.[4]

There was nothing in Hotze's physical countenance to set him apart from his peers. He was slight of statue, standing just over five feet, eight inches, and extremely nearsighted. The only known photograph of Hotze shows a baby-faced young man with wavy hair and a pale complexion. Nevertheless, he possessed several qualities that would eventually propel him into important positions both at home and abroad. As has already been mentioned, Hotze had an impressive mind with a remarkable penchant for reading and analyzing difficult material. His only complaint about his newfound Southern home was the "total absence of public libraries and the extreme rarity and scantiness of private." John Forsyth, the longtime editor of the *Mobile Register*, once remarked that "Mr. Hotze, though only a young man, is possessed of rare attainments in scholarship and a talent for steady labor and application which are bound to make their mark for him if his life is spared." A second trait, which would greatly enhance his career, was his uncanny ability to both meet and impress important people. Hotze apparently possessed a cosmopolitan charm and an air of sophistication (or what James M. McPherson described as a "suavity of manner and a style of witty understatement") that caught the attention of many of the elite members of society. By the time he was twenty-five, Hotze had cultivated lasting social contacts and, in many cases, solid friendships with men such as Nott, Forsyth, William Lowndes Yancey, Leroy Pope Walker, Judah P. Benjamin, Colin John McRae, and Jones M. Withers. These men, a mixture of social, political, and eventually military leaders, would be responsible for elevating him to various positions of responsibility.[5] The final "advantage" that helped Hotze along the road to notoriety involved his racial views. Hotze came to Mobile firmly convinced that race was the determining factor in the moral and intellectual potential of an individual—views which only became more entrenched as he mingled in Mobile's elite political and social circles. As one who could gracefully articulate such "racialism," Hotze was much in demand among the crowd that became his mentors and associates. It was through one of those mentors that Hotze embarked on the first step of his public journey.

Josiah Clark Nott was a well-known Mobile physician, scientist, writer, professor, and racial theorist. Educated in New York, Philadelphia, and Paris, Nott had dabbled in racial theory since at least 1843. As the pace of science and scientific discoveries increased—resulting in the amassing of increasing amounts of knowledge—Nott, like many of his fellow intellectuals, became obsessed with classifications. In Nott's case, the classifications centered on the division of mankind into distinct races springing from separate creations. In 1855, Nott collaborated with George R. Gliddon on a leading American text of human racial differences entitled *Types of Mankind.* A year earlier, Nott had become intrigued with the work of the French diplomat and writer Gobineau. In his famous *Essai,* Gobineau argued that mankind was divided into three races—white, yellow, and black. In Gobineau's opinion, these races were innately unequal and racial mixing had corrupted the pure form of civilization. Although Nott disagreed with parts of Gobineau's work— notably on the idea of single versus multiple creations (with Nott taking the latter view)—he found enough with which he did agree to warrant an English translation. Nott was particularly impressed with the way Gobineau had presented race as a theory of historical development. His emphasis on social evolution as opposed to materialist biology was used to demonstrate that race was the key factor in understanding the present and future as well. To undertake the translation project, Nott turned to his young protégé Henry Hotze. In the late fall of 1854, he contacted Hotze on a plantation near Montgomery where the young man had taken a position as a private tutor. It is not clear if Hotze was already familiar with Gobineau's work or if his first exposure came from Nott. In any event, he agreed to do the translation. In March 1855, Nott wrote to Gobineau that "I have a friend, a Swiss, Mr. Hotze now at work translating the first book of your work and shall have it published in the course of the year."[6]

Gobineau's *Essai* had a profound and lasting effect on Hotze. The *Essai* seemed to validate his already-held racial beliefs formed even before the young Swiss came to America. A year after completing the project, he wrote a personal letter to Gobineau in which he stated, "I have been several years in pursuit of the ray of light which your work afforded me. I have long been convinced of irradicable differences, mental as well as physical, among races. All that I wanted was to have the specific differences of civilizations clearly brought before my mind." He would later confide to Gobineau, "Your book reached me at a critical stage of my studies ... Here was the light I had sought for so earnestly and perseveringly, which had so often given me a transient gleam and left me more in the dark than ever."[7] Hotze completely immersed himself into his task; however, the version he produced took great liberties with the original. He changed the title to *Moral and Intellectual Diversity of Races* and added a subtitle—*with Particular Reference to Their Respective Influence in the Civil and Political History of Mankind.* What quickly becomes clear when reading his translated version is that Hotze (and Nott, who added his own appendix "containing a summary of the latest scientific facts bearing upon the question of unity or plurality of species") wanted to turn Gobineau's work into a political manifesto. Lest anyone might miss this purpose, Hotze added his own "Analytical Introduction and Copious Historical Notes" that ran over one hundred printed pages.[8]

The young "introducer" was certainly not bashful about expressing his own ideas in the "translation." Hotze set out to clearly define his own positions on several topics. His main concern focused on what he deemed to be the moral and intellectual distinctions of the various races. On this point, he was, for the most part, in agreement with Gobineau. Hotze pointed out that "Christ himself has recognized the diversity of intellectual gifts in his parable of the talents from which we borrow the very term to designate these gifts." He also concurred with the original author in his disdain for the concept of the "perfectibility" of man. Although not as pessimistic as Gobineau over man's ultimate destiny, Hotze scoffed at the "philanthropic" notion that any race could, with the right external forces, equal any other in moral and intellectual development. For Hotze, this was a crucial point because it could be used to refute the claims of the abolitionists that, given equal opportunities, the slave could one day take his rightful place among white society. There was one area of disagreement—however, one into which Hotze refused to be drawn. Nott and Gliddon promoted the idea of multiple creations (original diversity). Gobineau, on the other hand, believed in one creation with some subsequent external event as the explanation of racial inequalities. Gobineau saw the mixing of the races as both regenerative and degenerative, whereas, to Nott, the result could only lead to degeneration. Hotze took a position that obscured the real differnces: "Whether the races are a *distinct species* or *permanent varieties* only of the same, cannot affect the subject under investigation. In whatever manner the diversities among the branches of the human family may have originated, whither they are primordial or were produced by external causes; their permanency is now greatly admitted." Hotze believed that arguments over origin were distracting. The main point was that, regardless of when the differences originated, they had not disappeared in the last two millennia and no external device, no matter how well intentioned, could affect their future demise. The work of Nott and Gliddon, and now Hotze, had obvious proslavery implications. First, if the African was of a different species, then "all men are created equal" did not apply. Secondly, if the environment could not alter the moral and intellectual development of the black race, then slavery was its safest place. Finally, prejudice was elevated to the level of science.[9]

Predictably, Hotze's work received mixed reviews. Southern partisans tended to agree with his conclusions. Forsyth's *Mobile Register* called it a "bold, original, and learned work" and echoed Hotze's racial views by stating, "No change of circumstances can ever make the Negro look, think, or act like a white man." Not everyone was so supportive. Criticisms of the work centered on two main areas. The first was over what many felt was the excessive length of the introduction. Hotze's response, which sounded somewhat condescending, was, "The American mind is essentially averse to speculations, and to gain any large class of readers to the consideration of anything that savors of unpalatable ingredient, you must coax them by making the way as smooth and the ascent as gentle as possible." In his thinking, the "analytical introduction and copious historical notes" was "a sort of chart which should prevent the dullest mind from going astray." The more serious charge came from those who felt Hotze was overly zealous in his subjective editing of the original—conveniently ignoring passages that distracted from his own beliefs. One reviewer complained that "a common spirit of fairness . . . ought to have restrained him [Hotze] from taking so unwarrantable a liberty with Mr. Gobineau. An annotator surely cannot be justified in suppressing any portion of the text of his author, because he may happen to disagree with him in opinion." Gobineau himself felt that Hotze had only used the parts of his work that helped promote his own agenda. He was particularly concerned that Hotze had ignored his comments on "American decay generally and upon slaveholding in particular." Gobineau wrote a letter to a colleague in which he asked, "Do you not wonder at my friends the

Americans who believe that I am encouraging them to bludgeon their Negroes, who praise me to the skies for that, but who are unwilling to translate the part of the work which concerns them?"[10]

Apparently aware of similar sentiment, Hotze felt the need to pen two lengthy personal letters to Count Gobineau. In these communications he set out to explain why he had left out entire chapters of the original and modified still others. First, he claimed, the nature of the intended audience was a significant factor. The new American citizen again revealed a European prejudice when he noted: "Our reading public is a very different one—we are a nation of readers, but readers for the most part of limited or—what is worse—of superficial education." Hotze cited a chapter Gobineau had written on the history of the various language groups as one example of material that would not appeal to his American readers. A second defense concerned the relative importance of the subject of slavery and why he had devoted much of his introduction to that topic. Hotze correctly (and prophetically) pointed out that slavery, rather than being just a philosophical debate in the United States, was "the sore spot of the nation" and "the rock upon which the vessels of state will wreck one day, perhaps ere very long." Finally, in his American version, he was trying to avoid religious controversy. Although one of the major points of Gobineau's *Essai* was the degeneracy of mankind (caused by racial mixing), Hotze almost completely ignored it. Additionally the original versus subsequent diversity debate was avoided on religious grounds. Hotze informed Gobineau that "the United Protestant Churches, but especially the Presbyterian, are bitterly opposed to the slightest intimation of original diversity. The Calvinistic dogma of hereditary sin is thereby threatened and the authority of the Bible is impugned."[11]

The public reception of *Moral and Intellectual Diversity of Races* disappointed the brash translator/editor. Reviews, such as the one that labeled his work "suggestive, interesting, but nothing further," left Hotze feeling that he had failed to awaken the general populace to what he saw as the obvious and absolute truth of racial diversity. After all of his promotion and explanation, he was forced to concede to Gobineau that "your book has not, whether from faults of mine or other causes, met with a very brilliant reception on this side of the Atlantic. It has not produced the sensation I had rashly expected for it."[12] Although discouraged, Hotze was undeterred. For the next decade, his private and public writings showed that he never departed from his own racial views and the influence of Gobineau.

During the next three years, Hotze was involved in a number of governmental and private ventures. Mobile mayor Jones M. Withers appointed him to serve as a delegate to a Southern "Commercial" Convention. The meeting, which convened in Montgomery in May 1858, was attended by over five hundred representatives—hailing from nine southern states. While there, the young Mobilian listened to speeches given by firebrand partisans such as William L. Yancey and Edmund Ruffin. One of the main topics of the gathering—one that surely would have captured Hotze's attention—was the question of the potential for physical and religious improvement of the slaves. The assembly also spent much time and floor debate on the issue of the South's labor supply. Yancey made a motion to repeal congressional laws that had prohibited the foreign slave trade. The editors of the *Register* went even farther, stating, "Every Southern State should make a mutual agreement to remand the free Negroes to their former condition of slavery."[13] While there is no record that Hotze participated in any of the debates, there is also no reason to believe that he would disagree with any of the majority viewpoints.

Another opportunity—this time back in his native Europe—soon became available. President James Buchanan appointed General Elisha Y. Fair to serve as United States minister to Belgium. Again Mayor Withers proved to be a valuable contact. Withers secured a job for Hotze as the secretary for the legation. General Fair endorsed Hotze as a man "fitted by education and accomplishments for the position." Hotze would eventually serve as chargé d'affaires. In 1859 the mission ended when Congress refused to appropriate the necessary funds.[14] When he returned to Mobile, Hotze went to work in what would be his major profession for the rest of his life—journalism.

As a general rule, Hotze was not impressed with editors. He had earlier written that "editors, with few exceptions, are men who have no superior capacity or fitness for the task they assume, but nevertheless, pronounce ex-cathedra on all subjects and upon all occasions." One of those "exceptions" to the mold of which Hotze wrote was the man for whom he went to work—John Forsyth of the *Mobile Register*. Forsyth, the son of a former governor, U.S. senator, and secretary of state, was one of the South's most prominent editors. Forsyth had been at the helm of the *Register* on and off since 1837. As a leading figure in the state and national Democratic Party, Forsyth could indeed speak "ex-cathedra" on any number of political topics. Hotze came to the *Register* while Forsyth was in the middle of his personal campaign in favor of Illinois senator Stephen A. Douglas. Hotze worked closely with Forsyth during the controversial presidential election of 1860. During Forsyth's frequent absences, Hotze was left behind to manage the editorial department. Forsyth would later note that he was "largely indebted to his [Hotze's] industriousness and instructed pen for the rapid growth of the *Register* in the public confidence and appreciation."[15]

The alliance between Forsyth, Hotze, and the Northern Democracy was not as unusual as it might at first glance appear. Stephen A. Douglas was a champion of the Negrophobia of the Northern Democratic Party. The antebellum party practiced what some historians refer to as a "herrenvolk democracy"—democracy and equality for a master race or dominant ethnic group. For example, when northern Democrats opposed slavery expansion into the territories, they were simply trying to ensure a free white west. The white supremacy ideals of Forsyth and Hotze fit nicely into this philosophy.[16]

At least one Mobile editor was not as impressed with Hotze's work. The rival *Mobile Tribune* complained that Hotze was "nothing but a foreigner" and therefore had no business in American politics. It should be noted that Mobile had been a stronghold for the Know-Nothing and nativist movement, so non-Southerners such as Hotze tended to arouse resentment and suspicion. Hotze responded with a sarcastic rejoinder in which he offered an "apology." In his own defense, Hotze noted that his "offence" of foreign birth was remedied "as early as practicable after he was born, by coming to the South." He also pointed out that his native land "has a system of confederated government similar, if not identical, to that of the United States, and, if there be any mystic influences in such things, States Rights and Federal powers were discussed over his cradle as much as over that of the *Tribune*'s editor." Finally, Hotze observed with pride that he "felt it no disability to have been born of a race that never knew king nor feudal ruler, in the oldest republic in the world, the asylum of the fugitives of all creeds and all ranks on the Eastern Continent."[17]

After the election of Lincoln, the subsequent secession of the Southern states, and the formation of the Confederacy, Hotze began the more public phase of his career. As an appointed member of the Mobile Board of Harbor Commissioners, he became the spokesman for a group of citizens seeking the advice of the Confederate authorities over how to handle a potential military situation. Hotze sent a telegram to the new Confederate secretary of war Leroy Pope Walker regarding a scheme to capture the Union transport *Illinois,* currently docked at the Mobile wharf. The group wanted to make sure their action would not "conflict with the policy or plans of the President."

After the exchange of several messages, Walker gave Hotze's group authorization to "intercept and seize all transports carrying supplies and munitions of war for the Government of the United States." This authorization was important because, in the event of their capture, it would prevent them from being treated as pirates. The communication also promised them a share of any captured booty.[18]

With the firing on Fort Sumter, Hotze's life became much more hectic. Confederate president Jefferson Davis issued a call to the various Southern governors for volunteers. In Mobile, Captain Robert Sands, who happened to be in the local telegraph office when the appeal came through, immediately wrote to Governor Andrew B. Moore that "the Mobile Cadets tender their services and are waiting orders."[19] The Cadets, of which Hotze was a member, were organized in 1844. At that time, a number of boys from the "first families of the city . . . for the fun of the thing" had incorporated themselves into a soldier company. Due to their youth, the group had not been called to duty in the Mexican War. For the next few years, the Cadets survived as one of the more lively social clubs in town. After he joined, Hotze described their membership in this way: "Among their young men, almost every family of wealth and standing had its near and dear representative. Most of them had been raised in affluence; a very large proportion was college bred, many had already given promise of distinction at the bar, in literature, or in the higher sphere of commerce." An examination of the official roster of the Cadets shows a group made up of clerks, accountants, merchants, students, lawyers, jewelers, physicians, druggists, cotton brokers, and one journalist (Hotze).[20]

Nevertheless, the "sons of wealth and luxury," under the leadership of Captain Sands, prepared to enlist in the Confederate cause. On April 23, 1861—"A day long to be remembered in the local tradition of the city of Mobile"—the Cadets moved out. The scene was highlighted by "the solemn toll of church bells, the booming of salute guns, cheers after cheers from thousands of lungs, waving of hats and handkerchiefs." At the foot of Government Street, the band of brothers boarded the steamer *St. Nicholas* for the journey upriver to Montgomery and, eventually, to the Virginia battlefields. One of the group, Charles Forsyth (the youngest son of John Forsyth), noted that the men departed with "glad and cheerful feelings, ambitious as all were to be the first to strike for the sacred cause." The *Times* (London) offered a generic description of such mobilizations which could certainly be applied to this occasion: "When the young fashionables or the sober lawyers and merchants volunteer to march off anywhere for the defense of their country, there is a consciousness of doing something fine."[21]

A journalist by profession, Henry Hotze left us two firsthand accounts of his brief time in the service of the Confederate military. He sent a series of letters back to the *Mobile Register* under the name CADET. The CADET letters were written between May 29 and August 27, 1861, and published in the *Register* from June 7 to September 3. One year later, Hotze, by then working for the Confederate State Department in London (see below), published a series called "Three Months in the Confederate Army." This account covered events from the April 23 send-off through the end of June. This series appeared in the *Index* (London) from May 1 to October 23, 1862. Although the two accounts overlap, and some information appears in both, the careful reader recognizes that Hotze had a different purpose for each. The CADET letters dwell more on matters of purely local interest; for example, visitors, acknowledgment of gifts received from home, and how the young men were adapting to camp life. The "Three Months" installments, published for a foreign audience, tended to deal with the larger picture—the gallantry of the Southern soldier in general when compared to his Northern counterpart, the justness of the Southern cause, and the inaccuracy of Northern accounts of the war. In this journal, Hotze goes to great lengths to point out the aristocratic nature of his fellows. This would serve two purposes—it would appeal to the aristocratic leanings of his British readers, and it would dispel the prevailing notion of "the rich man's war and the poor man's fight." Hotze candidly admitted that the purpose of his "Three Months in the Confederate Army" was to "assist in bringing his countrymen and their just cause, more favorably before a foreign public than they and their cause had been brought through the representations of their enemies."[22]

The Cadets arrived in Montgomery on April 24. There the men, along with nine other companies, were formed into the Third Alabama Regiment with Jones M. Withers as colonel, Tennent Lomax of Montgomery as lieutenant colonel, and Cullen A. Battle of Tuskegee as major. Apparently a little dose of reality began to set in as Hotze noted that "most of us were a little disappointed on arriving here late last night. The *éclat* that had been given to our departure from Mobile caused us to expect some corresponding demonstration in our honor at Montgomery."[23]

The regiment left Montgomery by train en route to Virginia and much-anticipated glory. Their two-week journey took them through Dalton, Georgia; Knoxville, Tennessee; Lynchburg, Virginia; and finally to Norfolk. The only anxious moments on the trip came as they passed through east Tennessee—still a Unionist stronghold. They managed to get through without incident. At one point their cars pulled alongside a train in which rode Tennessee senator Andrew Johnson, who, in response to some unflattering catcalls, tipped his hat. They arrived in Lynchburg on May 1, finding a city that seemed "to have gone wild with joy." A member of the Mobile Rifles reported that "I never hope to see again such a general and heartfelt enthusiasm nor such a wholehearted welcome as we met." It was there on May 3 that the Mobile Cadets took their oath of service and were officially mustered into the Confederate army as Company A, Third Regiment, Alabama Volunteers—"volunteers for twelve months, unless sooner discharged." On May 5, the regiment finally reached Norfolk where it was assigned garrison duty near the old navy yard. The facility had been recently abandoned by the Federals, but it was generally assumed that they would soon return to reclaim the valuable ground.[24]

During his three months on active military duty, Hotze was never involved in any hostile action, and his two accounts are primarily filled with the routine aspects of camp life. Although Hotze does describe the hard work involved in setting up the camp, he, at least during the first few weeks of his tour, presents a description of a very lively social scene. The Third Alabama enjoyed fresh fruit, meat, vegetables, and tobacco courtesy of the local Virginia population. Baskets of champagne and boxes of claret were also plentiful. The men were pleased with the "numerous dinner invitations" offered by the appreciative townspeople. Several officers (including the just-married Charles Forsyth) brought along their wives. These ladies were popular guests at in-house dinner parties complete with servants, chefs, and butlers. Private Hotze proudly noted that his company had turned their tents into well-provisioned living quarters complete with hand-made furniture (crafted from lumber they had purchased in Norfolk), carpeted floors, and separate rooms for dining, reading, and writing. A steady stream of visitors from home, many bearing gifts of luxuries such as Cuban cigars, added to the comfortable atmosphere. One Virginia lady sent a letter to the *Mobile Register* in which she noted: "I have just returned from Camp Alabama. The station seems to retain its popularity as a place for resort for our city people, and it is not to be wondered at considering the courtesy and affability with which they are met by the gallant Alabamians of the 3rd Regiment."[25]

Even the routine drills and duties were, at first, a source of great pride for the regiment. Josiah Nott, while visiting the camp, boasted: "It is acknowledged everywhere that the 3rd Alabama Regiment has no superior in the field; their drills are the admiration of everyone who has seen them, and I have heard them spoken of in the most complimentary terms in every part of the state in which I have been." By the end of May, Hotze himself would pronounce, "Were the word given today to move northward, we would drive ten times our number before us like chaff before the wind, and never stop until Maryland was free and Philadelphia a hostage." During these heady days, Hotze had plenty of time to get some propaganda writing done. One of his favorite subjects was a comparison of the opposing armies. While the Confederacy was made up of "the representation of the best families in the land," the enemy was a band of "foreign mercenaries . . . wretched soldiers . . . the scum of every foreign clime, idle vagabonds unable to obtain their wages of labor in a country where labor is wealth."[26]

When the call to "move northward" was not forthcoming, Hotze and his compatriots grew restless. As professional soldiers throughout history have known, inactivity is a great foe. Hints of disillusionment began to creep into Hotze's journals. By the first week of July, he reported that "no event took place to cripple the stagnant surface of camp routine" and that "all of us shouldered the musket with the firm conviction that we would at once enter upon a campaign crowded with soul stirring events." In one of his CADET letters, he would complain, "Of all things that try human patience, to be condemned for months to be inactively under arms within sight of an enemy and within hearing of his guns, is the worst." Outside observers noticed the spirit of melancholy that was descending over the regiment. Dr. Nott reported that the men "only complained that they are condemned to inaction, when our country has so many wrongs to be avenged." Another correctly summed up the situation by writing, "They take it very hard that they cannot refresh themselves with a fight."[27]

In addition to the normal grumbling of the soldiers, two other results came from this period of inactivity. The first was a temporary breakdown of discipline. Hotze reported incidents of dueling, fights in the camp, and near-riots in the town between soldiers and locals as well as among regiments. Hotze had to admit that "despising the enemy, despairing of winning any glory in meeting him, or of having any serious work to do, disgusted with the dull routine of camp-life, we were gradually losing that stern sense of responsibility, that pride in our position, with which we had entered the ranks." Members of the regiment—including Hotze—began to ignore the rules. A humorous story illustrates this point. One day in Norfolk, a local lady spied a despondent Hotze walking the streets. In a conversation, Hotze lamented the fact that he would not be able to return to town for at least forty days unless he "ran away." Apparently, the temptation was too great and he did just that because the lady saw him pass her window the very next day. She later reported that a "gentleman from our vicinity visited the Alabamians that afternoon and found Monsieur H[otze] in the *guard tent,* not saying *pretty* words either."[28]

A second result of the boredom was that many members of the original Cadets left—either for home or, more likely, for some other duty. Hotze would note in July that his mess of twelve had only three original members left. Far from begrudging these departures, he defended his mates. Many had taken leaves to raise their own companies or to take commissions in other regiments. Others sought transfers to outfits with better prospects of "meeting the foe." After receiving word of the outcome of the First Battle of Bull Run (in which the *Fourth* Alabama Regiment saw action), many were afraid that the war would end before they had a chance to prove their mettle. Hotze, who had by now been appointed as a clerk in the adjutant general's regimental headquarters, also made plans to leave the Third Alabama. He had apparently talked with Colin J. McRae about help in securing an officer's commission.[29] On July 21, McRae wrote a letter to Secretary Walker, in which he mentioned, "I am personally acquainted with Mr. Hotze and know him to be a gentleman of ability and attainments." McRae also pointed out that Hotze was already doing the duty of a lieutenant—yet with the pay of a private. No word came back from this solicitation, so Hotze went home to Mobile on leave. When he returned to Virginia in August, he, "with great reluctance," again wrote to McRae. Hotze had to soon decide if he was going to stay with the regiment or seek some type of service elsewhere. He told McRae, "I have no talent and still less taste for the arts and tricks of professional office seekers. I cannot hunt down men in power and bore them into doing something for me for the purpose of getting rid of me."[30]

For a man with "no talents" for office seeking, Hotze was nonetheless a persistent seeker. He had been told that the army was no longer giving commissions to anyone from civilian life who did not have a proper military background. Hotze pointed out that a young man from a Louisiana regiment had just been commissioned who was "neither a West Pointer nor a graduate of any other military school." He requested that McRae try one more time and, if it still did not work out, "My pride shall be as it has always been to serve in the humblest capacity that a white man can serve it, and I shall endeavor not to feel it too bitterly that the Revolution of 1861 could find no better use for me than that of a common soldier." Walker did send one more letter recommending the "young gentleman of decided ability" as one who "is devoted to the cause of our independence." Appearing annoyed that his request was being ignored, McRae complained to Walker that it was "a pity that a man of his [Hotze's] attainments and patriotism should remain in the ranks as a private when so many inferior young men are being appointed to office."[31]

Hotze never did receive his commission. The Confederate officials had indeed found "a better use than that of a common soldier" for the confident young man. When he returned to Virginia, he was discharged from the army and presented a special assignment by Secretary Walker. Walker wanted Hotze to travel to Europe to communicate with Confederate agents already on the ground in Britain and France. Before Sumter, the Confederate provisional congress had sent William L. Yancey, Ambrose Dudley Mann, and Pierre A. Rost to Europe in pursuit of Confederate interests and recognition. Hotze's job was to try to speed up the purchase of war materials. This was a crucial task, because, according to Walker, the Confederates had "thousands of good and true men prepared for the field in camps of instruction, yet without arms." He was confident they could "bring into the field and maintain there with ease 500,000 men were arms and munitions sufficiently abundant." The department allowed Hotze to select his own method of passage to Europe. This process caused him no end of frustration. Hotze's plan was to enter Canada through Detroit and then make his way across the ocean. He ran into major delays in Indianapolis and Peru, Indiana (the latter described as a "wretched, struggling village"). His train ran off the track near Wabash—costing him another fourteen hours. He finally gave up on his original plan and ended up going through Buffalo. He did not reach Canada until September 14. By that time he was "tired, worried, and all out of patience."[32]

Hotze did use the long delays to record some observations about the Northern public. Everywhere he went, the war was the "exclusive topic." He believed the Northern people were perhaps overconfident of their chances in the unfolding contest. He described this feeling as an "overwhelming self-conceit, or a stolid ignorance as to the extent of the national danger." He was not very impressed with the soldiers he encountered—they "belonged apparently to the lowest walk of life. Where not foreigners, they seemed to be farm hands and helps." He was also stricken with the number of young civilian men he saw on the streets when the local newspapers were flooded with pleas for volunteers.[33] Assuming the role of a spy, Hotze sent back numerical counts of train cars headed east loaded with supplies for the armies.

The newly appointed Confederate agent finally arrived in Great Britain on October 4, 1861. He immediately met with his assigned contacts and fulfilled the routine aspects of his mission. He had not been a full week when he began to observe what he felt was even a bigger problem than the procurement of arms—the Confederacy needed a much stronger diplomatic and propaganda presence. Hotze was shocked at the unchallenged monopoly the Northern press had over the public opinion of the British people. Even at this early stage of the war, the Confederate diplomatic effort was, at best, ineffectual and, at worst, a disaster. Several problems had led to the chaotic situation. First, the South based nearly their entire diplomatic strategy on the principle of "King Cotton." This view held that the Europeans would quickly recognize and support the Confederate cause because of the strong economic interests. However, as one historian noted, "The view that cotton was king completely missed the mark and reflected a Southern appreciation of the commodity rather than its value to the Europeans." Along with this faulty approach, the Confederate leadership had employed inadequate diplomatic agents. Yancey, Mann, and Rost were, in the opinion of many, "inept diplomats and ill-equipped to deal with the problems and frustrations they encountered there." To complicate matters even more, there was a sizable contingent back in the states that felt diplomacy was unnecessary anyway— the Confederates could manage on their own. With an attitude that was not uncommon among Southern leaders, James M. Mason wrote, "Affairs look so promising at home that I am getting almost indifferent to the actions of the European powers." Military victories were needed more than European favor. Recognition would come only after success in the field. The propaganda machine that Hotze observed was likewise troubling. The North had an early advantage in the dissemination of information through the established press to the reading public. Hotze clearly recognized that the Confederacy needed an active propaganda office in Britain as a counterbalance. As a journalist, Hotze knew the power of a good press agency and distribution system. As he traveled back to a divided America, a scheme was hatching in his fertile mind.[34]

When Hotze returned to Richmond, he reported to the new Confederate secretary of war—Judah P. Benjamin. Hotze gave a two-fold report: The Confederacy needed a full-time propaganda agent in Europe and, moreover, he was just the man for such a post. The emergence of Benjamin was a fortunate break for Hotze and his plan. Benjamin, more than most of his colleagues, had long recognized the need for a propaganda organization in Europe. More than most Confederate leaders, Benjamin also knew the critical importance of European intervention. This intervention, which could take several forms, was crucial to any Confederate chance of success. A formal diplomatic recognition would provide instant legitimacy among the international community. A military intervention would provide needed manpower and supplies and be particularly useful in breaking the blockade. Even a European presence in the role as a mediator would give the South additional leverage.[35]

After meeting with Hotze, Benjamin was so impressed that he set up a meeting between the young Mobilian and Secretary of State Robert M. T. Hunter. Likewise intrigued, Hunter approved the plan and, on November 14, 1861, appointed Hotze as a Confederate "Commercial Agent" to London. In his official instructions, Hunter made it quite clear that Hotze's duties would have little to do with "commercial" interests. Hotze was to advise the CSA as to the tone of the English press, gauge the current of public sentiment, send back samples from public journals, convince the British public that the South could maintain its independence, and keep the "tyranny of the Lincoln government constantly before the people." All of this was to be accomplished on a yearly budget of only fifteen hundred dollars, which, according to one historian, was "a rather absurd price to pay for the good will of a whole continent." Even at this bargain price, many in the Confederate leadership (including President Davis) were skeptical of the mission. Critics believed that even this small amount was a waste of money since "King Cotton" was all the diplomacy and propaganda needed.[36]

After another lengthy period of delay, Hotze left Mobile on December 22, 1861. While stuck in the port city he collected coast surveys and harbor charts (which he would later use in Europe to assist blockade runners) and gathered as many Southern political works and newspapers as he could carry with him. Hotze reached Havana on December 31. From there he sailed to St. Thomas and, eventually, to Southampton. He arrived in London on January 29, 1862. For the first month of his new assignment, Hotze pretty much kept out of sight. He was, however, quietly doing what he did best—establishing contacts and making friends with important people. One historian noted that, during this period, Hotze was a "master-hand at dispensing good cigars and choice whiskey at the proper moment, and he became quite a favorite with all those whom he cultivated."[37] Hotze's most difficult task would be to judge the mood of both the general pubic as well as the British administration regarding intervention.

The opinion of the general British population that Hotze encountered appeared to be divided along socioeconomic as well as political lines. The nature and extent of this split has been the subject of a century of vigorous historical debate. The traditional view as expressed by E. D. Adams as well as Donaldson Jordan and Edwin J. Pratt held that the British aristocracy, upper middle class, and political conservatives supported the South while the radicals (proponents of popular democracy), lower middle class, and working classes (offended by slavery) favored the Union. Challenges to this view came from scholars ranging from Owsley, who claimed that slavery was not a crucial issue in diplomacy, to D. P. Crook, who felt that the British were ambivalent toward both sides. The most serious challenge to the traditional school came from Mary Ellison. In *Support for Succession: Lancashire and the American Civil War,* Ellison proposed that Confederate sympathy was more prevalent among all classes than previously believed. For example, the British middle class opposed the North for at least three reasons. First, many felt the war was misguided since secession would benefit both the North and South. Second, secession seemed justifiable according to precedent and the United States Constitution. Finally, given this legal status of secession, the North was pursuing an illegitimate war of conquest. Even the Lancashire mill workers—often cited as unselfish supporters of the Union in spite of personal hardships—cannot be viewed as firmly in the Northern camp. One simply cannot assume that a lack of agitation among the workers was a sign of support for the Lincoln government. According to Ellison, there was a "supreme determination to aid the South with at least moral backing while the North was viewed with a mistrust that deepened with the intensity of Lancashire's distress." More recent studies, including the work of Brian Jenkins, R. J. M. Blackett, and Duncan Campbell have tended to revert back more to the traditional view.[38]

Hotze's own reports seemed to give credence to the traditional view. In a letter to Benjamin, he reported: "The sympathies of the intelligent classes are now intensified into a feeling of sincere admiration to which even the few presses that continue hostile to us can not altogether withhold utterance. If it can not be said that this feeling is generally shared by the lower classes, it is at least certain that they also are swayed by that British instinct which hurrahs for the combatant who deals the hardest blows. There is only one class which as a class continues inimical to us—the Lancashire operatives. With them the unreasoning, it would perhaps be more accurate to say instinctive, aversion to our institutions is as firmly rooted as in any portion of New England, to the population of which they, indeed, bear a striking resemblance. They look upon us, and by a strange confusion of ideas upon slavery, as the author and source of their present miseries, and I am convinced that the astonishing fortitude and patience with which they endure these miseries is mainly due to a consciousness that by any other course they would promote our interests, a feeling which certain supposed emissaries of the Federal Government have worked zealously to confirm."[39]

Hotze also spent his first few weeks in London trying to evaluate British Parliamentary politics. This was certainly no easy endeavor as he was receiving mixed signals. Some reports coming from the European continent pointed out a consensus feeling that "it may be a question of time, but the governments of France and England have agreed on acknowledging the Confederate States of America."[40] He optimistically wrote Hunter that there were only two "men of weight" in the Parliament that were declared foes of the Southern cause—Earl Russell in the House of Lords and John Bright in the Commons. In his analysis, Hotze noted that Russell had "made himself the apologist of the Federal Government," while Bright, an opportunist, led "no party but himself."[41] The South did have a few strong allies—most notably Lord George D. Campbell and William H. Gregory. At one point, Hotze actually wrote a speech for Campbell, attacking the blockade, which Campbell delivered in the House of Lords. Perhaps the largest problem was not outright opposition, but rather unconcern, or, at least a preoccupation with other issues. Hotze thus summed up the current: "Not indeed, that public opinion is positively hostile to us, but it is cold and indifferent, seeing in the great war for a nation's life only a vexatious interruption to its wonted routine of thoughts and pursuits."[42]

An examination of the political realities of the situation points out the dilemma faced by the Palmerston ministry. Presiding over a shaky coalition in his own cabinet—precariously balanced between the liberal Earl of Derby and the conservative Benjamin Disraeli—Prime Minister Lord Palmerston had to weigh several important considerations, not the least of which was whether to follow principle (based on one's view of slavery) or pragmatism based on the flow of events. As noted in a letter written by Henry Brooks Adams to the editor of the *New York Times*, "the first overt act will be the signal for a conflict that will probably destroy the cabinet and bring a tremendous struggle on the parliament and the people." Perhaps the most delicate question was deciding when a section in revolt could be considered to have actually won independence. As pointed out by historian Howard Jones, the bottom line was that at no time did the British government feel that support for the South outweighed the consequences of going to war with the United States.[43]

The first major propaganda coup came on February 22. One of the first contacts Hotze had made was with the editor of the *Morning Post* (London), the official organ of Lord Palmerston. Hotze arranged for an editorial (called a "leader" in Britain) to be inserted in the *Post.* In this writing, he presented the "most impressive evidence of the unanimity of our resistance" and the justification of the Southern right to recognition. This editorial, printed almost verbatim, had, according to Hotze, great effect. Many who read the *Post* were convinced that the words either came from Lord Palmerston himself, or, at the very least, with his endorsement. After this breakthrough, Hotze reported, "The columns of the journals to which I most desired access are open to me; and with this I have acquired the secret of the 'open sesame' of the others I may need." In March, Hotze used this newfound access to contribute a series of four letters to the *Morning Post.* Under the title of "The Question of Recognition of the Confederate States," Hotze (writing under the name of "Moderator") gave a detailed political treatise on the legality, necessity, practicality, and desirability of Southern independence and European recognition. In subsequent weeks, he was contributing pieces to the *Times,* the *Standard,* the *Herald,* and the *Money Market Review.*[44]

Despite the encouragement of this early success, Hotze was uneasy over the general attitude he was encountering in Britain. When it came to the American struggle, apathy, the greatest enemy of the propagandist, appeared to be rampant among the British leadership. Hotze was concerned that the official political parties were content to take neither side. He grasped that most would like to see the United States divided, but not enough to come to the aid of the Confederacy. Hotze had to agree with the assessment of Yancey who, after a meeting with a top British official, described the government policy as "cautious and non-committed." Even the trump card—the cotton supply—was not having the desired effect. The manufacturing sector was actually benefiting from the blockade due to the high prices they were getting for the large surplus of cotton already in the country. Larger companies were happy to see smaller companies go by the wayside. These factors plus the emergence of a substitute supply from India served to "delude a large and influential class and render it blind to its true interest." Lord John

Russell, the British foreign minister, wrote to Lord Richard Lyons, the British minister to the United States, that "there is no longer any excitement here upon the question of America." It should be noted that, even at this early stage, many in the Confederacy recognized this lethargy and felt that to continue to pursue European aid was fruitless and degrading. At the time of Hotze's first European trip, a writer in the *New Orleans Delta* had stated: "Further persistence of the Confederate States of America in the endeavor to obtain the recognition of our nationality is useless." Mary Boykin Chesnut perhaps best summarized the frustration of the South when she commented, "The Lord help us, since England and France wont."[45]

By the end of April, Hotze had made the most important decision of his foreign tenure. He informed his government that he had "after mature deliberations concluded to establish a newspaper wholly devoted to our own interests."[46] Taking his propaganda efforts to a new level, Hotze had three purposes in branching out in this (unauthorized) fashion. First, he would use the organ to reach the British cabinet. He would present the Confederate cause in a nonconfrontational way. Second, the newspaper would create a source of information for the British press concerning all things vital to the South. Since it was common for newspapers to "clip" information from other publications, Hotze's work would be an available resource. Finally, Hotze hoped to recruit important journalists and leader writers into the Confederate camp. The new editor began to secure both financing and talent for his fledging venture. Neither task was simple—at first, Hotze compared himself to "the leader of an orchestra who has himself to play every instrument." With monetary backing from H. O. Brewer of Mobile and Auguste P. Wettner of Savannah, as well as with his own funds, Hotze was confident he could produce (at least for three months) a paper "worthy of the cause, beyond the possibility of failure, even if every copy had to be given away during that time."[47] Again fortune was on Hotze's side. His old friend and supporter, Judah P. Benjamin, had, in March 1862, replaced Hunter as secretary of state.

The first issue of the *Index* appeared on May 1, 1862. Even the chosen title of the publication had a propaganda purpose. The name had two symbolic meanings. In the first place, the newspaper would serve as a compass. In the opening issue, Hotze wrote: "If the *Index* should be fortunate enough to point the way to a more speedy settlement of the unfortunate American war, or if it should serve as a guide to a better understanding of the real character of a greatly calumniated people, we might well congratulate ourselves on the choice of our title." In the second explanation, Hotze claimed that, as far as awareness of the Southern cause was concerned, the "intelligence of Europe" was like a sealed book. The *Index* could "awake the interest of an indifferent reader, and induce him to turn over the pages."[48]

During its three years of publication, Hotze used the *Index* to hammer several themes home to the British government and people. One of the major ideas was the material advantage to be gained by Great Britain in supporting the Confederacy. Hotze pointed out that not only would a divided Union weaken a potential industrial rival, but also that the Confederacy offered a chance at free trade as opposed to one restricted by a system of high tariffs. Another theme involved the illegal and ineffective nature of the Federal blockade. The *Index* sought to appeal to the pride and honor of the British in not succumbing to such an arbitrary system. One of the major goals of Hotze and his editorial staff was to give a balanced account of military activities during the war. To his credit, Hotze was surprisingly candid in his assessment of the military situation, although he did at times try to downplay the significance of Southern defeats. Another constant refrain involved arguments over the nature and legality of secession. Hotze went to great lengths to point out that secession was not only legal, but its purpose was independence—not the prolongation of slavery. Finally, as we shall see, Hotze returned to scientific racialism in an attempt to prove the inequality of the races and that slavery was the natural state of the black race.[49]

In his first year of editing the *Index,* Hotze experienced the ebb and flow of public sentiment. After four months in London, during which time he was "zealously devoted to studying and influencing" public opinion, Hotze lamented that he was "convinced that though it has been swayed to and fro by events of the war, its center of gravity is still the same." At one point Hotze wrote to William Gregory that "things appear to me to look brighter for the Confederate cause on this as well as the other side of the Atlantic." A year later he would, however, complain that "the public mind has settled down into a state of quiescence on American affairs which resembles stagnation. Everybody wishes well to the Confederate cause, but nobody now speaks of recognition; nobody thinks about it; nobody even writes pamphlets about it." At certain times, it appeared that the fickle mainstream of opinion had turned in the favor of the American South. After the Confederate military successes of 1862, the emotional outpouring following the death of Stonewall Jackson, and, most notably, during the debate over the ill-fated Roebuck Motion for recognition, Hotze expressed optimism that British support might at last be forthcoming. The preliminary Emancipation Proclamation also raised Southern expectations. Although many textbooks today point to the Proclamation as the ultimate guarantee of British neutrality, when released, it actually made intervention *more* likely. In October 1862, the *Times* (London) noted that "Mr. Lincoln will, on the first of next January, do his best to excite a servile war in the States which he cannot occupy with his armies." Likewise, the *Saturday Review* labeled the plan as an "audacious and lawless strategy of arbitrary prerogative." Many in Britain felt that since the abolition of slavery had not seemed an important goal of President Lincoln at the start of the war, any such attempt at this late date was merely a desperate military measure.[50]

Confederate optimism was, however, short-lived. A series of British cabinet meetings in October and November 1862 doomed, for all practical purposes, any hope of involvement. By this time Lord Russell (as well as the French emperor Napoleon III) was increasingly leaning toward some form of intervention in American affairs and sought to bring Palmerston along with him. Russell saw in the Emancipation Proclamation a portent of servile insurrection which would disrupt social and economic stability on both sides of the Atlantic. Thus for a combination of humanitarian as well as financial concerns, Russell felt Southern independence was a "fair price to pay for peace." As Russell attempted to nurture the intervention momentum among his fellow cabinet members, a dose of reality in the form of a memo appeared. In this document, the British secretary for war, George Cornewall Lewis, put forth three convincing arguments against any form of formal involvement: (1) the South had not yet achieved independence; (2) intervention in any form almost certainly meant war against the Federal Union; and (3) the British had no sustainable plan for a postwar peace. During the cabinet debate of November 11–12, the sobering assessment of Lewis held sway. Hotze could only complain that "the action of the Government on the American question has thus far depended on persons rather than on parties." The "illogical speech" of Lewis had, in his mind, influenced the cabinet to go against the will of the majority.[51]

Any faint hope of recognition and support ended in July 1863. Before Hotze received word of its disastrous results, he wrote Benjamin that "the news of General Lee's advance has been received with great satisfaction here." Gathering up one last burst of confidence, Hotze noted that "the apathy of the masses of the Northern population under actual invasion of their soil, and the helplessness of the Washington Government, are the objects of contemptuous sneer." After the results of the fighting in Pennsylvania, along with the events on the Mississippi River, became evident, one can see the hopelessness of the situation begin to surface in Hotze's reports. On July 23 he wrote, "The news of the check sustained by our forces at Gettysburg, coupled with the reported fall of Vicksburg, was so unexpected as to spread very general dismay not only among the active sympathizers with our cause, but even more among those who take merely a selfish interest in the great struggle." Benjamin himself realized that recognition was probably a lost cause. He could only bitterly surmise, "How unwise the course of Great Britain has been will become more and more apparent as the war progresses." By the next year, he was referring to European diplomatic efforts in the past tense: "Our judgment is now finally made up that the British cabinet deemed it best for Great Britain that some hundreds of thousands of human beings should be slaughtered on this continent that her people might reap profits and become more powerful."[52]

With the prospect of British intervention exhausted, Hotze began to formulate a plan of action that would involve two new strategies. The first would be an expansion into new territories. In March 1864, he wrote to Benjamin, "I may undertake a task in which the chances of failure greatly exceed those of success. I refer to the attempt of favorably influencing the French press." Hotze, like many Confederates, was convinced that Emperor Napoleon III was willing to commit to the American conflict, but only in concert with Great Britain. Perhaps a swell in French public opinion would push the timid Napoleon to either act alone or force him to exert more pressure on Palmerston's government to come along. Hotze briefly toyed with the idea of starting a French version of the *Index*. Working in harmony with John Slidell, Hotze was successful in making great inroads into the French inner circle of journalism. He lined up an impressive network of writers (many of whom he was already employing for the *Index*) to submit pro-Confederacy material into the major French publications. Despite his great organizational skills and his ability to secure important contacts, the French government did not budge when it came to any kind of formal recognition or support. Although Hotze could claim a "dominant and almost impregnable position in both the French and English Press," he had to admit to Benjamin that "I cannot blind myself to the fact that the immediate object toward which our efforts were directed have failed, and whatever may be our triumphs in the area of public opinion, we no longer expect the political action of the governments of Western Europe to have any direct influence upon the issue or duration of the war."[53]

Although uncharacteristically discouraged, Hotze was not completely ready to give up on the idea of foreign help. He now formulated a scheme to take his mission into Germany. According to Hotze, the Confederacy had "interest to protect in Germany of vastly greater importance than either in England or France," because "it is from Germany that the enemy must next spring recruit another army; it is upon Germany that he relies for the gold to carry on the war and to bolster up a fictitious value of greenbacks and bonds." He appealed to Benjamin to send a special agent with duties similar to his own to operate exclusively in Germany. The strategy in this new field would differ somewhat from what had been attempted in Britain or France. Rather than trying to provoke direct governmental action, the goal would be to attack the material supplies of the enemy. Hotze even went so far as to nominate the agent that should be sent—Auguste P. Wettner—one of the primary financiers of the *Index*. This was actually the first time one of Hotze's ideas received an unfavorable response. Officials in the Confederate state department explained to him that no money was available for such a project and that Hotze should just stick to his original concerns. After this slight rebuff, Hotze conceded that "the German mind is now so much occupied with the Danish War, that we can have but scanty hope of attracting serious attention to our cause."[54]

The second major shift centered on the editorial stances taken by Hotze in the *Index* regarding the issue of the African American. From the earliest issues of the *Index,* Hotze had certainly addressed the issue of slavery and the slave. His comments had tended to center on defending slavery on religious grounds as the best possible fate of the black race. In one of his first leaders on the subject, Hotze had noted that "the institution of slavery was for the South a solemn and Providential trust, for the faithful discharge of which they are individually, and as a nation, accountable before the judgment seat of Heaven." Rather than attacking the South and her institutions, "The true philanthropist should congratulate himself that the people most immediately concerned in it [slavery] hold themselves accountable to God and to their fellowman for the conscientious discharge of solemn duties." To Hotze then, slavery was a paternalistic, benevolent, divinely ordained system in which the slave looked to the white man as his "friend, teacher, and protector."[55]

Two events in the summer of 1863 caused the radical change in the focus of Hotze's writings. The first was the aforementioned military disasters that the Southern armies had experienced. The editor accepted, before many of his countrymen, the fact that slavery was on the verge of collapse. He was now forced to ponder what would be the nature of Southern society if faced by the forced emancipation of the slaves. The second major event was his association with the newly formed Anthropological Society of London (ASL). Hotze returned to his fascination with Gobineau's work and shifted his emphasis from religious to scientific racism. If the "divinely sanctioned" institution was doomed, it could be replaced with a scientifically sanctioned form of white supremacy. Thus his editorial focus moved from slavery to race.[56]

In 1863, the Ethnological Society of London split over the issue of slavery and the debate over single versus multiple creations. The breakaway group, led by Dr. James Hunt, became the Anthropological Society. While the Ethnological Society dealt with science and humanitarian concerns, the splinter group delved more into political issues—specifically, how science could be used to justify slavery and racism. Apparently aware of Hotze's racial views, Hunt contacted him about the new organization, offering the Southerner a seat on his fourteen-member council. To Hotze he communicated: "You should and must take a strong interest in our objects, for in us is your only hope that the Negro's place in nature will ever be scientifically ascertained and fearlessly explained."[57] Hotze eagerly embraced the new organization by accepting the council offer as well as providing editorial and financial support. Hotze devoted space in two issues of the *Index* to reprint and enthusiastically endorse Hunt's presidential address before the ASL. In this virulent diatribe, Hunt sought to prove that "the highest type of the Negro race is at present to be found in the so-called slaves states of America" and "nowhere does the Negro character shine as highly as it does in his childish and fond attachment to his master and his family." In the address, Hunt gave "scientific" evidence to back up his points. At one stage he noted: "It can not be doubted that the brain of the Negro bears a great resemblance to a European woman or child's brain, and this approaches the ape far more than the European, while the Negro approaches still more to the ape." In a published review of the speech, Hotze heartily endorsed these claims. Thus he wrote: "It will be conceded that women are less intellectual than men and that physically, politically, and even socially, they are subordinate to the sex which is physically and intellectually stronger. But are women, therefore, unhappy? Would women be happier if the Yankee notion of the equality of the sexes was carried out? On the contrary, society would suffer from women being taken from the proper sphere of subordination, and women would be less happy." Hotze also agreed that "the Negro's place in nature is in subordination to the white man," but, he added, "let us be glad, that subordination, the result of intellectual inferiority, does not preclude happiness in the world."[58] The implication here was obvious. Slavery was the natural state of the black man. But if outside interference led to the extinction of the slave system, then at least *racial* subordination must remain in its place. In Hunt, the young Hotze had found his second Gobineau.

From 1863 to 1865 the *Index* contained an increasing amount of venomous racial propaganda or what was referred to at that time as "scientific racialism." In one writing, entitled "The Natural History of Man," Hotze echoed what he had stated nearly a decade earlier in his introduction to Gobineau's work: "The most dangerous dogma of modern times, and that which, unconsciously, to the majority of those who accept it, underlies nearly every social, political, and religious heresy which mars our civilization, is the dogma of the equality of man." At least one of his leaders caught the attention of Confederate officials on the other side of the Atlantic. In "Arming the Negroes," Hotze opined about the possibility of enlisting slaves in the Confederate army. He claimed that "what the Negro lacks in that intelligence, which characterizes the white American volunteer, he more than supplies by implicit obedience and insensibility to danger." Such a plan of conscription could actually be used as a precursor to eventual emancipation. The idea drew a swift response from Hotze's old benefactor, Colin J. McRae—by now the Confederacy's chief European financial officer. McRae wrote, "The policy of arming the Negro has not, and in my opinion, will not be adopted by our Government. The Negro can be made of great value in the war but not as soldiers." To drive home his point, McRae explained to Hotze that the CSA was having enough trouble supplying the men they had—"Why therefore talk of putting 400,000 inefficient Negro troops in the field when we cannot properly feed and clothe 300,000 of the best white troops in the world?"[59]

As the war came to a close, Hotze's racialist writings correctly predicted the problems that the freedmen would face during Reconstruction. In his mind, regardless of the fall of institutional slavery, the African American as well as society as a whole must understand that "the relation of the inferior to the dominant race in the Confederate States has not its origin or reason in municipal laws, but in a decree of nature." Hotze clearly saw what he felt to be the need for restrictions on the rights of the freedmen. Just after

Appomattox, in a leader ominously entitled "The Impending Revolution," Hotze noted that "Emancipation settles no questions; it simply opens that which slavery had practically, or at least temporarily solved. How is the Negro to be fed, to be clothed, to be kept from idleness, pauperism, and crime? If he is to enjoy political equality, it will be necessary to discover the average amount of liberty which can consistently, with social order, attach to the common citizenship of enfranchised African Anglo-American freemen." Hotze correctly predicted two of the more tragic outgrowths of Reconstruction—the Black Codes and violence. Of the former, he noted: "No doubt stringent laws and severe penalties will be necessary. The Negro must be taught that it is more painful to break a contract than to perform his allotted task. The punishment for vagabondism must be of such a nature that the Negro will dread it and avoid it." Regarding the latter, he foresaw a violent clash between the races and warned that "the Negro race, numerically as one against two, and weaker in every other respect, will perish in such a war."[60]

From the summer of 1864 until the surrender, Hotze struggled with two major thorns—the first being his mental and physical well-being. The many months of what Edwin DeLeon had once termed the "thankless and terrible labor, as the conduct of the *Index* involves," had indeed taken a toll. After repeatedly seeing his best efforts fail to gain their desired result, Hotze, who normally prided himself on his "buoyant temperament," complained to a friend that "the hill of despondency is as familiar to me as if I had been born in it." Physically, his eyesight was still his most serious ailment. He reported at one point that he had "endured for more than two years the awful certainty of rapidly approaching blindness." The second major concern was the financial plight of the *Index*. Although never designed to be a revenue-producing venture, the paper still had to generate enough money to pay the bills—a need more important during the latter stages of the war when monetary advances from Richmond were, at best, inconsistent. By the spring of 1864 a large part of Hotze's correspondence dealt with financial matters. He was forced to cancel or cut back many of his prized correspondents. To one he wrote, "I am in the conduct of the *Index* under the peculiar obligation of strict economy." To another, the excuse was that the "demands upon my contingent fund are now so numerous and heavy, that at least for a month or two, I shall scarcely be warranted, in prudence, in incurring any new expenses." Complaining to Benjamin that his work was being hampered by the lack of adequate funds, he noted, "I already see the bottom of my purse." Things grew progressively worse in the first few months of 1865. On a single March day, Hotze composed letters to his correspondents in Germany, New York, and Manchester—each informing the recipient that his services could no longer be supported. He could only regrettably explain that he was "adapting my plans to the emergency, and practicing the most strict economy."[61]

With the end of the conflict in April 1865, Hotze made an important decision. He would try to keep the *Index* afloat in a revised form. Actually he had two contingencies. In the first, he would continue the *Index* as a political organ with much the same focus. He was not yet ready to accept the finality of the Confederate defeat. To Joel Cook he explained: "I am of the opinion that when the passion of war has subsided, the practical good sense of the American people will again come into the ascendant, and sternly decide against the party in power the question whether the 'reconstructed' Union should be Africanized or a white man's government. This question may or may not be settled in the North, but it certainly contains the seeds of civil war, and in any event, journalism will have an important play in it." Hotze proposed to publish a special American edition of the *Index* to "vindicate the true history of the struggle and the principles which though overcome by force still survive."[62]

Another, perhaps more practical, idea for saving the paper was to convert it from a political propaganda organ to one of economic information. With this concept in mind, the tireless Hotze wrote to a contact in Alabama requesting "information which at the moment is of exceeding importance to businessmen connected with the cotton and the American trade generally." Specifically, he asked for intelligence on eight areas:

1. The condition of the plantations
2. The extent of the cotton already sown
3. The possibility of getting the Negroes to work and under what system
4. The extent to which the cotton plantations had changed hands during the war
5. Could the damage be repaired during the current year
6. The state of the currency and trade in general
7. Military and civil measures adopted to preserve tranquility
8. Personal news about the principle property owners.

At the same time, Hotze was asking his British contacts for lists of businessmen who might have a use for the information he was gathering in America. If this scheme worked, he could tout the *Index* as a publication "less exclusively Southern than before" and one that would "devote a larger space to commercial and literary material."[63]

Hotze and the *Index* limped along for four months after the war's end. Try as he might, even the South's most effective foreign agent had to admit, "Unfortunately we find our usefulness marred by the general impression that the journal had been nothing more than a Confederate organ." On August 12, 1865, the 172nd and final issue of the *Index* was printed. In his last leader, simply entitled "Our Farewell," Hotze was still somewhat defiant: "It did not, and indeed does not, occur to us that the downfall of the Confederacy deprived us of a field of usefulness. On the contrary, we thought, and still think, that there are many problems in course of solution in America in which such a journal as the *Index* might assist by disseminating information." However, as a practical businessperson, he had to concede that "it is impossible not to see that the public on both sides of the Atlantic regard the *Index* as a kind of protest against the decrees of Providence."[64] Hotze closed his public career with this benediction:

> The South has been conquered and is afflicted, but as long as she preserves the tradition of her glory she cannot be enslaved. The Southern Confederacy has fallen, but her gallant sons have not died in vain. Whatever flag flies over her capitals, the South will be free. Under whatever Government her people live, their influence will be felt. As yet the land is desolate. As yet the women mourn for those who have died for their country. But time will obliterate the ravages of the fierce conflict, and the South, chastened by the will of God, and exalted by her chastening, will yet be happy and prosperous as in bygone days. To nations, as to individuals, tribulation is often the herald of blessings. We are confident it will be so with the South, and therefore it is with a good heart, though with personal pain, we bid our Southern friends farewell.[65]

With the suspension of the *Index,* Hotze quickly faded from public view. Very little can be discovered regarding his final twenty years. Although he apparently kept his U.S. citizenship, Hotze never returned to America. He obviously kept writing in some form as his obituary made mention of the fact that in his later years, he "received various decorations from foreign governments for services as a publicist." In 1868 he married a daughter of Felix Senac, the Confederate paymaster in Europe. His wife, Ruby, was a cousin of Robert Sands, his captain in the Mobile Cadets during his brief army days. Hotze moved several times between London and Paris until, after a long period of illness, he died in Zug, Switzerland, on April 19, 1887.[66]

How then should we evaluate the brief career of Henry Hotze? Historians have tended to compartmentalize Hotze's work into exclusively military, diplomatic, or racial spheres. Richard E. Bonner is correct when he notes that "only by taking the long view can Henry Hotze's Civil War mission be appreciated as something more than a relatively minor, albeit intriguing, aspect of Confederate foreign policy." A proper review must indeed take into account his work as both an editor with a diplomatic purpose, but also as a racial propagandist advocating a social model. To properly understand the correct significance of Henry Hotze and the *Index,* one must realize that the successive phases of his writings are not mutually exclusive; rather the opposite is true—they are intimately linked. His military service, diplomatic work, and racialist activities were all related to the "enlightenment" brought about by Gobineau's *Essai.*[67]

Since the *Index* was, in his own words, his "little kingdom," this must be the starting point and major focus of any assessment. Hotze once wrote to a colleague that "I have for the *Index* the same weakness that a man has for his estate which he has amassed by his own industry and perseverance."[68] Hotze did indeed build his "estate" from literally nothing into a well-respected and fairly effective journalistic venture. However, from its inception, critics of the enterprise could be found. Major complaints fell into several categories— from Edwin DeLeon, who felt money and time could have been better appropriated elsewhere, to Clement C. Clay, who believed the *Index* did not address the correct issues, to even Slidell, who felt that Hotze was simply not tough enough on the British. It was this last complaint that seemed to be the most recurring. Hotze's most outspoken adversary, Paul Pecquet du Bellet, focused almost entirely on this perceived shortcoming.

Du Bellet, a New Orleans lawyer and unofficial Confederate agent who had lived in France during the war, had tried unsuccessfully to get the Confederacy to concentrate more effort on trying to secure French recognition. He would later write a memoir entitled *The Diplomacy of the Confederate Cabinet of Richmond and Its Agents Abroad* wherein he vented his frustrations at the various CSA European operatives. Du Bellet blamed the Confederates in general and Hotze in particular for a variety of diplomatic failures. He especially felt that Hotze's mission to Britain and, moreover, the establishment of the *Index* had been a terrible plan: "Never probably since the beginning of the world was such a political blunder committed by men who assumed to lead a revolution and to control the destinies of a nation." Du Bellet believed that Hotze had been much too cozy with his British hosts. He stated, "The social position of the chief editor of the *Index* in London must have been a very comfortable one thus to fill his heart with the milk of human kindness and to give him the patience to temporize with the enemies of his adopted land." In condemning tones, Du Bellet concluded that the *Index* "was useless, for it could do nothing to England and would in no case compete with the ability and talents of the existing political organs of London."[69]

Throughout the lifespan of the *Index,* Hotze had refused to be drawn into "newspaper controversies." He had determined not to fall into the trap of many editors who, in his mind, were guilty of "mistaking forcible words for forcible ideas." Indeed, one of his main goals in establishing his own newspaper had been to "draw a marked contrast between the *Index* and the popular idea of an American paper." Hotze had, on more than one occasion, rejected material sent for publication on the grounds that it would "weary and prejudice the reading public." Du Bellet printed a personal letter in which Hotze had rejected a piece he had submitted to the *Index.* Hotze had written: "Sincerely speaking, I could not use your correspondence because it was violent in tone and language . . . The English are an unimpressionable people and I understand them well. You set them against you the moment you show them any strong feeling."[70] Although Hotze knew such a position would be "mistaken by many of our countrymen for lukewarmness, timidity, or lack of spirit," he pressed on toward a higher goal. Even though he had only been an editor for less than five years, Hotze had a pretty good idea of what his duties were. To be successful, the editor must possess a certain amount of genius, skill, and art. The genius was to "know what his readers wanted to know and to find it out for them." The skill was in "dressing the information he has to give in the most attractive manner, and to display it in the most accessible way." Finally, his art was to "leave always something in his bill of fare which tempts the appetite of the public, and to display it conspicuously."[71] To depart from his "tone of studied moderation" merely to please critics such as Du Bellet would have been inconsistent with his expressed vision.

The praise for Hotze's diplomatic endeavors far outweighs any complaints. Historians over the years have tended to be kind to Hotze in their evaluation of his work. Burton J. Hendrick described him as one who "possessed a suavity, a subtlety, and silence in method that would have distinguished an experienced diplomat." Charles C. Cullop echoed these comments when he stated that Hotze, "with his admirable intellectual equipment and intense drive . . . could have won a distinguished position in an able and experienced diplomatic corps." In his seminal study of Confederate diplomacy, Frank L. Owsley gave perhaps the best summary of the overall effectiveness of Hotze's mission: "As able as any agent who went abroad during the Civil War. He showed more insight into public opinion and tendencies than did either Mason or Slidell, and his fastidiousness, his deftness, and his lightness of touch in a delicate situation were remarkable. His resourcefulness had a masterly finesse that would have done honor to Cavour or Bismarck. Finally, he was intellectually honest and unafraid to face the facts."[72]

Once when describing what he considered to be the standard for an editor, Hotze appeared to be describing himself: the proper journalist, he wrote, must learn "to be cosmopolitan and yet have a country; to be miscellaneous and yet to have an object; to be tolerant and yet not indifferent; to be moderate and yet to have strong convictions; to be instructive and yet not dull; to be entertaining and yet not frivolous." One is hard pressed to argue with his self-assessment that the "*Index* has obtained a historic position in the great American revolution" or with that of Douglas Southall Freeman, who referred to the *Index* as a "remarkable publication, into which every student of Confederate history should dip."[73]

However, any assessment of Henry Hotze without reference to the impact of the racial philosophy to which he adhered is, at best, incomplete and, at worst, highly selective. As the most cosmopolitan of the Confederate foreign agents, Hotze played an important role in spreading the American version of racialism across the ocean. Bonner pointed out that "Its [racialism's] articulation depended on individuals who were capable of forging cosmopolitan intellectual connections between different societies." Surely Hotze was the most active and effective Confederate in this area. If, as Hotze desired, racism could be given the status of "science," then national borders or cultures made no difference. This "pseudoscientific" idea became the basis for the racist societies that we would later see in Europe, in South Africa, and in the Jim Crow American South.[74]

In Europe, Gobineau's racial theory enjoyed renewed popularity after the explosion of German pan-nationalism resulting from the Franco-Prussian War. The Civil War writings of Hotze obviously gave proponents of racial inequality much ammunition. In 1894, Ludwig Schemann, a member of the board of the Pan-German League, founded the Gobineau Society. This organization was devoted to the advancement of the ideas of racial diversity and inequality. In 1910, Schemann published a book entitled *Gobineau's Rassenwerk*, in which he included two personal letters from Hotze to Gobineau. Hotze's name thus became linked with the German version of racial theory. It should be noted that the Nazis later appointed Schemann to the *Reichinstitute* for modern history and awarded him the Goethe Medal for service to the nation and race. Hotze began his aforementioned "Natural History of Man" by stating: "The most dangerous dogma of modern times . . . is the dogma of the equality of man." It does not take a very active imagination to see the same philosophy expressed in the opening sentence of a 1937 Hitler Youth manual: "The foundation of the National Socialist worldview is the knowledge of human inequality." The "moral and intellectual diversity" of Gobineau, Nott, and Hotze would take the shape of the "white man's burden" in the late nineteenth century, the master race theory of the 1930s and 1940s, and segregation and apartheid in the middle to late twentieth century. A century after the American Civil War, racial ideas promoted by men such as Hotze were still causing violence and death from Durban to Birmingham.[75]

Part One

"A Consciousness of Doing Something Fine"

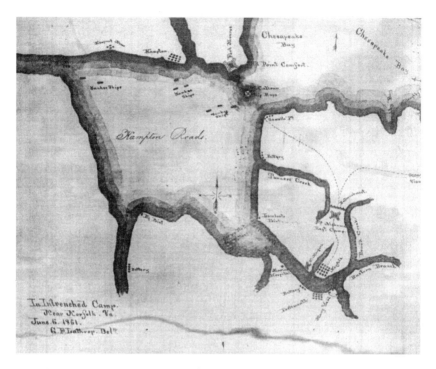

Map of the Norfolk area drawn by a member of the Third Alabama Regiment, 1861.
(Alabama Department of Archives and History)

Three Months in the Confederate Army[1]

OFF TO THE WARS

The twenty-third of April, 1861, is a day long to be remembered in the local traditions of the city of Mobile. About noon the rumor had flashed through the town that the Governor of Alabama had accepted the services of the Mobile Cadets, and of another volunteer company, and had summoned both to repair instantly to the capital of the state, then also the provisional capital of the new-born Confederacy.[2] Four hours are a brief space of time for preparation and leave-taking to men who are suddenly summoned from home and family and business to battle-fields a thousand miles away. Yet at four in the afternoon a vast multitude had already collected before the city arsenal, where the public arms were deposited, and in the capacious hall of which the two companies were then forming. An hour later the doors were thrown open, and forth stepped, with measured tread, Mobile's first contingent to the War of Independence. It was not now a holiday parade, such as had often enlivened the streets of the peaceful city. The showy uniforms in which, in happier times, harmless citizens delighted to play at soldiering, had been left behind, and officers and men were clad in a stout, serviceable gray, specially selected for a rough campaign. There was something, too, in the countenances of the men, their carriage and bearing, that would have indicated to a mere stranger more impressively than the swelling knapsack and the heavy blanket strapped to it, that the youths before him were animated by a stern resolve in the discharge of a patriotic duty.

At the wharf a halt and a "rest" were ordered, and then came the last leave-taking of mothers, sisters, sweethearts, wives; the hand-shakings of friends and companions, the blessings of old men, the final exhortation of father to son, the sobs and tears of agonized women. There was a feeling of relief when the command "Attention" cut short the painful scene. A few minutes later, the two companies had formed again on the upper deck of the steamer, overlooking the agitated sea of human beings that overflowed the wharves and all approaches to them; for the whole population of Mobile had assembled to bid "God speed" to the brave young hearts that day departing, many of them never to return. And now the shrill whistle of the steamer, the splash of revolving wheels, the solemn toll of church bells, the booming of salute guns, cheers after cheers from thousands of lungs, waving of hats and handkerchiefs—and the city of Mobile had lost the *elite* of her youth.

Two hundred young men occupy a small space, numerically, in the population of a large commercial city; but among these young men, almost every family of wealth and social standing had its near and dear representative. Most of them had been raised in affluence; a very large proportion was college bred; many had already given promise of distinction at the bar, in literature, or in the higher spheres of commerce. Now they had become common soldiers—mere unthinking machines—whose places, some said, might as well and better have been taken by men less valuable to the community. But the young men thought otherwise. They felt that in the struggle in which their country was engaged, every odd was arrayed against it. They felt that in a war for a nation's existence it was a privilege to be allowed to bear the first brunt; and that it became them, sons of wealth and luxury, to set an example of self-sacrifice, of cheerful devotion, of patient endurance, of orderly demeanor, and true soldierly discipline, to those less favored by fortune. They did not wait for commissions, so tempting, to youthful vanity and even more mature ambitions; but, with a full sense of the consequences, they stepped into the ranks as "enlisted men" for a term of twelve months.

The Mobile Cadets, being the oldest organized volunteer company in the state, claimed the honor of being the first in having their services accepted for actual duty in the field.[3] When the proclamation of President Lincoln destroyed the faint hopes of peace which had sprung up during the month of his hesitation, the company decided by a vast majority, to place itself upon a war footing, and tender its services in the proper quarter. The small minority, whom circumstances prevented from joining their comrades were honorably excused, their places supplied by a most fastidious system of balloting among a large number of applicants, a simple and serviceable campaign uniform procured, all deficiencies in equipment and accoutrement supplied, daily morning and evening drill instituted; and in less than ten days a troop of young men, originally united for purpose of military amusement, had been transformed into a well-officered, well disciplined company of soldiers. Nor were the Cadets the only company which pursued this course. In Mobile, and in other cities of the Cotton States, as also in the rural districts, companies similarly situated acted in a similar manner, without awaiting each other's example. There was at first some doubt whether the authorities would receive this class of volunteers, and many weighty objections were raised against it, chiefly on the ground that these young men could be more useful to the state in less humble capacities. But the necessity of promptly pouring upon the exposed frontier of Virginia, then but a few days previously acquired to the Confederacy, troops having already at least the elements of effective organization, and a certain proficiency of drill, prevailed over all other reasons; and thus, on the 23rd of April, five days after the secession of Virginia, the Mobile Cadets received their marching orders to the "Old Dominion." The first levies of the South were exclusively among the gentlemen of the South.

A set of hurried notes, written at irregular intervals, mostly with no better desk than a camp-stool, or a knapsack laid on the grass, can scarcely deserve the name of journal. They were intended to reproduce more vividly at some future day the impressions of the hour to the writer's mind, rather than to serve as a record of adventures, of which, indeed, his connection with the company was singularly barren. Battles and sieges and hair-breadth escapes, therefore, the reader will not find in them, nor even the stories of painful marches or harassing retreats, or much if any of the soldier's stern work. Hardships and fatigues there undoubtedly were, but so light compared to those so bravely borne by others more fortunate in the field of action assigned to them, that memory refuses to chronicle them. The most these unpretending notes can promise is a glimpse into the interior of the armies of the young Republic while it was collecting its resources and gathering strength to resist the blow aimed at its vitals. The creation of an army of 400,000 men scattered over a territory of near a million square miles, within a space of less than twelve months, in the face of an enemy overwhelming in numbers, as in the appliances of war, by a Government scarcely formed, and dating but of yesterday, is a spectacle so novel and so replete with interest, that even the feeblest effort to throw light upon it may not go altogether unrewarded.

The writer's sole object, he frankly admits in advance, is to assist in bringing his countrymen, and their just cause, more favorably before a foreign public than they and their cause have been brought through the representations of their enemies. But he will not seek to further this object by falsifying facts or investing them with a fanciful coloring. To impartiality he does not pretend. No man thoroughly and earnestly enlisted in any cause, right or wrong, can honestly do so. Writing in a distant place of safety about companions in arms, who are still undergoing every hardship and privation for their country's sake; it would be difficult not to treat them with that loving-kindness and forbearance which, when he was among them, all imposed upon themselves the duty of practicing toward each other. But if this bias may sometimes bear him to a more favorable judgment than a stranger would have pronounced, at least he can venture to promise that he will say naught he himself does not believe true, nor suppress anything that is necessary to form a correct opinion. For this reason he has thought it better to leave his notes, rough as they are, without material alterations or emendations, and to be sparing of post-dated comments, except where such are absolutely needed for the intelligence of the reader.

EN ROUTE FOR VIRGINIA[4]

On board steamer St. Nicholas, Alabama River, April 25, 1861

The scene before me deserves a record, though my shoulder is strained, and my fore and middle fingers ache with "Carry Arms." Here, on the floor of the vast saloon lie some 300 men, so closely packed that it is actually impossible to tread through or between them. The folding doors of the ladies' saloon (for we have ladies on board, and not a little proud of them we are—the young wives of our second Lieutenant and of our Orderly Sergeant, accompanied by two unmarried sisters of the latter) have been closed, and though it is not nine o'clock yet, every one that does not wish to stand up during the night, has been compelled to occupy his considerably less than "three by six" on the saloon floor. I have been one of three lucky ones to whom the Captain has given a berth in his "state room," and I further enjoy a little corner at the first clerk's desk, whereon to write.

Fun and merriment run riot in the saloon, for "taps" has not beat yet. It is amusing to watch the good temper and real wit with which men defend their heads against some other men's legs, and the sham battles which are waged between inconveniently shortened antipodes. But even more pleasing is the cheerful readiness with which a place is sought and given to some luckless struggler who has neither cabin berth nor floor room. The more the merrier is the motto, and the saloon floor, omnibus-like, is never full, though I expect very shortly they will lie in strata like salt herrings.

Not a quarrel has yet occurred nor even a high word spoken, though there has been so much drinking that the officers threatened to shut up the steamboat bar. Strange enough, there has, however, been no drunkenness, the mental excitement apparently preponderating over the physical.

At various landings we have taken in other companies from the rural districts; stalwart, good-looking fellows, a little rougher in their manners and appearance than our city-bred gentlemen, but lacking in no essential of courtesy and good-breeding. In their green hunting shirts, for the country companies have not yet had time to uniform themselves, they have much the appearance of good-humored savages. But they represent the best families in the land, and are most of them young planters, with a sprinkling of lawyers and doctors, and one or two editors among them. Our fraternization with them would not have been out of place among the scenes of the French Revolution, so exuberantly enthusiastic have been the demonstrations on both sides, though I doubt whether as much of the blood of the grape was shed on those bygone occasions as there was whiskey in these. Well why not? In a day more we shall be under the rigid discipline of common soldiers. Everybody believes that our destination is Western Virginia, and perhaps a bit of Pennsylvania, and that in ten days we shall "have a chance at the Yankees."

We drill six hours a day on the upper deck, and the sun is excruciating. Many of us are "green" in the manual, and each of the older members acts as instructor to an "awkward squad." One or two of the most awkward ones were discovered late last night, long after "taps," rehearsing, in solitary despair, the hard-learned lessons of the day. The thing was too ludicrous and, besides, too well-intentioned to provoke more than a formal reprimand from the officer of the guard.

Yesterday the two Mobile Companies held a meeting with one of the Captains in the chair, and one of the privates as Secretary, to pass complimentary resolutions to the owners and officers of the steamer *St. Nicholas*. The reason was that while the Governor paid only for deck passage and soldiers' rations, we, as well as the other companies, had all received first-class passage and saloon fare. Though 500 men, in rotation of companies, sat down to each meal, the tables from morning to night groaned under the weight of good cheer, and even the stock of fresh milk and butter and of ice, so scanty on crowded river steamers, had never given out. The resolutions were passed, and a collection made, amounting to 263 dollars, for the purpose of purchasing a suitable testimonial to the Captain and first clerk of the liberal steamer.

Tomorrow, our third day from Mobile, we shall be at the capital, there to be formed into a regiment, and then "on to Washington!"

A FAMINE AND A FEAST[5]

Montgomery, Alabama, April 25, 1861

Most of us were a little disappointed on arriving here late last night. The éclat that had been given to our departure from Mobile caused us to expect some corresponding demonstration in our honor at Montgomery. Instead of this we found the city dark and silent, the wharves deserted, and neither quarters nor commissariat stores provided for us at the end of a short but tedious march to the "Fair Ground," about two miles from the city. It was not until after midnight that we were able to wrap ourselves in our blankets, supperless, on the rough plank floor of the Exhibition building. The excitement of the leave-taking from home and friends, and of the gay trip up the river, had now subsided, and the first lesson learned, though a wholesome, was not a pleasant one—that in leaving home we have also left behind the individual and collective importance our youthful vanity had tempted us to ascribe to ourselves. This morning the State Commissary sent us for breakfast twenty pounds of soap, which is suggestive but not nourishing. Hungry stomachs, however, refuse to appreciate the point of the joke, and prefer the barrels of salt pork and ship biscuit which the officers have sent for from the city. Blunders of this sort are no doubt inseparable from a quartermaster's and commissary's department, which are as yet improvised, rather than organized; but though every man of us would be ashamed of complaining, yet human nature cannot be expected to abstain from comments which are not always complimentary to his Excellency the Governor and his military staff. Our officers have determined to take the commissariat into their own hands until we shall enter the service of the Confederacy, whether the Governor allows a commutation for our rations or not.

The pork and biscuit breakfast was not, however, without some features of the picturesque. There was not much room for cookery, and even such as there was had to be performed without apparatus or utensils of any sort. The few that had pans fared no better than those who had only sticks with which to toast their bacon; and every device to make the pork less salt, or the biscuit less hard, ended in signal failure. The bill of fare afforded no other choice than between burnt bacon and raw bacon. But when breakfast was over, no one could fail to perceive the foresight of the commissary, who had sent us so timely and bountiful a supply of soap.

During the day we have been either drilling or putting things to right in our temporary barracks. Our drill-ground is a large enclosure used for the annual cattle show or State Agricultural Fair; and the frame building, devoted to the exhibition of specimens of home industry, serves as barracks. A considerable amount of cleaning up and some carpentering has made the latter comparatively comfortable. Our city youths are not much used to the broom or the besom,[6] nor to the axe and saw; but each one's awkwardness and grotesqueness of appearance affords merriment to all the rest, and, upon the whole, the task is moderately well performed.

This afternoon a huge board appeared at the barrack-door, on which was inscribed the pathetic notice which follows:

LOST.
Late on Thursday night, on leaving the steamer
St. Nicholas, between the wharf and the fair
ground.
My Military Enthusiasm.
The honest finder is earnestly entreated to return
the same to the disconsolate loser, and will have
the consciousness of a good action for his reward.

Montgomery, 27th April

I much fear that we have done great injustice to the beautiful city of Montgomery, and its hospitable inhabitants. Our chill reception is rather fancied than real. For three months past the town has been the theatre of events so grave and stern, that it could not well be expected to go into ecstasies over the arrival of a few volunteer companies, however high the social standing of those composing them. Hereafter, every steamer's whistle will announce the arrival of others quite as deserving as we of pompous demonstrations, if such demonstrations were really in good taste at so critical a moment. Besides, Montgomery is fitting out her own young men, to send them to the Northern frontier; and these young men are full as dear to fathers and mothers, and sisters, and sweethearts, as we are to ours.

In genuine kindly hospitality, the town has not been lacking. Ever since the soap story was bruited, hampers and baskets, filled with the choicest of the larder and the barn-yard, have continued to arrive in uninterrupted succession. The barracks look more like the resting-place of a gay picnic party, and if we had a famine yesterday, we have a surfeit of feasts today. Some of the messes, even, have been favored with baskets of champagne and boxes of claret, and a generous-minded grocer has sent out a whole barrel of whiskey—genuine old Bourbon—a present of which the officers have already shown their high appreciation by giving it a guard of honor.

On the way to town is a little Baptist Church, of which the ladies of the city have taken possession, and there they lie in ambush, sallying forth and capturing the groups of soldiers that loiter town-ward, to offer them the services of their busy needles. Our uniforms, though simple, were made by the best tailors, and as yet not a button has had time to come off. But the fair patriots will not be disappointed, and so each one of us has been presented with a sort of fatigue cap of red flannel, with a jaunty yellow tassel, which the boys now wear under their kepis, in honor of the donors. We have also a sort of Havelock of white linen, not unlike the hood of a Sister of Charity, to protect us against the hot sun, imitated from the pictures of Zouaves in the Algerian war: and when our wags wear red cap, kepis, and hood, all at the same time, the effect is irresistibly comical.

Permits are freely granted today to visit town and avail ourselves of the numerous dinner invitations, which pour in upon us. But attendance at drill hour is pitilessly insisted on, and it is deemed dishonorable to be absent without formal permission. To attend a brilliant dinner party, clad with ostentatious modesty in a private's gray jacket, to be made a hero of by admiring friends, and linger over the wine and the kind farewell wishes of the company, is all pleasant enough. But to hurry out to camp, to have barely time to seize firelock, and step into line before the first sergeant commands "front," then to go through the weary manual, and "double, quick" with the bountiful meal still weighing heavily on the conscience, over a mile or so of uneven ground, is more amusing to the spectator than to the performer. It is high time that this anomalous mixture of incongruous characters should cease, and that we should become soldiers in good earnest, or return home to play the fine gentlemen.

All wonder what detains us here so long, summoned as we were in such hot haste. Two full days have now elapsed, and yet no preparation seems to have been made to form us into a regiment, although companies enough have joined us, and to spare. Some will have it that the Governor wishes to impose upon us a favorite of his as colonel, and waits for companies who are sure to vote according to his wishes. The matter has been a prominent topic for discussion ever since we left Mobile, and I much fear that ill-feeling will spring from it before it is settled. There are few who would not gladly leave the choice of a commander to the President; but we are still in the service of the State, and according to the law of Alabama, must elect all our regimental officers.

A MILITARY ELECTION

Montgomery, Alabama, Sunday, April 28, 1861

Early this morning the order came to hold an election for colonel. The following companies were included in the order, and now form the regiment, which is to be called the "3rd Alabama Volunteers," although we are, in fact, the first regiment formed in the State since the declaration of war by Lincoln's proclamation:[7]

The Mobile Cadets,
The Mobile Rifles,
The Washington Light Infantry,
The Gulf City Guards,
The Montgomery True Blues,
The Metropolitan Rifles,
The Tuskegee Light Infantry,
The Wetumpka Light Guards,
The Beauregard Rifles,
The Southern Rifles.

Instantly on the receipt of the order, the officers of all these companies met in secret consultation to select proper candidates, which the men had pledged themselves in advance to accept. Meanwhile each company was drawn up in line by its Orderly-sergeant, and the result of the officers' consultations awaited in silent and somewhat anxious expectation. After about an hour's delay, the officers assumed their commands. A little shed served as poll, the senior captain acted as judge of election. Each company was then arranged in single file, according to the muster-roll, a slip of paper handed to each man on entering at the poll, to be delivered to the returning officer with his name. As each man took his place again on the other side of the shed he could only surmise who he had voted for. As soon as the last man of the last company had deposited his vote, three hearty cheers announced the unanimous election of Jones M. Withers of Mobile, as colonel of the first and finest regiment Alabama had ever mustered for actual bloody service. The same ceremony was twice more repeated for the election of a lieutenant-colonel and one major, and the organization of the 3rd Alabama Volunteers was complete.[8]

To the uninitiated, this election must appear a passing strange one. To one who had a glimpse behind scenes, it is a capital piece of good management and clever tact. Perhaps a majority of the Mobile Volunteers were, from principles, opposed to the election of field-officers by the men, thinking it bad precedent; copied, with many other ultra-democratic vices from our late Northern allies and now enemies.[9] At the same time, none were willing to leave the selection to the Governor, who, as a civilian, was supposed incompetent for the task, and whose appointments to the small regular army raised by the State a short time previous had aroused some dissatisfaction and derogatory comments. President Davis, to whom all would have cheerfully left the arbitration of the difficult choice, had no power under the laws to act in the matter.

In the ranks of the Mobile companies were men not unacquainted with the tricks of the questionable game of politics, and, thanks to them, an ingeniously devised plan was at once put into successful operation. It was decided that as there were four Mobile companies, two from Montgomery, and four from the country districts, in the regiment, the favorite of Mobile should have the first rank, the favorite of Montgomery the second, and the favorite of the country companies the third. It was further laid down, as a sine qua non, that the colonel should be a man, not only of practical military experience, but a regularly educated officer, who had won his first epaulettes at West Point. The better to harmonize conflicting interests, some of the companies set the example, which the others, in very self-respect, were compelled to follow, of voluntarily resigning without reserve of their vote to their officers. Not a little "log-rolling" and electioneering, and cunning play upon local and individual *amour propre* was necessary to bring about the desired result, without sowing the seeds of future misunderstandings and jealousies in a regiment combining so many local interests.

The most difficult task was to induce the four Mobile companies to unite upon a candidate. The name proposed was that of an officer of acknowledged military ability, the senior graduate from the State of Alabama at the United States' Military Academy at West Point, and who had filled posts of great trust and responsibility in the Mexican war. For several years back he had occupied, and was still occupying, the chair of Chief Magistrate of the city of Mobile, and during his administration the most important and expensive public works had been initiated and energetically prosecuted. Like most men of very decided character, he had arrayed violent personal antipathies against him, and among the 400 Mobilians upon whom he was to be imposed as their first and last and only choice, the number of his personal and political enemies, perhaps, greatly exceeded that of his friends. Yet, strange to say, the honest conviction of his eminent fitness, and probably, also, a little local pride, prevailed over other considerations, which, under different circumstances, would have been conclusive; and it is worth mentioning that the chief electioneering argument urged in his favor, was his reputation as a stern, if not a cruel, disciplinarian, and a natural disposition, which those who only imperfectly know him, call self-willed, and harsh to despotism. Thus it is that the 3rd Alabama Regiment voluntarily and knowingly have this day chosen between King Stork and King Log, and crowned the former.[10] I have a thousand reasons for being gratified at today's election; yet, with a full knowledge of all the springs that were set in motion, and the wires that were pulled, I have not yet recovered from my surprise.

Our own and another company have this moment received orders to leave tomorrow by train for Lynchburg, in Virginia, and as fast as rolling stock can be procured, the others are to follow after.

OUR FIRST ADVENTURE[11]

Dalton, Georgia, April 29, 1861

Delayed here by want of rolling stock, as it is said, to carry off that vast northward flowing tide which gathers volume at every wayside station. Some say we are delayed to await orders from Montgomery, as there are dark rumors afloat that Tennessee has forbidden the passage of Confederate troops through her territory, in the same manner as she has emphatically refused that passage to the Northern forces intending to invade the South. I believe these reports to be malignantly circulated by emissaries of the enemy, to produce ill-feeling and mutual distrust where harmony of thought and action is so essential. In a few days, if not hours, Tennessee will assuredly be a member of the Confederacy, for none but cowards can be neutral in such a contest as is now approaching and none but fools can hope to stay it by conciliatory attitude. The North has drawn the sword; we must force, not beg her to sheath it again. Some men in Tennessee may still talk to "impartiality," and of "keeping her soil sacred from the tread of hostile armies;" but the heart of the people is sound, and its beatings cannot be repressed by a few would-be leaders.

There are several regiments forming here, most of them from Georgia, but one or two from Alabama. They have given quite an animated appearance to this little village just struggling into life by virtue of its being the point of intersection of several railroads. In one of the half-built houses, upon which the village rests its title to be called a village at all, I have just seen one of the prettiest and most novel sights that I ever added to my memory album. The ladies, for thirty miles around, have collected here in an improvised sewing society, busy with needles and sewing machines in working for the soldiers. Where they have found so many sewing machines I cannot imagine, unless they have emptied the store of some enterprising dealer in "Yankee notions," who may have speculated upon the future grandeur of this still unborn city. At all events, never have these useful contrivances of Northern ingenuity served a better purpose than they now are, in making tents for those who go forth to defend their homesteads against Northern covetousness and rapacity. Few of the companies here have uniforms, most of the men being still in their civilian clothes, and ours is, I believe, the only company which has its own tents and camp equipage. These ladies are truly engaged in a patriotic service, for without them, many of our enthusiastic youths here must go into the field without a change of clothes, or a tent to sleep under. It is a strange sight, this large hall filled with high-bred dames and damsels, all bent with an industry which they never knew before, upon a toil which, but for its object, would be as repulsive to them as it is new. Most of them are accompanied by their black attendants, and mistress and maid vie with each other in the amount of work each can do. And real work they do, indeed, for ever and anon a lot of jackets, or of trousers, or underlinen, or a set of tents, is handed over to the quartermaster's officers, who, but for these ladies, would have no stores to dispense.

There is a guard at the entrance of the hall to screen their fair workwomen from the intrusion of the merely curious; but some of us have found access, under various pretences, the most unscrupulous of which is in the case of a member of our company, who cut off several buttons from his new jacket to have the pleasure of having them sewed on again by the delicate fingers of a beautiful young girl, whom the wretch deliberately made the unsuspecting victim of his guile. There was at first a suggestion that the mutilated jacket should be sent in without its wearer; but how can a soldier be expected to have a choice of wardrobe ready for a change at the bidding of an impertinent sentinel? The young lady seamstress, who sewed the button on again is, strange enough, a niece of Mrs. Lincoln, a Kentucky belle, on a visit to friends here. Mrs. Lincoln, it appears, is like her husband, a Kentuckian by birth.

Eight o'clock, p.m.

Orders have just arrived. We are to leave here at one o'clock tonight. The rumors of this morning seem unfortunately only too well founded. Eastern Tennessee, through which we must pass on our way to Virginia, is in a state of excitement, which may already have broken out into open insurrection. There is good reason to believe that the railroad bridges are held by armed bands of Union men, and that the first blood we may have to shed will be on Southern soil. We are to have fifteen rounds of ammunition served out, and the unexpected need for this proves to be the true cause for our detention here. The bitterness of feeling among our men is intense, and I fear if we have to fight our way through to Virginia, it will be difficult to restrain them from excesses which they would never have thought of committing on a Northern foe. I must still believe that the reports are grossly exaggerated. East Tennessee, I know, is inhabited by a population widely differing from that of the middle and western portions of the state in origin, in interests, in manners, and pursuits. A large portion of it is a mountainous country, with a sterile soil, settled by small farmers more resembling the peasantry of Europe than the planters of the South. Such a people could not, perhaps, be expected to appreciate and understand the great change which has, to them suddenly, come over the country. The great issues at stake are unknown to them, except through the willful perversions of leaders like Parson Brownslow, men whose very existence is a plague-spot to any community.[12] But I cannot think so ill even of the East Tennesseans as that they would take for their model one whose chief delight is to blaspheme his Maker in the very robes of His servants, and in the very place of His worship; one whose masterpiece of pulpit eloquence was in saying, "that he should fight Secession until hell froze over, and then fight the Secessionists on the ice."

Knoxville, Tennessee, April 30th

Our first adventure is at an end, and would be amusing if it were not for the real hardships of our journey hither. We left Dalton at one o'clock last night, in no better conveyance than cattle cars, thirty men in each, closely packed on the floor, and with no ventilation except that afforded by the fissures in the sides. The doors, for some unexplained reason, were closed, and we kept in the full enjoyment of the atmosphere left behind by the sheep and pigs that had preceded us as passengers. A series of forced marches would have been preferable to this railway journey in a dark foul prison, momentarily expecting an attack, against which we would have been helpless. We had ten rounds of ammunition served out to us on leaving Dalton, with strict injunctions, repeated to each man in person by the company officers, not to fire or even load without express orders. About an hour after daylight this morning, the train stopped for wood and water. Thanks to our frantic beating against the walls of our prison, and our united yells many times repeated, the doors were thrown open, and we had once more a glimpse of light and a mouthful of fresh air. I believe if we had continued in this locomotive Black Hole some of us would have died.

On looking out it was discovered, with amazement, that we were the only live freight on board. During the night, the train being too heavy for the engine, had been divided, and that portion on which the troops were, left to follow. Nothing in the appearance of our car indicating the presence of human beings, and a cattle car resembling in all respects a luggage van, we were, by a not unaccountable mistake, sent on with the heavy freight. When the discovery was made we were within an hour's run of Knoxville. A consultation was at once held, and there being neither officer nor non-commissioned officer among us, the first step was to find a leader. To avoid even the appearance of an election, which we all condemn in principle, the unanimous voice of our little forlorn hope gave the command to one who had on several occasions acted as corporal in company drills. The engineer informed us that the railway bridges which we had passed were indeed held by Tennessee troops, but they were troops under the orders of the governor, sent to protect them against the malignity of disaffected individuals. It was therefore decided to go on to Knoxville, there quietly to await the arrival of our companions. If insults were offered us, we were ordered to bear them with dignified silence; if violence by a greatly superior force, to make no resistance. It was an anxious half-hour, that last one before making the chief city of East Tennessee.

So here we are, in the town of Parson Brownslow, the place which had been represented to us as the hot-bed of disloyalty to our sacred cause. Thirty men at the mercy of any band of his followers who may choose to insult us, or do worse. But neither Brownslow nor any of his men can be seen or heard of. On approaching the station, we descried the United States' flag waving from a huge staff, but reversed, and with the banner of the Confederacy floating triumphantly over it. So soon as the cars stopped, we were greeted with a loud "Hurrah for Jeff Davis," and surrounded by men who cordially took us by the hand, and offered us the hospitalities of the city, in the shape of unlimited drinks at the neighboring bar-rooms. They seemed mortified when we informed them of the suspicions we had entertained, and assured us that though "there might be a few d——d scoundrels of traitors in their midst, they dared not show their faces, and would be 'eaten up' if they did," and that even the blasphemous parson kept prudently silent. In a short time all apprehension was removed, and we obtained leave to disperse in various directions to take a look at this really beautiful town.

A TRIUMPHAL MARCH

Lynchburg, Virginia, May 1, 1861

If we were a band of conquering heroes returning home with well-won laurels, instead of a set of youths who have yet to win their spurs in their country's cause, we might more appropriately have accepted the ovations we have received ever since we left Knoxville, and, indeed, even since we left Montgomery. We have been pelted with bouquets at almost every village we passed, and scarcely a man of us that has not secured his own individual trophy. Many of the bouquets have cards attached to them, with patriotic prose or verse written in dainty ladies' hands. My own reads: "God speed ye, patriotic sons of the South. Our hearts follow you to your battle-fields, and our prayers shall strengthen your arms in your sacred duty. Conquer, or die in the attempt; but let none return so long as a Northern foe threatens our homes."

Another which I am permitted to copy by the happy recipient, is, if possible, still more enthusiastic:

Hail! Brave defenders of a holy cause. Our heartfelt wishes, our constant prayers, attend you whithersoever you go to search the hated foe. Let no Yankee footsteps pollute the native soil of free men and free women. Your memory will be sacred to us if you fall, our smiles shall reward you if you return victorious. Better death than disgrace. God defend the right!

The younger members vow that when the war is over, they "will come back and find out these noble girls that write such pretty notes." Each one thinks that which fell to his share the most eloquent, and hugs the conceit that it was specially intended for him. Wherever the train stops, bevies of girls of all classes of society crowd the depot, and the more enterprising of the gay volunteers generally manage to leave the cars, and make the best use of the few minutes the locomotive is willing to allow to their flirtations. Men we seldom see in any large numbers; they are all drilling and making ready to follow us. The only place, besides Knoxville, where we received the greetings of our own sex, was near Marietta, in Georgia, where 400 commissioned officers of the Georgia militia had been formed into a camp of instruction under the personal supervision of the Governor.

The ladies, however, are not unmindful of our material wants, and know that we cannot feed on the rose leaves of their nosegays. At Greenville, in Tennessee, we found a substantial lunch prepared by them for the whole regiment, and good hot coffee enough for two regiments. We were agreeably surprised at this, because we had been led to consider this locality the most disaffected in all East Tennessee. It is the home of Senator Andy Johnson, over whose house still waved the Stars and Stripes, as if in defiance to the Secession ensign displayed from the flagstaff at the station. The Senator himself we had passed a few hours before in a train going towards Knoxville. He looked pale and suffering. A few of the men were sufficiently lacking in self-respect to groan as the two trains stopped by the side of each other, to which he replied by taking his hat off. The offenders were severely reprimanded by the officers, and their conduct condemned by the whole regiment. It is, however, a remarkable forbearance on the part of our people to let this man, as well as Brownslow, go at large. Johnson was actually on his way to make a Union speech at some place on the road. He is said to be an eloquent orator, and to have unbounded influence among the people of the mountains.

At Whitville, a small hamlet marking the boundary of Virginia and Tennessee, we found no breakfast, except for some twenty or thirty of us, for the few hospitable private houses could accommodate no more; but we were welcomed to Virginia by a speech of no moderate pretensions. Among the privates of our company is a barrister of note, whom we appointed orator of the occasion. Unfortunately, in the midst of his eloquent peroration, the whistle sounded, and orator and audience had to scamper, *sauve qui peut,*[13] to jump on the moving train.

At Liberty, some 300 ladies had assembled, and with their own hands prepared us dinner. Ours and another company, perhaps because we were the best dressed, had a table allotted us overlooked by a low back gallery thronged by our fair entertainers, thus enjoying the advantage of hearing their comments on the appearance, individually and collectively, of our modest selves. The repast came near having a tragic termination, for a portion of the frail balcony gave way, though, thanks to the prompt rush in assistance, without more serious consequence than the display of a well-turned ankle or two.

Whatever had been the enthusiasm of our reception on the way, it is exceeded by our welcome to Lynchburg. The city seems to have gone mad with joy. As the regiment marched through its whole length (for the regiment is now together, the various companies having overtaken us during our different stoppages), we seemed passing through a city on fire, so continuous were the flashes of fireworks, and so dazzling the blaze of light. We were leaving the suburbs for our camp-ground, a few miles further off, when the telegraph announced the passage of an ordinance of Secession by the Legislature of Tennessee. Though we are punctilious sticklers for military discipline, no sooner had the news been passed by the officers along the line, than the regiment burst forth in cheer after cheer, joined in by the thousands in the streets and windows: "Hurrah for Tennessee!" "Hurrah for the Southern Confederacy!" "Hurrah for Jeff Davis!"

TAKING THE OATH[14]

Lynchburg, Virginia, May 2, 1861

From this day we are, not in theory only, but in sober fact, common soldiers— "enlisted men" for the term of twelve months, under the Rules and Articles of War of the Confederate States, which are identical, bating the change of an adjective, with those for the regular army of the United States. This morning a Confederate officer arrived at Lynchburg, authorized to muster us into the service and administer the oath. The ceremony was an imposing one, and there was not, I truly believe, a man in all the ten companies that did not feel the solemnity of the occasion, and of the obligations he was assuming. Had any one regretted, or even hesitated, it was yet time to withdraw before taking the final step, for up to that moment the authority of our officers rested solely upon our own voluntary consent, and we were private gentlemen in military clothes, subject to no law, beyond our own wills, which did not apply to all other citizens alike. Now, in the discharge of the highest duty of citizenship, that of defending our country, we have abjured all its rights and privileges, nay, even the slightest claim to personal freedom of thought or action. Surely it is a hard sacrifice for gentlemen to make, but it has been cheerfully and unreservedly made.

It had often occurred to me how harsh are the military regulations of the United States' standing army; how much more like a transcript from medieval days than like the military code of a modern nation. The death penalty occurs in them more frequently than in either the French or English regulations, and corporal punishment, once abolished, has been reinstituted within the last few years by an Act of Congress. The gulf between officer and private is wider than in any other army, excepting, perhaps, the Austrian; and instead of aiming to elevate the self-respect of the man, these regulations systematically and intentionally tend to degrade him in his own estimation. There is a strange anomaly in this, when it is considered that these are the military institutions of a country whose political institutions are based upon universal equality, universal suffrage, and an assumed universal capacity for collective and individual self-government. But the reason was plain, and, perhaps, sufficient. In other countries the regular army, in whatsoever manner raised, whether by voluntary enlistment, or by conscription, consists of the natives of the country. Not so with the small regular army of the United States, which is composed, without exception, of foreign mercenaries, principally Irish and Germans, the only native element in it being the commissioned officers. Between these, educated at one of the best military schools in the world, and representing, as a class, the most genuine social respectability of the land, and the wretched soldiers, there does not even exist the tie of a common country, nor, in a majority of instances, a common language. This little army, moreover, at no period exceeding 13,000 men, was designed for the protection of a remote and illimitable frontier, scattered into little posts and detachments, far from the region of civilized life, amid the Red Indians, and white men scarcely less savage. No wonder, then, that a stern, and even cruel, code should be devised for such an army, so composed and so circumstanced.

But it would be difficult to imagine a system of legislation less adapted to our necessities, and more directly opposed to all common sense deductions from existing facts. Instead of being the scum of every foreign clime, idle vagabonds unable to obtain the wages of labor in a country where labor is wealth, we are the representatives of the best families in the land, many of our number men of vast wealth, all possessed of some means, and none devoid of the essentials of a superior education. Instead of seeking a miserable livelihood, we all are sacrificing private interests to what we cherish as a sacred cause and a bounden duty. While among the "regulars" of the United States' services, not an instance is on record of a man having risen from the ranks to a commission, the right of election, which with such strange inconsistency, is thrust upon us, may convert the private soldier of today into the commander of a regiment tomorrow. Instead of being broken up into small frontier posts, thousands of miles away from civilization, we are about being massed into huge armies, and our battles will, for the most part, no doubt, be on our own soil and under the eyes of those whose approbation and praise we value.

This is not grumbling. I write it to one of the leading journals of the South, in the hope that it may direct the eyes of the authorities to the absurdities and glaring inconsistencies of a system which, in the progress of the year now commencing, might work serious mischief.[15] The habit of command is acquired by the Southerner from his earliest childhood; the habit of obedience to lawful authority is the correlative of the habit of command. I believe there is no people more easily ruled than ours, no people that has, to the same extent, the instinct of discipline. But the rule must be one which their reason approves, and its discipline must be free from arbitrary and useless annoyances. No troops will bear hardships and privations more cheerfully than ours, and they will not even inquire the cause, so long as they believe that there is a good cause for them; but no troops, also, will sooner rebel indignantly against wanton exactions or imbecile commands. Now, these army regulations, no doubt admirably adapted to the purposes for which they were devised, are so strangely unsuited to the volunteer system that if they are enforced they will be felt as cruel and wanton injustice; if they are not enforced, then it will leave us without any systematic discipline whatever. Thus we shall combine the worst features of a regular army with those of loosely-organized volunteer troops.

Among other things we have lost this day are our high-sounding company names. Henceforth, the Mobile Cadets will simply be "Co. A 3rd Reg. Ala. Vol." The most usual style will be to call each company by the name of its captain. When Company A was mustered in this morning, it was found to contain three men more than the military laws of the Confederate States allow. Each company is entitled to four company officers, viz: captain, one first and two second lieutenants, four sergeants, four corporals, one drummer, and 100 privates; a total of 109, or an aggregate of 113. While the company retained its right of balloting for members, several urgent applicants, who had overtaken us on our way, had been added without a very close inspection of the muster roll. Some awkward disputes might have arisen from its redundancy, which, however, was wisely obviated by our captain, who at once ordered three of the oldest members to the rear, whereupon the remainder mustered in without them.[16] They are to follow us as supernumeraries, without pay or rations, but subject to all the duties and penalties of privates, and will take their places in the ranks again, so soon as vacancies occur either by death or promotion. This is not exactly regular; in fact, it is decidedly irregular. But the mustering officer knows nothing of it, and we shall take good care not to obtrude our excess of numbers on the knowledge of the Confederate authorities. A less difficulty is presented by our fifth sergeant. He will still be respected and obeyed as a non-commissioned officer, but reported on the books as a private, and draw pay as such; that is, if any of us ever draw pay at all.

THE FIRST CAMP

Lynchburg, Virginia, May 3, 1861

Our first quarters at Lynchburg were on the Fair Grounds, and the stalls used for the annual cattle show served us as barracks. On the evening of the 1st., however, we pitched our tents in a beautiful oak forest, wholly free from undergrowth, on the brow of a lofty hill, in full view of the majestic Blue Ridge. To many in the regiment the sight of a vast range of mountains is a novel one, and as interesting as would be our boundless plains and low swamps to the inhabitants of a mountainous region.

The rapidity with which this lively canvas town rose seemed the work of magic. It would have done credit to the oldest veterans of any European army. Within little more than an hour from the word of command every tent was pitched, and not carelessly or slovenly, but with geometrical accuracy of lines, and according to the minutest requirements of the books. Two-thirds of the companies are old, established volunteer companies, and the other third have seen some service in the occupation of Pensacola before the war broke out. A fair majority of the members of each are, therefore, not altogether novices in camp life, and have now an opportunity of practicing in earnest the lessons learned, more for amusement than instruction, in the gay annual encampments of the happy days of peace.

To me it is a strangely new experience. Being unskilled in the art and science of pitching tents, I, with others equally in the way, have been set to a task more ignoble, but not less useful. A layer of dead leaves, several inches thick, covers the ground, and this we set resolutely to work to remove. In default of proper instruments, we raked it together with our hands and feet, and then swept the earth with branches of trees. The next day the work was resumed on a grander scale, to clean up our company parade ground, and our share of the regimental parade. On that occasion we managed to procure some garden tools, but hands and feet still remained the only substitutes most of us had for them. The absurdity of our respective postures, and the novelty of the occupation, in a measure compensated for the fatigue, but there are several concomitants of this sort of work which are decidedly disagreeable. The dirt is the slightest of them, for water and soap can remove that. But this layer of dead leaves is inhabited by millions of little creatures, familiarly called the "red bug"—I do not know its scientific name—a small insect, almost invisible to the naked eye, which buries itself in the skin and causes painful inflammations, and sometimes serious sores. The ingenuity of our volunteers has already discovered a specific against these vicious vermin, viz.—bathing affected limbs in whiskey, but this precious beverage is too scarce to be thus wasted, as it has to be smuggled into camp surreptitiously, and experiments are now on foot, on an extensive scale, to discover whether its internal application might not prove equally efficacious.

Yesterday a large lot of lumber arrived, which we had sent to the city to purchase at our individual expense. This we are still busily converting into tables, benches, and gun-racks, and already the camp begins to wear an aspect of comparative comfort. It is wonderful how quickly all of us are adapting ourselves to the requirements of this al fresco[17] existence; the city companies apparently more quickly than those from the rural districts, but their readiness of invention serves as example to the others. A number of coarse cheap carpets have been bought to spread on our tent floors, to protect us from the moisture and cold which we, accustomed to a milder climate, feel severely.

On the day after we took the oath, we had our first regimental parade, with half the female population of Lynchburg as admiring spectators. The impression we produced must have been highly favorable, for ever since our camp has been thronged with lady visitors every evening. At first they scarcely ventured a glimpse into the interior of the tents, but they have already become so far familiar with our soldiers' ways that they now accept our gallant invitations to partake of our fare, admire our "carpets," and rest as comfortably upon the unplaned benches of our own rude construction as upon their own sofas. Hams and tongues, hot rolls and buckwheat cakes, roast turkeys, loaves of fresh bread, and similar welcome donations pour in upon us with delightful profusion; and some of the messes have had whole breakfasts sent out to them served on fine china and plates. Invitations to dinner are not wanting either, only the officers are less liberal of furloughs than they were in Montgomery.

This is the great centre of the tobacco region, and the chief emporium of that great staple. So bountifully has the generosity of the citizens supplied us with the choicest brands of the narcotic weed, that a fair division among the whole regiment, would give every man at least ten pounds of tobacco, which a prince need not disdain to smoke.

Lynchburg, May 4, 1861

Just as we are becoming quite comfortable at Lynchburg, and making acquaintance both with the picturesque town and its hospitable inhabitants, we are ordered off again. Tomorrow, at daylight, we are to strike our tents, and proceed by special train to Norfolk. The navy yard has been precipitately abandoned by Prendergast [sic],[18] after a vain attempt to blow up the dry dock. The *Merrimac* has been partly burnt and sunk, the old *States,* and *Pennsylvania,* of glorious memory, destroyed. The Yankees are expected to return in force, as they can never abandon without a desperate struggle a place so important to them and to us. So we are to have a brush with them as soon as we expected, though in a different quarter. We are proud of being selected for the post of honor, as Norfolk, unquestionably, will be the scene of the first great battle.

THE TUNE OF DIXIE[19]

Norfolk, May 5, 1861

We arrived here at daylight this morning in two special trains, after nearly twenty hours continued but slow traveling. Our conveyances were again, as for the greater part of our many days journey, cattle-cars, or box-cars, as they are termed; but these had been well aired and cleaned, a sort of rough benches fitted into them, and the sliding side-doors kept open, so that our situation, if not comfortable, was at least endurable. One passenger car was attached to each train for the officers and sick, of which latter we have already a goodly number, owing to the sudden change of climate, and of water and food though no serious cases. The officers, for the most part, remained in the box-cars among the men, sharing their discomforts, and assisting in turning them into subjects of merriment.

The scenes on the way were a repetition of those we had witnessed in Georgia and Tennessee. Bevies of girls to greet us wherever the train stopped for wood and water, and gifts of flowers, cakes, and early fruit by the enthusiastic fair. Our "boys" have composed a set of doggerel rhymes to the tune of "Dixie," commemorative of the recent accession of Virginia and Tennessee to the Confederacy, and especially complimentary to the former. This they sing on every appropriate occasion, with marked effect upon the hearts of the Virginian beauties. Such was the popularity of the song at Norfolk, where it originated, that some considerate persons bethought themselves of having it printed on little slips of paper, as "The Song of Dixie, sung by the 3rd Regiment of Alabama Volunteers, on their passage through Virginia." These slips have been plentifully distributed on the road, and, I doubt not, will be preserved as historical relics, when the pretty girls who welcomed us shall have become grandmothers, and relate to the wondering little ones about the times when the first troops of Confederate volunteers came from the far South to fight the Yankees on Virginian soil.

Oh have you heard the joyful news?
Virginia does old Abe refuse,
Hurrah! Hurrah! Hurrah!
And Tennessee and brave Kentuck
Will show the North their Southern pluck,
Hurrah! Hurrah!

and so on, through a dozen stanzas, each of which ends with the patriotic refrain:

"We'll die for old Virginia."

It is marvelous with what wild-fire rapidity this tune of "Dixie" has spread over the whole South. Considered as an intolerable nuisance when first the streets re-echoed it from the repertoire of wandering minstrels, it now bids fair to become the musical symbol of a new nationality, and we shall be fortunate if it does not impose its very name on our country. Whether by coincidence simply accidental, or from some of those mysterious cause which escape our limited intelligence, its appearance in its present form was the knell of the American Republic, and as such it seems to have been instantaneously received by the masses in the South everywhere. What magic potency is there in those rude, incoherent words, which lend themselves to so many parodies, of which the poorest is an improvement on the original? What spell is there in the wild strain that it should be made to betoken the stern determination of a nation resolved to achieve its independence? I cannot tell.

Most persons believe it to be of recent origin, first introduced during the last Presidential contest by an "Ethiopian minstrels'" troop performing in New Orleans. This is only partially true; its real origin is of much older date. Those who have traveled much on Western rivers must often have heard it, in various forms, among the firemen and deck-hands of the river steamers. For years the free negroes of the North, especially those employed on board the streamers on the Western rivers making periodical voyages South, have cheered their labors with this favorite song:

I wish I was in Dixie;
In Dixie's land
I'll take my stand,
And live and die in Dixie,
Away, away,
Away down South in Dixie—

expressed the negro's preference for his more genial and sunny native clime, the land which is the negro's true home, and the only land where he is happy and contented, despite the morbid imaginings of ill-informed or misguided philanthropists.

The word "Dixie" is an abbreviation of "Mason and Dixon's line," as the line separating Maryland and Pennsylvania is called, and which, both geographically and rhetorically, has expressed the Northern frontier of the South ever since the line was drawn by the surveyors whose names it immortalizes. Years before I heard the tune I have heard negroes in the North use the word "Dixie" in that sense, as familiarly as we do the more lengthy phrase from which it is derived.

ON THE SCENE OF ACTION

Norfolk, May 7, 1861

There can be no doubt that this is to be the field on which we must win our spurs in the country's service. I have accordingly seized with avidity the opportunity afforded me by a friend on the staff of the commanding general, for obtaining an intelligent comprehension of what must unquestionably be the first battle-field of the revolution. A small military map traced from the latest United States' Coast Surveys, has been of material assistance to me in this respect. I now more fully understand the hot haste with which we were summoned hither. My anxious prayer is that the enemy may allow us the time for those defenses without which we must fall a useless sacrifice. On the other hand, I marvel at the imbecility which caused the precipitate abandonment of so important a place.

It now appears that Commander Prendergast [*sic*] was frightened away by a ruse which almost passes credence that it should have produced such results. Mr. Malone, the President of the Seaboard and Roanoke Railroad, had heavy trains passing over that road all the day, and until late into the night of the 23rd ult. The noise of these trains could be plainly heard at the Navy Yard, as also the cheers which rent the air when each of them arrived. By the Federals they were supposed to convey large masses of troops, while, in truth, they were employed, and had been run purposely, to create that impression, and prevent any closer inspection into the condition of the town. All communication between the latter and the Navy Yard had for several days past been prevented by the authorities, aided by a Vigilance Committee truly deserving the name. Norfolk, however, besides its own citizens armed as best they could, had at the time but 500 troops, who had hastened from Petersburg to its assistance. On the same night the powder magazine, at some distance from the yard, had been surprised and seized. This corroborated the fears of the Federals that they would be attacked, and some show of placing obstructions in the channel of the river inspired the further fear that their retreat would soon be cut off. I have the testimony of my own eyes to the panic with which they abandoned the place, without even giving themselves time for its destruction. The *Merrimac,* which, with immense stores of powder on her, they set on fire and scuttled, is already raised and the ammunition in her hold is uninjured. She sank before the fire reached below the gun deck, and her hull and machinery are as serviceable as ever.[20] The old frigate *United States* is also but little injured. None but the sheds, officers' quarters, and a few of the minor buildings, are consumed by the flames. All that is essential for our use remains. The explosion of the dry-dock is said to have been prevented by one of their own men, who managed, in the confusion of departure, to get away and turn the water on, thus extinguishing the train. When we, in turn, must abandon the place, which, in all probability, will be before long, we shall set about the work of destruction more deliberately, and more successfully. For this we are now preparing, even while working day and night at the defenses; for it is almost too much to hope that the Federals, recovered from their panic, will allow us to complete the latter. Much of the rich booty has already been removed to Richmond. Some 1100 naval guns of various sizes, and considerable stores of provisions, and ammunition still remains, including some 30,000 shells. When all shall have been removed to a place of safety, I shall breathe more freely.

At present I can see nothing to prevent the Federal fleet from returning. Elizabeth River might be hotly contested at Sewall's Point and Craney Island; but at the former we are only just building a battery, and at the latter we have only a few guns. Both will be tenable in about a month, but not sooner. The approach by land is more difficult, but yet practicable. Norfolk is enclosed, as by a pair of forceps, between two deep, marshy creeks, or rather tide-water inlets,—Tanner's Creek and Broad Creek—the heads of which are only one and a-half miles apart. The bridge which spans the former is ready for the torch at the first signal of alarm. The only other practicable road to Norfolk, when this is burned, lies between the heads of the two creeks; and there it is now our first and most pressing duty to erect breastworks—also a work requiring with the utmost zeal and diligence, at least four or five weeks. If the enemy grant us that time we may defy him by land and by water. It will be a wonderful good fortune on our part, and unpardonable stupidity on his, if he does.

Several regiments from Georgia, Louisiana, and North Carolina have joined us here already, making in all about 4000 men. A recent copy of the *New York Herald* estimates our number at 20,000, upon the authority of a correspondent purporting to write from here.

MY MESSMATES[21]

The pages of my note book will not serve me here. The jest which beguiled an idle hour of camp life sounds ghastly now when it conjures up the image of a dear friend bleeding and dying on a battle-field. The rough sketches of my companions, made while we all were together, though the idea of death, separation was not absent from them, jar painfully on my feelings. Alas! of these companions many a one no longer answers when the roll is called.

The first who fell was Major R. B. Armistead—there is no indelicacy in naming the heroic dead. He was a barrister of eminence in Mobile, past the first flush of youth, and on the platform, as in the forum, an orator of no mean repute. He was an accomplished gentleman, a true friend, but neither by nature nor taste fitted for a soldier. Rather predisposed by temper and pursuits in favor of all established order, he saw with regret the disruption of the magnificent Republic, and acquiesced in Secession only as a sad necessity. But when his native State (Virginia) after long hesitation and anxious deliberation, dissolved her connection with the Federal Government, and solemnly united her fortunes to those of the Gulf States, he stepped into the ranks of the first Mobile Company dispatched to the seat of war. I doubt whether before that period he had ever shouldered a musket, and his portly figure was the mark of many a good-natured joke in the squad of raw recruits; yet a few weeks sufficed to make him one of the best drilled men in the company. When we were mustered into the Confederate service, our corps having more than the legal quota of members, Private Armistead was one of the three whom the captain, to prevent dispute, selected to forego their claims to membership. These three never left the company, and remained subject to all its regulations and duties, but without pay or rations, until some vacancy in the ranks should enable them to step in again. Such was Private Armistead of Mess No. 5, and few more efficient soldiers were there in Company A. When off duty, he was a diligent student of "Hardie's Tactics;"[22] and as we had daily opportunities for practicing the lessons of this admirable textbook, both as automata in the drill of our own battalion, and as criticizing spectators of the drill of the other, it need not excite much surprise that a well-trained mind like Mr. Armistead became in a few months respectably proficient in the tactical knowledge required of a regimental officer. When, therefore, on the authorization of the new levies, subsequent to the battle of Manassas (Bull Run), Private Armistead was invited by the Secretary of War to raise, in conjunction with another gentleman, a new Alabama Regiment, he was not quite unprepared for the responsible duties devolving upon him. The regiment was soon raised, and placed, fully armed and equipped, at the disposal of the Government. Private Armistead was to become Major Armistead of the 22nd Alabama, the lieutenant-colonelcy having been declined by him in favor of a West Point graduate. In the great battle of Shiloh, where every Southerner did his duty, no regiment won brighter or more dearly-bought laurels than the 22nd Alabama Volunteers. The second day of the battle found Major Armistead in command of this corps, and while leading it on to victory he was shot through a vital part. Quietly dismounting from his horse, he walked to the rear; with hands convulsed in the agonies of death, he wrote a brief farewell to those he had dearest in the world, and a few hours after expired without a groan. There was something so quiet, so unassuming, so truly manly, in the brief military career of this man, there was such a stern heroism in his death, that among the many martyrs Mobile has given to the cause the memory of none is more dearly cherished than that of Major Robert B. Armistead, of the 22nd Alabama.

The head of our mess was Sergeant James Broune. He was well descended, and connected with some of the most aristocratic families of Alabama and South Carolina. His pride consisted in being the best non-commissioned officer in the regiment, and to repeated offers of a commission he used to reply, "No, no, leave me where I am; I know what I am fit for, but I don't know whether a lieutenancy would fit me." An excellent drill-officer he certainly was, and a strict one, as I have occasion to remember, whenever my musket was not up to his standard of dazzling brightness, or when luck placed me in the rear rank at the "march in line." If Sergeant Broune had any military ambition, it was to be the color-bearer of our regiment; and no taller or handsomer man for the post could have been selected. "I should be sure to be killed, the Yankees could never miss me," he was in the habit of saying, half jestingly, half seriously, when discussing his prospects for the coveted appointment. On the expiration of the twelve months' term, he re-enlisted with his regiment; at the battle of Seven Pines, near Richmond, he bore aloft the riddled flag of the 3rd Alabama, and fell shot through the heart.

The lists of killed and wounded which chance has from time to time, brought to this land of peace—these fragmentary leaves torn out of the awful record of death and mutilation—are seldom without a name of one of my messmates, and there is not one of them of whom I can confidently speak as being still in the world of the living. We were twelve in number before the country's service called us, one after another, to different fields of duty, higher and more distinguished than those we then had, but surely not more honorable. During the three months that we were crowded together under the same tent there never was an unkind word spoken to or of each other. Nearly every profession, and certainly every variety of natural temperament, was represented in the mess. I well remember how "at taps" we were wont to huddle together in our narrow quarters, each man's knapsack serving for his pillow, and with what a sense of relief we counted upon the nights when, in the alphabetical order of the roll, one or two of our number should be detailed for guard duty, and leave breathing space for the rest. Beside me, nearest the opening of the tent, lay a well-to-do cotton broker of middle age, whose epicurean experience and practical culinary accomplishments added largely to our material comforts; who eat well and slept well, and who never seemed sad, save when a letter from home brought more vividly to his mind the thought of a young wife and child a thousand miles away. Just opposite to me, on the other side of the tent, our legs fitting carefully between each other, was a planter's son, a dashing, singularly handsome youth, whom we never should have suspected of a serious idea, or a pang of care, had we not surprised him once or twice pensively poring over a photograph, which no profane eye was permitted to see. Poor fellow! His wedding day had been fixed when the summons of war dispelled his dreams of happiness. Those who were in his confidence knew his boisterous gaiety to be seldom genuine. At my left lay a young physician who, after a brilliant graduation in the best medical school in America, was perfecting his professional education in Europe when the revolution called him home to take his place in the ranks also. When off duty he found time to assist the surgeons of the regiment, and in one instance, at least, gave evidence of more than ordinary skill in his profession; but for himself, he firmly declined the appointments on the medical staff, which were more than once urged upon him. At a later period of the war, he raised a company, and at the head of it won the honorable mention of General Beauregard.

This brief sketch of some of my messmates has carried me far beyond the period embraced in my notes. The reader will pardon the anachronism, and return with me to the camp near Norfolk in the early part of May, 1861.

SOLDIERS DUTIES

Camp near Norfolk, May 11

Yesterday was my first detail for guard duty since we have been subjected to the rigid discipline of a camp in presence of the enemy. As I write, now released from guard, exempt from drill for the rest of the day, to record my first impressions, it is difficult for me to distinguish between the ludicrousness; and the extremely disagreeable nature of some of my duties during the last twenty-four hours. I rather enjoy the recollection of the night passed shelter-less under a heavy rain; for the guard tents, which have been promised us these eight days back have not yet gladdened our sight. Thanks to my India-rubber cloak, I slept tolerably well during the better part of the four hours "off guard;" and the two "on," the wind and rain notwithstanding, were rendered less dreary by the novelty of the position. It is during the daytime that I don't know whether to be amused or ashamed at my curious predicament. As luck would have it, the post of all other posts which I should not have selected fell to me, post No. 1 at the entrance of the camp, my sole duty being to enforce the police regulations. Our officers appear to have no fear of spies, and freely permit visitors of respectable appearance to pass through the camp. So far so good, though I did feel a little awkward at first in my new attitude towards my lady acquaintances at Norfolk, and I pride myself that no sentinel ever more politely yet firmly refused admittance to a carriage attempting to trespass. My duties towards the smugglers of illegal commodities were not so easily discharged. All fruits, shell-fish, cakes, but especially all ardent spirits, were rigidly prohibited. A pitiless refusal to the vendors of the former wares was generally sufficient; but experience had taught me what wonderful resources of ingenuity were brought into the service of the last-named. As my general instructions on this head were specially sharpened by the officer of the guard, who happened to be a professor of temperance in the strictest sense, I could not conscientiously let a laundress pass without a scrupulous examination of the contents of her basket. Then I knew the jugs labeled "vinegar" or "molasses" to be extremely suspicious vessels. Nor was it always safe to permit the owner to pass after he had produced a sample of treacle on his finger from the mouth of the jug.[23] Canteens, also, could not be trusted, even after a specimen of water had been poured from them. A still more irksome duty was the arrest of every luckless wight who presented himself at the entrance of camp a few minutes after the hour fixed in his furlough. No excuse in such a case is valid, though there is not a man in the regiment who would not rather be shot than sent home, much less think of deserting. What makes the regulation appear so absurd is that our camp is filled with negroes, either hired from town by the different messes, or brought with us from home. These negroes, not coming within the cognizance of the military code, have free ingress and egress at all hours between reveille and tattoo. They enjoy amazingly being able to pass unquestioned where their masters cannot pass without written permits, and then only on strictly defined conditions. They no doubt wonder at our scrupulous obedience; for the most severe rules to which any of them have been accustomed are lenient compared to those which govern us.

Despite these disagreeable incidents, the day was not without amusement. I have a prejudice in favor of strawberries and cream at this season, and after a narrow construction of the rules, I did not feel myself compelled to interfere when thirst suggested to some of my companions the expedient of negotiating for the purchase of these luxuries across the line which I was entrusted to guard. Provided the consumer kept on one side of the boundary and the vendor on the other, I paced my watch with dignified indifference to the evasive transaction. Nay, when a kind corporal of the guard consented to relieve me for a few moments, I seized the opportunity of refreshing myself from the rapidly disappearing supply. Inveterate disciplinarian as was our colonel, who at that moment rode up, he could not, probably, help feeling amused at the spectacle of a couple of score of soldiers kneeling on one side of a little path, with a row of fruit mongers ranged opposite them. At all events, no notice was taken, though I was fully prepared for an extra turn of twenty-four hours of guard duty wherein to digest my strawberries.

The next humorous incident occurred at the forming of the first relief for the night-guard. The officer, determined to carry out to the letter the regulations for the instruction of illiterate recruits, made us repeat after him the different calls or replies to be made by us on our post under every conceivable circumstance. The rehearsal of our lessons, singly and collectively, was much after the fashion of a geography lesson in an olden-time country school. The instructor being a mustachioed officer, and the scholars a set of strapping fellows with muskets in their arms, made the analogy only the more amusing. Yet I may add, I think to our credit, that each man of us appreciated the motive, and no one attempted to give the rehearsal a more comic turn than it inherently possessed. We all felt that though the thing was unnecessary and ridiculous in our case it might not be in others, and that it was better our officers should err in this direction than in the opposite one. Upon the whole, now that I have put on paper my first experience "on guard," the pleasant recollection predominates over the unpleasant one, and I feel conscious that I am not insensible to the compliment just paid me by one of the officers of having been an efficient sentinel, though a few weeks ago I certainly did not think that I would earn praise in that capacity.

THE FIRST VISIT OF DEATH[24]

Camp 3rd Ala. Vol., near Norfolk, May 1861

Last night, some time after "taps" had sounded, the tent lantern put out, and we were composing ourselves to sleep, the report of a musket broke upon the deep stillness of the camp. Was it an alarm? Was the enemy approaching? The conjecture was improbable, for no enemy was so near that the first signal of his approach should be given by our own sentinels. Every man was instantly upon his feet; from all the tents rose the buzz of excited conversation, when the stern voice of the orderly-sergeant ordered "Silence! No man to leave his tent." The conviction at once flashed through our minds that some dreadful accident had occurred. A few minutes afterwards a corporal rushed to our tent, with orders for Drs. ——— and ———, privates in our mess, to proceed with all possible haste to guard quarters, where the regimental surgeons required their assistance. A lieutenant has been shot—was dying at that very moment—this was the hurried information of the breathless messenger, in answer to our anxious inquiry. He did not know the name or corps of the dying man—we had not been long enough together for each of the subaltern officers to become personally known to all the men—could only say that he was slight of figure, and fair in complexion. The imperfect description applied to the brevet-lieutenant of our own company—a general favorite, and on guard this very day—and a simultaneous rush was made to the opening of the tent. But the order, "No man to leave quarters," again thundered forth, and we were fain to obey. The suspense was fearful, and became agonizing when presently a special detail was noiselessly made from each tent in the company for what purpose was not told. The oldest members of the messes had been selected: they were not to load: the bayonet alone was to be used; above all the most absolute silence was enjoined and preserved. Again, all sounds were hushed in the excited camp, save only the distant tramp of rapidly marching men, which from time to time our ears, closely pressed to the earth, could catch. Thus we lay for hours, some surmise more dreadful than the rest being occasionally communicated in a low whisper from neighbor to neighbor.

At last one of our medical messmates returned. It was not our lieutenant that had been shot, but an officer of a country company in the left wing. He had expired after brief suffering; his last words, "That I should die thus—not on a battlefield." The murderer was a sentinel.[25] His own company disowned him; no one had any personal knowledge of him; he had joined on the way to Virginia, since the company was formed. Was considered an intruder, an unfit associate. There were ugly rumors about his antecedents. A fearful excitement prevailed in the murdered officer's company; the remaining officers would not answer for the men; some of the hotheaded youths had sworn summary vengeance upon the murdered. A strong guard, drawn close to the inner lines of the camp, alone prevented them from at once attempting their mad design. The criminal himself was protected by a picked guard. Patrols intercepted all unauthorized communication between the inner and outer lines. Such was the statement of our messmate, and we had not finished our whispered comments upon it when the reveille summoned us to our morning duty.

This morning, after the first drill, and before the order of "break ranks" was given, the captain briefly related to us the tragic events of the night. He enjoined us to form no rash opinions, and especially to abstain from comments, either among ourselves or with others, assuring us that the offender would be tried by the proper authorities, and that, in all probability, his crime, though great, was not intentional. There is, of course, but one topic of earnest conversation throughout the regiment; but expressions are more temperate. A feeling of pity, even, is manifested for the unfortunate man who, perhaps, is guilty only of stupidity or gross awkwardness. His friendless condition in his own company, which with some raises such grave suspicions against him, is urged by others as a claim on our sympathies, and a private in our ranks who has earned a high reputation at the bar volunteers to be his counsel, if the colonel will grant permission. In the Wetumpka Guards the excitement has also much abated since the object of their wrath is removed to the city. Some few still sullenly speak of reaching him even there; but, upon the whole, the sense of justice and the spirit of discipline predominate, and no trouble is apprehended. They have certainly sustained a great loss, for Lieutenant Storrs was an officer of great promise, and in his private life a gentleman of high social respectability, esteemed for many excellent qualities of head and heart.[26]

This evening, at dress parade, the death of Lieutenant Storrs was officially announced at the head of the regiment, and the customary mourning ordered. A few feeling words of eulogy on the deceased and of sympathy with the bereavement of his company followed the announcement, but no allusion whatever was made to the manner of his death, except that "he died on duty." The city papers, which have just reached camp, briefly chronicle the occurrence, and attribute the fatality to the "accidental discharge of a gun."

To the surprise of the entire regiment, the homicide was never tried by a court-martial. Though the offence had been committed within the lines of a military camp, and in time of war, it was argued that in the absence of any formal proclamation of martial law, the offender was amenable only to the law of Virginia, and to the authorities of that State he was accordingly handed over. Undoubtedly, our military superiors gladly availed themselves of this pretext, if pretext it was, to avoid the necessity of applying the sterner code of war, and also to remove beyond the camps a topic of constant and, perhaps, dangerous irritation. The trial, which took place some weeks afterwards, was conducted with the time-honored formality and solemnity that distinguish a Virginian court of justice, and the imposing scene, so novel to us from the more southerly States, produced a wholesome impression upon the entire regiment. The fate of the prisoner remained for a time doubtful, though he was defended by most able counsel—the barrister who is mentioned in the preceding note as having volunteered his services—but it being proved that his musket, although a new one, had a fault of construction, he was acquitted of any worse crime than gross carelessness, and escaped with a term of imprisonment. Months afterwards, when he had paid the penalty of the law, the poor friendless man made a last visit to the regiment to receive his dismissal from service; and in honor to frail humanity be it said, no one thought of insulting him by word or gesture.

A DINNER PARTY IN CAMP

May 1861

Up to this time we had been under command of our Lieutenant-Colonel, Tenant Lomax, of Montgomery, Colonel Withers, being at the time of his election, Mayor of the City of Mobile, a few weeks elapsed before he would transfer the city government to his successor.[27] Last Friday the announcement that he had arrived at Norfolk, and would, within a few days, assume the command, caused some little trepidation in the regiment, for if our present commander is strict in discipline, the new one has the reputation of being stern to severity. The rural companies especially, who are familiar with many more or less apocryphal stories of the summary dealings of the Mayor of Mobile, look to his advent as their colonel with something very much like awe. His first unofficial visit to camp, and the complimentary remarks he is said to have made to the officers upon the appearance of the regiment at the review, have softened this harsh impression, and it is generally admitted that, though he may be a severe disciplinarian, he appears to be a just and generous man, who will not unnecessarily resort to harshness. That he is an officer of tried capacity, the most inveterate prejudice cannot deny. He is a soldier by education and graduated with highest distinction at West Point. In the Mexican war he won the rank of colonel, and was appointed by the commander-in-chief civil and military governor of an important province. The rumor is already current that he will not command us long as colonel, but will soon be appointed by the President a brigadier.

With the colonel arrived two ladies upon whom our company has special claims, and looks upon almost as members. One is the bride of our second-lieutenant, married only a few days before we received our marching orders; the other, the young wife of our orderly sergeant, and the daughter of the colonel himself.[28] Both these ladies accompanied us from Mobile as far as Montgomery, where they remained until our destination should be ascertained, and our location comparatively permanent. They will now take up their residence in Norfolk, where it is probable some of us may soon need them as nurses—that is, if the Federals have not so utterly lost their senses as to leave us undisturbed in our present untenable position. We are not a little proud of our lady members, and they, in return, are not a little proud of us. Almost every man in the company is a friendly acquaintance of long standing to one or both, and it may be that among the younger members of the company there are those who once contended for the prizes which our lieutenant and orderly sergeant have drawn. In fact, the roll of Company A might almost serve as the list of male visitors at their respective homes.

Their appearance in camp was quite a holiday. We did the honors of our humble tents; they peeped, looked, and wondered at our improvised housekeeping arrangements, and had a thousand questions to ask. They laughed heartily when some young gentleman whom they had known for his care and taste in dressing came up in undress uniform, laden with a pile of the ration bread, which kept tumbling down when he caught a glimpse of the unexpected visitors; another struggling under a load of ration pork, or jauntily swaggering along with a bucket of water in each hand; still another surprised, broom in hand, with head tied up in a handkerchief, sweeping the space before the mess-tent. Upon the whole, the domestic inspection was favorable to us; they could not understand how we managed to live so comfortably, left all to ourselves; and we, elated by the compliments, invited them to dinner. The invitation was accepted, and yesterday, Sunday, fixed for the grand occasion. There being no battalion drill that day, and Divine Service not held until after dress parade, we had nearly the whole afternoon free. Two o'clock was accordingly the appointed hour.

The inviters were my mess, No. 5. The guests invited, besides the ladies themselves, their husbands, the captain of our company, the colonel, who considered himself sufficiently represented by his daughter, and the general commanding, who sent his aide-de-camp, a personal friend of several members of our mess. Altogether, it was thought throughout the regiment to be the most impudent thing that ever was done by a set of mere privates; but there being nothing in the military code to prevent privates from giving dinner parties which did not interfere with their duties, and the social position of all concerned being established beyond a doubt, the affair was humored by those in authority. The captain even lent us his commodious tent. A deal table of sufficient size was quickly constructed by amateur mechanics, and its rough surface concealed under several layers of table cloths. Crockery, napkins, and other essentials were sent for from town, either hired or bought, as the case might be. Wines and provisions were judiciously selected by the caterer of the mess; our own black cook, the servant of one of our messmates, was entrusted, under the superintendence of a committee of one, with the details of the cuisine. Another of our number was appointed butler, another gentleman-waiter; and thus the memorable dinner came on. In an artistic point of view it was not, perhaps, a perfect success; there were, unquestionably, some of the discomforts of a picnic; there were also some discoveries of things forgotten which ought to have been there, and of others thought of which might well have been dispensed with; but I venture to say that none of the twelve that yesterday sat down to the table ever before knew how much enjoyment might be derived from a dinner. The zest was heightened by the dull boom of the enemy's cannon, which interrupted our desert, but alarmed no one, not even the ladies, to whom we soon explained that it proceeded from Fort Calhoun, familiarly called "the Rip Raps," on a rock half way between Fortress Monroe and Sewell's Point. Upon this rock the Federals have recently placed a long-range gun, called the Sawyer gun, with which they practice every afternoon upon our out-posts, but without much chance of ever hurting any one, for several of their shells, which have been dug up, were found to be filled with sawdust instead of powder, probably through some treachery among the operatives of their arsenals.

The novel banquet was brought to a sudden close, after a duration of four hours, by the tap of the drum, which called us to dress-parade. Leaving the mere fortunate ones of the party, whose rank exempted them from this duty, to entertain the ladies, and exacting a promise that our fair guests would not leave until we had had the honor of escorting them to their carriages after parade was dismissed, we were soon in our places in the ranks—twelve months "enlisted men" once more. Much as life in the extreme South habituates one to strange contrasts, this trifling event is so out of keeping with our position and its duties, and is so strikingly characteristic of the composition of the army on which the fate of our young Republic rests, that it deserves a conspicuous place in my note-book.

THE FIRST FIGHT[29]

Camp, 3rd Alabama Volunteers, near Norfolk, May 1861

The monotony of camp life has been enlivened during the past week. Last Sunday, an unusual number of furloughs had been given to visit the city, and strong detachments from each company of our regiment were just sitting down to the well-supplied public table of the Atlantic Hotel, when a preemptory summons arrived for our immediate return to camp. We were to strike tents in two hours. Several of the regiments had received marching orders. Rumors of mysterious movements on the part of the enemy were already circulating in the streets. Hastily leaving our untasted meal, we hurried towards camp in such conveyances as the offer of extravagant prices could procure. The whole regiment was in a buzz of preparation. Comrades had already packed our knapsacks. The tents were stripped of their contents, ready to fall at the order to strike. Our negro followers were busy cooking three days' rations, or packing the superfluous baggage upon carts sent for from town. Soon each company was drawn up in line on the company parade grounds—the roll called—no one was missing. Several non-commissioned officers now passed up and down the line, dealing out from huge baskets, cartridges, conical balls, and caps thirty rounds to each man. "Rest" was then ordered. Buoyant with the hope of a speedy meeting with the hated foe, feverish with impatience, we waited for two weary hours. Meanwhile orderlies galloped in from headquarters. The officers stood in little groups conversing in low tones. After all, we were doomed to disappointment. At 6 o'clock the usual dress-parade was held; we were then dismissed to our quarters; cautioned to sleep on our arms; and, at all events, to be prepared for an early start in the morning.

That night we slept in our now naked tents without being disturbed by any alarm. At 4 the order to "strike tents," was given, and the canvas-built town fell, as if by magic, to the ground. At half-past 4 the regiment was in line of march—whither, none of us as yet knew. After a march of about three hours we halted upon a broad expanse of fallow land, and there, we now learned, we were to pitch our new camp. It was not in human nature to abstain from grumbling after such repeated disappointments, nor was our ill-humor mollified by finding, a few hours later, that our baggage had taken the wrong way, and we would not be able to pitch our tents before nightfall. The whole of that long day we were exposed to a broiling sun, with not so much as a shrub for a shelter, and with no food nor water except what our haver-sacks and canteens afforded. Trifling though it was, it was the first hardship we have been called upon to endure, and appearing to us utterly purposeless, we grumbled accordingly.

May 1861

A few days have shown that the alarms of Sunday were not altogether ground-less. Day before yesterday, the Federal steamer *Monticello,* a merchant vessel converted into a gunboat, appeared before our unfinished battery at Sewall's Point, and from a distance of about one mile and a-half, commenced a brisk fire of shells and round shot, which was promptly and effectively answered by the four guns already in position. The steamer, after firing 125 rounds, was forced to signal for some tugs to haul her off, having been struck in some part of her machinery.

Yesterday, I had an opportunity for visiting the scene of the conflict. The only damage sustained by the battery, from a fire of several hours, consisted of two embrasures being knocked into one, and this trifling injury was repaired during the night; not a man was hurt, except one very slightly wounded by a splinter from a tree. The result of this, the first engagement since war has been openly declared, is truly wonderful. The battery was defended by the Columbus City Guards, ninety-eight men, under Captain Colquitt. They have not been above a week at their present post, and as they were organized as an infantry company, have had but an exceedingly imperfect drill at the guns. The captain is an old artillery officer; and assisted by three practiced gunners, who act as instructors to the company, he has been able to defend this rude and unfinished structure of turf and sandbags against a most for-midable attack. Though the men were for the first time under fire, they be-haved, not indeed with the coolness of veterans, but with a reckless daring amounting to foolhardiness. After each discharge some of them sprang upon the guns, waving their hats and shouting defiance at the Yankee craft. Cap-tain Colquitt told us that he felt himself unable to restrain their mad enthu-siasm. "The boys must be allowed a little frolic this time," he added, "after another brush or two they will sober down." The trees in the rear of the bat-tery are literally mowed down, and the fields behind are thickly strewn with shell and shot. Few of the former exploded; the nearest within about twenty paces of the battery. Some have been found filled with sawdust instead of powder; a fact which argues ill for the faithfulness of the operatives in the Federal arsenals.

It was suspected in Norfolk that the attack of the *Monticello* might be intended to cover a landing in the rear of the battery, and a battalion of infantry had been hastily dispatched to foil this intention. The ill success which had attended the steamer seems to have caused its abandonment, if it was ever entertained. The work is now continued with renewed energy, and in the course of a week fourteen heavy guns will command the channel, and defy the assault of any ordinary force.

It was not until several weeks after the occurrence of this little affair that the Northern accounts of it reached us. We were then amused to learn that the engagement was one of immense importance, that the rebel battery had been utterly demolished, that the rebels themselves had been seen rushing into the woods like flocks of scared sheep, and that foremost among the fugitives was an officer of high rank described galloping away in wild haste. Such a success was cheaply purchased at the cost of a few lives on board of the steamer and the crippling of its machinery. It was long a question among us whether these ludicrous falsehoods were wholly due to the inventive genius for which the Yankee nation is celebrated, or whether the poor scribblers had so lost their heads through fear that they believed at least a part of what they wrote.[30] Thus the fugitive officer of high rank might have been the mounted vidette dispatched to Norfolk with the news of the attack; the frightened rebels rushing wildly into the woods might have been the gang of negroes employed upon the works, who, at the discharge of the first gun, scampered away to the ditch dug for their protection in anticipation of such an emergency. On another occasion, when a young lady[31] waved her handkerchief at the harmless pyrotechnic display with which we are favored every afternoon by their great "Sawyer gun" at Fort Calhoun, the correspondents of the New York papers gravely reported that a white flag had been raised by the rebels at Sewall's Point.

LUXURIOUS LIVING

During the last week in May, and nearly the whole month of June, no event took place to ripple the stagnant surface of camp routine. The roll-calls, the company and battalion drills, the dress parade, became almost as dull as the long intervals between them. All of us had shouldered the musket with the firm conviction that we would at once enter upon a campaign crowded with soul-stirring events, but which would be necessarily short. To men accustomed to mix in the busy pursuits of life—men who at a heavy sacrifice of interests and feelings left business and family behind them—no trial of patience can be more severe than to spend week after week in compulsory idleness approaching to inanition, and varied only by periodically performing the part of unthinking machines.

If material comforts could have compensated us, we should have had no reason to complain, for however much we might claim sympathy in other respects, we could not in this. Norfolk had been in times of peace the great market garden of New York and Philadelphia, and as the blockade cut off its ordinary customers, we became the beneficiaries of its abundance and lived literally on the fat of the land. Excellent beef and mutton was furnished at much more reasonable prices than we of the Gulf States were accustomed to. Fowls, including the largest and fattest of turkeys, were correspondingly cheap. The choicest vegetables could be obtained for almost nothing; indeed, several of the market gardeners in the neighborhood gave us a free entrance to their teeming gardens, on no other condition than the unnecessary one, that we should take nothing save what we wanted for our own use, nor should waste anything wantonly. It will afford some idea of the cheapness of the place, that fresh eggs, as many as we could consume, were brought at 5d per dozen; butter, far superior in quality to the best procurable in Mobile or New Orleans, cost from 7 1/2 to 10d. per lb. Strawberries, during the month of May, were sold by the quart, at 5d. In June, melons took their place at even cheaper rates; soft shell crabs, which in the cities on the Gulf are deemed a very rare and expensive luxury, had here a mere nominal value, and were ultimately excluded from the camp, as well as some other over-abundant luxuries, for sanitary reasons. Thus we were enabled, at the small rate of a shilling a day per head, to supply our mess table, very much after the manner of a well-regulated household. Coffee, salt meat, rice, and bread, were furnished as rations, but formed the least part of our meals. On Sundays, to give still greater variety to our bill of fare, we had what we termed our birthday dinners, when each member of the mess in turn became the host of the others. On such occasions, some special delicacy in the shape of game and wines was provided, and guests invited from among the different regiments or from the city. Most of the messes had substituted crockery for the rude tin ware that came from the quartermaster's store. All had constructed deal tables and benches for their use, which were mostly sheltered from sun or rain by rough sheds. In our weary leisure hours, we amused ourselves with amateur carpentering, and each tent could boast of a gun rack, or a set of shelves, or some other testimony of the ingenuity and industry of its inmates. Long before the authorities furnished us lumber for the purpose, most of the messes had, at their own expense, planked the floors of their tents. Cheap carpets even were introduced, and in individual cases, buffalo robes and heavy rugs ensured a still more comfortable couch to the owners. In course of time our company purchased three additional tents, which it had received permission to pitch upon its allotted ground, and then we could boast of having a chapel, a dining room, and a writing room of our own during the daytime, besides the sleeping space so much needed during the sultry summer nights.

There was never any lack of money. Our brevet second-lieutenant, who acted as quartermaster, and also as banker, for the company, brought with him about six hundred pounds in gold, partly the original property of the company, partly made up by contributions from some of the moneyed institutions of Mobile, as well as some of the parents or relatives of members. This sum was devoted to general company purposes, and also to the cashing of our individual drafts, within reasonable limits. For a long time we were able to make a considerable premium upon our drafts, as the Mobile banks did not suspend specie payment until a much later period, when compelled by an injunction by the Governor for political reasons. Our custom was therefore eagerly sought by the local banks of Norfolk. The further fact that an advertisement was inserted by our captain in the city papers, stating that all debts contracted by members of the company would be promptly paid on presentation to him, gave to us all an almost unlimited individual credit. In thus putting us upon our honor, Captain Sands ran but little risk, for each man in his command had a good name and his social respectability at stake, as the company proudly and justly claimed to be composed of the elite of the youth of Mobile. Inequalities of wealth indeed exist among us; comparatively few enjoy an income which can be properly called independent; by far the greater number depend upon parents, upon the proceeds of a business more or less damaged by their absence, or upon employers. Where the latter is the case, the salaries are nearly all continued, either in whole or in part. Still there are in our company, as well as in others, some instances of men who, in leaving home, have deprived themselves of all their pecuniary resources. It is for those cases that our company fund is especially useful, and it is a maxim in the application of that fund that no member should want for anything he really needs. Besides, the rich share freely their surplus with less favored companions. Where a member of a mess is not quite able to bear his share of the expense, he is never asked for it, nor is the matter ever alluded to. Were we a company of strangers, thrown together by some caprice of fortune, this species of communism would be a practical impossibility. Lifelong acquaintances as we nearly all are, each mess composed of old friends, it serves only as another tie to bind us more closely together in the bonds of brotherhood.

MISCHIEF AND ITS CURE[32]

The luxurious ease, in which we whiled away the idle weeks of May and June, had its proverbial effect upon our military morals and soldierly character. Day by day our duties, and the engagements we had entered into with our country, appeared less solemn and less serious to our eyes. It seemed ridiculous to think or speak of stern resolves and heroic self-devotion where there was nothing to do but to eat well, to drink well, to sleep well, and to wax fat upon an admirably hygienic system of moderate exercise and calm repose. The daily drill had become intolerably monotonous, and puerile. No pet guard of some martinet monarch could march more regularly than we, none with greater ease and accuracy execute the various maneuvers which extort applause at a holiday review. At dress parade no regiment could form a more exact line, and at the order "parade rest," the row of white gloved hands was a geometrical marvel to behold. All this, we knew, was very well in its place, but we felt also, and felt it keenly, that it was not the true school of the soldier. Of foot-sore marches, such as our brethren in North and Western Virginia had, of privations which should harden us into veterans, of outpost duties, of skirmishes with the enemy, we had none, nor did it seem likely that we ever would have any at our present post. Every day rendered an attack on Norfolk less probable, for battery after battery had been quietly erected to defend the approaches by water, and elaborate field-works ensured us even more completely against a land attack.

About this time an affair occurred which impressed us with an indescribable contempt of the enemy, and strengthened the already rapidly growing conviction that there was "no fight in him." General Magruder, whose small corps d'armee was stationed on the opposite side of the James River, in the vicinity of Yorktown, had for some time "felt" the Federal army at and around Fortress Monroe, and tempted General Butler, in command there, by sending out foraging parties, almost up to the very walls of the fortress.[33] One of these foraging parties or outposts, consisting of a part of a Georgian regiment, and a part of a North Carolina regiment, under Colonel Hill, and a company of Virginia howitzers, with five pieces—in all less than 1100 men strong—was suddenly attacked by four Federal regiments of infantry, and a considerable force of regular artillery. The surprise was so complete that retreat upon the main body, some twelve miles distant, was out of the question. According to all military probabilities, the little force should have been annihilated. Instead of this, with no better defense than a hastily thrown up breastwork, it repulsed and routed the vastly superior odds of the assailants, suffering a loss of only one killed and one wounded; and killing, wounding, and taking prisoners some 300 of the enemy. The details of this engagement, known as the "battle" of Great Bethel, are so incredible that we would not fully believe them until the most ample confirmation had been received.[34] It then appeared that the attack was made in a solid column, which our few pieces could rake at every discharge; that in no single instance could the Federals be induced to charge up to our breastwork; but each time broke and ran after one volley of our musketry. Finally, the whole body fled in wild disorder, strewing the roads with arms and knapsacks, hundreds of which were sent as trophies to Norfolk and Richmond. In the annals of warfare a more disgraceful tale of gross imbecility on the part of the commanders, and arrant cowardice on the part of the men, had never been told. There was one redeeming feature, indeed, and only one. Every man in a Confederate uniform spoke respectfully of Major Winthrop, a member of a distinguished New York family, who was shot through the heart by a North Carolinian rifleman while springing forward, sword in hand, vainly encouraging his men to follow.[35] Sincerely did we pity him for being thrown by fate among such a gang of slinking vagabonds. When the Northern account of the affair reached us, we learned, for the first time, that before coming up with us, two of the attaching regiments had, in the darkness of the night, mistaken each other for enemies. One, a regiment of Germans, fired upon the other, a New York militia regiment, nine rounds of musketry, with as many discharges from a field-piece, at a distance of 150 yards, killing two and wounding five; whereupon the latter regiment broke and ran. The New York press, with a cynicism that added to our disgust, remarked that the Germans had proved themselves stauncher men than the natives, but very poor shots.

The affair of Great Bethel, though an important success for our arms, did us harm. When men are already restless and discontented by inactivity, it is not well for them to learn to underrate and despise their enemy. General Butler, who had planned the expedition, became a by-word and a mockery among us. We punned upon the initials of his name, and he was generally known as "Bethel Failure Butler." The "masked rebel batteries," by which he accounted for his disgrace, and the other preposterous lies which made up his official report of the engagement, were a standing joke with us. We accepted the raw undisciplined rabble we had so easily routed as a fair specimen of all the Federal armies present and prospective, and we found it impossible to believe that a people could seriously contemplate a long war, which received the news of so indelible disgrace in the manner the Northern people seemed to have done. We, had the same thing happened to us, should have been disposed to exaggerate our loss as an extenuation of the disgrace; they, at the very time that we buried eighty-seven of their dead, published their loss to the world as eighteen killed and thirty-seven wounded, apparently without perceiving how their own figures added to their shame that any body of troops should flee in disorder before one-fourth of their number after so trifling a loss.

Despising the enemy, despairing of winning any glory in meeting him, or of having any serious work to do, disgusted with the dull routine of camp life, we were gradually losing that stern sense of responsibility, that pride in our position, with which we had entered the ranks. A sort of demoralization, not in the worst meaning of the word, but still serious enough to be painfully felt, was spreading through the regiment. Men began to look upon it as a clever thing to slip through the lines after "taps," spend the night in town, and return without detection before roll-call in the morning. If detected, the extra twenty-four hours of guard duty was not deemed a punishment, because the public opinion of the regiment no longer considered it a disgrace. Cases of "sleeping on post" also began to occur, partly because extra guard duty had become too frequent a punishment, and partly because of our fancied security from any danger whatever. Idleness had bred silly camp gossip, which in turn gave rise to petty jealousies among the different companies, and even quarrels among individuals. An unfortunate editor in our mess, who had been plagued into writing, sorely against his will, letters from camp to his paper at home, became suddenly the object of almost universal enmity, for no better reason than a typographical blunder.[36] He had written of his own company that only one other excelled it in drill, and none in gentlemanly behavior. The types had substituted the word equaled for excelled, and forthwith every other company considered itself insulted in the most sensitive chord of its self-respect, and individual members felt themselves called upon to resent the insult. More serious quarrels arose. One day a member of one of the Mobile companies was found shot through both thighs in the vicinity of the camp. As neither he nor any of the parties in the secret ever divulged a word that could give a cue to the cause of the accident, the official inquiries resulted in nothing; but it was evident that a duel had been fought—one of the most serious crimes according to the military code.[37] Nor were the disturbances confined to our own regiment. Men, when in town, whether with or without furloughs, had several times come into collision with members of other corps. Intemperance—always the cause of such disputes—had once or twice resulted in bloodshed. On one occasion a serious riot was imminent between the Alabamians and Virginians in the city, when, fortunately, the major of our regiment rode up to the spot, and without inquiring into the cause, ordered "every member of the 3rd Alabama at once to camp;" an order which was instantly obeyed. It is but fair to add that the esprit de corps of the regiment never failed to severely condemn the offenders or even the participators in such disturbances. Not quite so decided was our public opinion, however, in a less serious occurrence. A captain of our regiment had knocked down a saucy Norfolk bookseller, for some offensive personal remark. It was thought a very shabby thing of the colonel to do, to order the captain into arrest for his summary resentment of an insult, and even to make him answer before the Mayor for the offence, like any ordinary civil disturber of the peace.

During the period to which I refer, our colonel was appointed a brigadier-general. I presume he must have been deeply impressed with the truth of the old adage about Satan and idle hands, for he suddenly found us so much work to do, that Satan would have been sorely puzzled to find any idle hands among us. Our comfortable camp, whose broad smooth avenues looked like the streets of a well-regulated city, was summarily transferred into a dense pine forest. From sunrise to sunset the men were now busy felling the huge trees. To clear a space large enough for the camp of 1100 men, with ten ample company parade grounds, and one regimental parade sufficient for two battalions to drill at once, was neither small nor easy work. When the trees were felled and burned—branches, leaves, and undergrowth—the "stumps" or roots had to be dug up, hewn into firewood, and the cavities filled with solidly trodden earth. This on Southern plantations is called "grubbing," and is about as severe and back-straining an employment as fashionable young gentlemen ever undertook. Next came digging and draining, more clearing of the forest, and lastly there were guard barracks to be erected, and our newly-acquired carpenters' skill came into play. Lest all these various tasks allotted each day to each company should not sufficiently employ us, the general discovered that he had urgent need of some thousands of fascines for the entrenchments. The spade and shovel have never in the Confederate army been deemed fit implements for the soldiers, except in a case of sudden emergency, and thus our field-works had been thrown up by a gang of several hundred negroes, hired from, or gratuitously furnished by, their owners for this purpose. But fascine-making was, in the general's opinion, quite suitable work for his intelligent and industrious command, and fascines we did make, at the rate of about 100 a day to each company.[38]

Besides this dose of "hard labor" administered to the whole regiment, the general had special remedies for individual cases. A few summary dismissals by Courts Martial—bodies which were singularly deaf to the eloquence of counsel, and stolid to influence of the social position and family—were read from the head of the regiment with very salutary effect. One or two officers were rumored to have been compelled to send in their resignations to be accepted on the slightest lache on their part. Measures even more severe were reported from other regiments. A whole company had been deprived of their arms, and placed under arrest, for venturing upon a remonstrance against some order they considered unjust. In another instance the penalty of death was decreed for "sleeping on post," but commuted by the general into the wearing of "the ball and chain." The hand of justice evidently was heavy upon us, and the reins of discipline were drawn tight. Increased guard duty also came. There were details for provost marshal's guard, for brigade headquarter guard, fortification guard, special duty; patrols, which added to our own regimental guard, required daily nearly one-third of our effective strength.

Strange to say, and yet perhaps naturally enough, with the inauguration of this new regime all discontent, if not all grumbling, ceased. There was no more restlessness of inactivity; we were happier, healthier, and we might fairly claim—what was freely accorded to us by staff officers who visited us from time to time—to be the best disciplined, most efficient, and smartest-looking brigade in the service, and a credit to any army, either of the Old or the New World.

CONCLUSION

Towards the end of June and commencement of July, it was noticed in the regiment with what ease long furloughs to visit home and honorable discharges were obtained.[39] An application for either, if made in due form, was almost always certain to be successful. It is true that every discharge was made contingent upon the condition that a substitute should be furnished;

but this condition was in practice a merely nominal one, since a number of applicants was always ready and eager to fill any vacancy in our ranks. Many of these applicants were constantly waiting in Norfolk, courting popularity in the regiment, and watching their opportunity to enter. Admission into our company was specially sought after. It therefore became optional with any of us to continue in the ranks or to leave them. The matter at first created no little surprise, and gave rise to some severe comments, but in course of time came the explanation, and proved that the policy of the Government was wise and farsighted. New levies on a far larger scale were already then in contemplation. The regiments then in the field were drawn from the flower of the Southern youth. Ours, for instance, was composed almost exclusively of men who in any society might claim the rank of gentlemen. These men had had two or three months' practical experience of active service; they had most of them qualified themselves in the school of obedience for the duties of command. The military ambition aroused in them, seconded by their personal and family influence at home, were valuable auxiliaries to the Government in promptly raising to a reasonable standard of efficiency the 300 new regiments which, a month later, were authorized by Congress.

With scarcely an exception, the young men who obtained long furloughs to visit home profited by them to raise companies of their own, which were afterwards tended to the Government; in many cases fully equipped, and even armed, at individual expense. Sometimes two or three combined together to raise a company, dividing among themselves the commands, according to the amount of money or the number of recruits which each had contributed. Battalions, and even whole regiments, were thus formed and organized. As a rule, and unless some special grounds for rejection existed, troops thus raised were accepted by the War Department, and those who tendered them received suitable commissions. Recruiting was easy, and every young man of respectable social position, and a moderate degree of popularity in his town or country, found little difficulty in obtaining the complement of men he required. Father or guardian would furnish the means to feed them until the formal acceptance of the command; for the Government, except where special authorization had been given, allowed neither pay nor rations until the whole regiment, fully organized, was mustered into service and its officers were commissioned. Female relatives would assist the aspirant to military honors with blankets for his recruits, stripped from the family bedsteads, and with clothing made by themselves and their servants. At a later period, and where unusually large means were requisite, the ladies would club together to give amateur entertainments—concerts, masks, and charades—which never failed to yield large proceeds to be devoted to the necessities of this or that newly-formed or forming regiment. It is not, probably, an exaggerated average to estimate that every man of the first levies, relieved from his enlistment, came back into the service with a company. It was thus that, at comparatively little cost to the Confederate Treasury, the 300,000 men called for after the battle of Manassas (Bull Run) were ready to hand as soon as wanted. By a judicious policy, bringing into play individual ambitions, and individual wealth and talents, the Government was saved the expense of a system of recruiting, the delay of drilling raw recruits; and it, moreover, accomplished that most difficult of all tasks with a suddenly improvised army—securing a respectable social status and military proficiency in the distribution of the subaltern commissions. Comparatively few of the officers in the present Confederate armies, who are not graduates of a military college, received their appointments before they had served some time at least in the ranks.

At first, before we understood the secret motives which prompted the policy of easy discharges, we were little disposed to take advantage of it. Many disdained commissions and claimed that the place of honor was in the ranks. All felt that we had no right to wantonly absolve ourselves from a solemn obligation into which we had voluntarily entered; all dreaded the judgment of public opinion at home. At first one or two in the regiment, who had families dependent upon them, went home, allowing unmarried brothers to take their places. The scramble for commissions, however, did not commence until our general gave us, as it were, the signal. In organizing his staff, he made his selections, with one exception, from the rank and file. Our company supplied him an assistant adjutant-general and two aides-de-camp; the rest of the regiment a brigadier-quartermaster and a number of minor staff *employees.* These sudden promotions spread the taste for military titles. It was not in human nature to see the messmate of today, on the morrow gallop into camp on a handsome charger, giving orders, without desiring to follow in the same rapid path of promotion. Three months after the period of which I write our mess of twelve had only three of the original members left; and these could not be tempted by gold lace. The company—still numbering its old effective strength—had furnished to the army one major, five captains of infantry, one of artillery, one of cavalry—in all, forty-three commissioned officers. It is only fair to those who thus exchanged the musket for the sword to say, that youthful ambition, though a strong, was not the strongest, motive for the exchange. The mere garrisoning of a fortified place without prospect of meeting the foe, had become distasteful to them, and they longed to seek danger and win glory on more exciting fields. All of them found the danger they sought, and most of them have purchased the glory with their lives. Nor were the comrades they left behind destined to spend their lives in inglorious inactivity, or felling trees, "grubbing" stumps, ditching, and fascine-making. In the battles before Richmond no regiment earned a more enduring fame than the 3rd Alabama Volunteers. They have been repeatedly decimated; they have lost seven-eighths of their effective strength; yet they have never broken, never faltered, never for a moment lost their regimental organization even in the deadliest of the fight.

My notes are now drawing to a close. The full details of the battle at Manassas reached us on the 23rd of July, exactly three months after we had left Mobile for the war. A court-martial was in session at the time at our brigade headquarters. An unfortunate member of a North Carolina regiment was being tried for sleeping on post. The proceedings were suspended, and when the Recorder had read the details of the great victory, the President rose and said, "Oh this day no Confederate soldier shall be tried for his life. The Judge-Advocate will withdraw the charge. The Court is adjourned." At the same time a civil tribunal was in session at Norfolk to try some soldiers for a broil in the streets. There also the proceedings were suspended, to allow the reading of the news. The State Attorney entered a *nolle prosequi*.[40] The disputants shook hands. Everybody shook hands. The commanders of the corps between which feuds had obtained, made mutual apologies. Alabamians and North Carolinians and Virginians pledged each other to everlasting friendship, and to stand by each other like brothers in defense of the sacred cause. From that day, I believe no silly State feuds or rivalries ever disturbed the friendly goodwill among the Confederates from the wild Southwest, from the cities of the Gulf, and from the older States of the Atlantic seaboard.

My military experiences did not end with the date of the battle of Manassas; but from that date I ceased to shoulder the musket as a private in the ranks.[41] The object of these rude sketches has been to throw some light upon the formation of our first armies. With the period at which these sketches end, begins a new system of military organization on a far larger, but less interesting scale. The efficiency of that system requires no illustration from my pen, it is illumined by the lurid glare of many a well-fought battle in the East, in the West, in the North, and in the South, of the new-born Confederate Republic.

The CADET *Letters to the* Mobile Register[42]

CAMP, THIRD ALABAMA VOLUNTEER REGIMENT.
NEAR NORFOLK

May 29, 1861

It will be gratifying to our friends at home to know how comfortably situated we are. To say that we *are* comfortable may not perhaps convey a strictly correct idea, but we *feel* so, which amounts to the same thing. Comfort, like all others, is a relative term, and Providence has blessed man with a power of adapting himself to circumstances, to cultivate which is the great secret of human happiness. We, for instance, had been so long camping in old cornfields, without verdure or shade, that we have come to regard pine trees as the most luxurious of shelters and their straw the most delightful of beds. If at home we were compelled to sleep twelve in a narrow room, it would appear as intolerable hardship, but here we lie, twelve of us, closely wedged together, and legs dove-tailed, in a space of twelve by fifteen, quite contented, if we ever kick the extremities of our antipodes into comparative quiet. And when, in a twenty-four hours' tour of duty, we pace our night watches, perhaps in rain, wind, and cold, we think of the sleepers in that crowded space with envy. Thus, by contrast, hardships become comforts, and absolute necessaries, luxuries.

In truth, however, we have everything that supplies the natural wants of man, as the good health of our regiment so sufficiently attests. Provisions are abundant. We have tolerably good water, both from springs and wells, and we have excellent salt water bathing at our very doors. Nothing can be more picturesque than this city of tents, its streets and broad avenues, its throngs of negro cooks, hucksters, and laundresses, strikingly contrasting with the

martial sounds and sights everywhere, companies and squads drilling, sentinels walking their posts, groups of loungers, police squads busy with hoe and
shovel, and pick-axe and spade. The whole space covered by the camp had to
be cleared with our own hands, and while I write I hear the ring of axes, just
felling the last trees and grubbing the stumps on our parade ground, which
extends two hundred yards in width along the whole front of the camp. The
"boys" rather like this work, new to most of them, but candor compels the
admission that the country companies, if not commencing their tasks with
the same frolicsome enthusiasm, usually perform it more steadily and do it
better than we city soldiers.

The discipline is excellent, the camp being under the strict military rules
of war. No soldier is allowed to pass the chain of sentries which closely
girdles the camp, without permission from his immediate commanding officer, countersigned by the officer of the guard, and these permits are given
to only three of each company in any one day. Even then, they are never extended except for special reasons, to an absence over night, so that few of us
have slept more than once or twice, if at all, in what the civilized world calls
a bed since we left home. I myself tried the experiment and found that this
much boasted luxury of civilization is a humbug, a plank, if one knows how
to distinguish the "soft side," being decidedly more conducive to sleep, and
after some practice, the bare ground with an extra blanket (or in wet weather
an oil-cloth cloak) spread thereon, being still better. I have also found that a
knapsack, judiciously packed, makes a capital pillow. In all such matters, the
enjoyment depends on knowing how to make them, and I assure you that I
have felt more convenience from a cross pole laid upon two forked sticks in-
side the wall of the tent than from the most sumptuous wardrobe and toilet
table that ever was at my service. In addition to this convenience, a few feet
of lumber, bought at any place where we are likely to remain a few days, become, under our ingenious hands, musket racks, benches and tables. Truly,
"man wants but little here below."[43]

The only real inconvenience, a small one indeed, for sometime was the
want of a place for writing. My handwriting, never remarkable for its beauty,
has consequently not improved either in that or in legibility, as I have painful evidence in the strange perversions the types make of what little sense
I can squeeze into my sentences under the circumstances. The same letter,
about which I found it necessary to write you a special correction, contained
other errors equally annoying.[44] The same types which, by substitution of
the word "equals" for "excels" made me appear guilty of arrogance and bad

taste, that I would not have pardoned in another and never dreamed of myself, converted an allusion to the weather into a reflection on an officer in command, and that by printing *unreasonable* where *unseasonable* had been written.

Of a more ludicrous character, though equally puzzling to those who think well enough of the writer to believe that he means sense, was that blundering precision by which *few* professors of total abstinence were stated as *five* in number. Much speculation has been excited in camp who the *five* were. I do not profess to have such statistical information. Do not imagine that it is a wounded *amour propre*[45] which causes me again to refer to this subject. Had the typographical errors, to only a few of which have I alluded, been only of the ridiculous order, I should have laughed and said nothing about it. But by strange fatality they were, at least one of them, precisely of a nature to disturb the good feeling that existed among the different companies of the regiment. Ignorantly and, perhaps, in some cases malignantly circulated as intentional, the matter has created an impression the extent of which amazes me. There are probably several hundred in this regiment who, hearing only an oral version and never have seen the delinquent paragraphs, who honestly believe that I have published that there are no gentlemen here except the Cadets, and that such is the spirit and feeling which animates the company to which I belong.

CADET

ENTRENCHED CAMP, NEAR NORFOLK

May 30, 1861[46]

Ere this letter can reach you, the Confederate States will have assumed control of the mail service, a change which I should have gladly seen sooner. Thus disappears the last trace of the role of a Government which has become our deadliest enemy. I had hoped that before Abe Lincoln could give full effect to his blockading scheme, arrangements might be perfected to continue our connection with Europe by what has always been the natural and most direct route for the extreme South, namely, by way of the West Indies. There are at least five regular Spanish and English mail steamers during the month from Cuba and St. Thomas, besides those which sail in the intervals between the regular days. In default of any postal treaties with these Governments, mail agents traveling as passengers, or stationed at various points of departure of European steamers, might temporarily serve the purpose. I do not believe that the most rigid blockade could effectively obstruct the operation of such arrangement, and an uninterrupted communication with the Old World is more important to us the longer the war continues.

That the war will be a long one, purposely by the Northern Government, appears from many indications to be the opinion of those in authority. The opinion has in its favor the presumption that the North can scarcely expect by force of arms to conquer a country equal in territorial expanse but little inferior in available population, and that therefore the probable plan of the enemy is to harass us by innumerable feints, to vex and exhaust us by blockades and to force us to keep large bodies of troops constantly on foot. That such a policy is the only one which affords even the slimmest chance of partial success, I can readily conceive, but will it be left to the enemy to follow the policy of their own selection? From our point of view, here in camp, this seems incredible.

What we earnestly desire, we readily believe, says the Latin Proverb, and thus it is the confident expectation of the troops here, that our military authorities will soon assume the offensive, if the enemy do not soon attack us. It is the well nigh unanimous opinion, that in such a case we have everything to gain and but little to lose. Our people are better suited for rapid and brilliant exploits, than for a Fabian policy of cautious moves on the military chessboard.[47] A few victories would make the Southern Republic that "*fait accompli*" in the eyes of the world which would warrant and indeed compel the European powers to step in as authoritative mediators. A defeat would only spur us to greater exertions and be soon wiped out with Northern blood. The troops against whom we are opposed are, for the most part volunteers like ourselves with less natural adaptability for the use of arms than we, and over whom we have, moreover, the advantage of immense moral superiority. They need time to make them soldiers, we are soldiers already. The class to which they belong is not missed at home. We cannot easily be spared for the field. Such is the temper of our volunteer armies that, were the word given today to march Northward, we would drive ten times our number before us like chaff before the wind, and never stop until Maryland was free and Philadelphia a hostage. With our advanced guard in Harrisburg and our headquarters in the city of Penn, we might dictate a peace. Awaiting the enemy on our soil, no matter how skillful the combination which entices him to destruction, we lose many of the advantages which result from the genius of our people and the character of our armies.

In these speculations I simply reproduce the opinions or rather the hopes most prevalent among us. To those hopes the removal of the Capital to Richmond has given additional probability. This removal can scarcely be intended as permanent, and it is supposed to have for its principal reason to facilitate the assumption of offensive operations at the first favorable opportunity. Be this as it may, there were never troops since the days of the first Napoleon who had a more implicit and unwavering trust in the skill and fortunes of their commanders. A hundred reverses could not abate this confidence, which amounts to devotion, and it is bestowed not only upon the President, who is regarded as the guardian spirit of the Republic, but upon all whom he honors with his confidence. Here is another element of success which has seldom failed in the history of warfare.

The health of our Regiment continues excellent, and we are daily making ourselves more comfortable as far as circumstances will permit. As the discipline becomes still stricter, our hopes of a speedy engagement with the enemy increases and we submit with buoyant spirits. The entrenchment is rapidly approaching to completion. Some six hundred negroes, mostly railroad hands accustomed to similar work, and under their own overseers, being constantly employed on them. Should it become necessary, four thousand strong arms more used to the rifle and the minnie than the spade, are ready to take up the less familiar weapons.

I cannot conclude this letter, which like most of its predecessors is forced to a premature close by other duties, without acknowledging the numerous tokens of friendly recollections which we have received from Mobile since reaching here. Most especially did your correspondent and his messmates enjoy a luxury for which we were indebted to Mr. Theo Guesnard, in the shape of several boxes of excellent Conchas, the equal of which we have seldom smoked, even in Mobile where good cigars are plenty.[48] Here, where none are to be procured, either for love or money, and where, in fact, a good cigar is worth ten times its weight in gold, it becomes an act of disinterested friendship and heroic self-sacrifice in the happy possessor to offer one, and the height of epicurean luxury to smoke it. Those of us that ever get back to Mobile will not forget Mr. Guesnard, and I shall have an additional reason for gratitude for thanks to his very acceptable present. My mess have almost forgiven me for publishing in the *Register* among the names of the messes, the jesting surname which was once jokingly given it. More anon.

CADET

ENTRENCHED CAMP, NEAR NORFOLK

June 5, 1861[49]

This morning occurred another of those sharp cannonades in the outer harbor, to which our ears have now become so accustomed, that the heavy roll of the broadsides scarcely elicits a passing remark. This time it was the *Harriet Lane* which ventured too near to the battery on Pig's Point (one of the mouths of the James River), and after receiving several shots, was compelled to beat a precipitate retreat. This much we learn by signals; whether anyone on our side is hurt, I cannot ascertain until the arrival of the courier. As I write, the report of heavy guns is again heard, but the intervals are too long to make it likely that the engagement has been renewed.

Nothing can be more perfect than the system of signals by which communication is maintained with all of the principal points of defense, and by means of which the slightest movements of the enemy, whether by day or night, are known at headquarters with more than electric rapidity. I was an ocular witness of the efficiency of the system the other night, happening to be, at a late hour, at the General's headquarters, where the principal officers of the Adjutant General's Department sleep, so, as to be ready at a moment's warning.[50] It was a rainy, stormy night, the very night for a surprise attack, and just such a night when the magnetic telegraph would have been useless. A party of us was sitting chatting about the war and incidental topics, when a flash of what seemed to be red lightning, but which none of us for an instant mistook, passed through the window. In a moment, the Chief Inspector of the signals, Capt. Milligan, was at his post, and two minutes later, we knew that "an armed schooner is passing up the James River," and resumed our pipes and conversation. Had the information portended mischief, every regiment and post within fifteen miles of Norfolk would have known it almost as soon as ourselves, and been ready for action.

I forget whether I told you that Colonel Seibel's Division has been increased by another regiment, the Second North Carolina Regiment of Volunteers, commanded by Col. Sol Williams. They number a little over one thousand, and are the hardest, finest looking set of men I almost ever saw, somewhat raw in drill as yet, but just such material as a couple of weeks will transform into the best soldiers that any army had. Their Colonel is quite a young man, scarcely over twenty-six or twenty-seven, a soldier by education and profession, handsome, dashing, and of gallant bearing, just such a man as I should have selected to command such a Regiment. Colonel Withers' Division is now composed of six Regiments (his own being the first, the other four from Virginia), one Battalion of Georgia Volunteers, under command of Maj. [Charles] Hardeman, besides several detached cavalry and artillery companies, the former performing vidette and scout duties, the latter manning the various batteries along the river and coast. You will be surprised to learn that the Division is officially styled the First Division of Virginia Volunteer Forces, and that therefore we are not yet in the service of the Confederate States properly, but in that of Virginia, a fact which I did not know until quite recently. Several Mobilians serve on Colonel Withers' temporary staff, while acting as Major General. Dan B. Huger of the Mobile Cadets acts as Aide-de-Camp, Mr. Henry Hotze, of the same company, acts as assistant to the Adjutant General of the Division, Major [Allred] Cummings, C.S.A. Mr. John W. Gooden, of the Mobile Rifles, acts as Quartermaster General of the division with Mr. W. B. Hamilton (also of the Cadets) as Assistant. Dr. D. D. Childs (of the Rifles) acts as Surgeon of the laboring forces employed in the entrenchment, now consisting of some six or seven hundred negroes under competent overseers and superintendents.

A prominent topic of camp conversation now is the election of a successor to Colonel Withers, as it is thought improbable that he will much longer continue to discharge the onerous duties of a higher grade without the rank and emoluments pertaining thereto, though it is known that he considers himself under a self-imposed obligation not to leave the Regiment which elected him. Besides, there is a pretty general impression that the Regiment, derived, I suppose, from home letters, that he will probably be called to the gubernatorial chair by the August election. At all events, pubic opinion in camp has gradually become familiarized with the idea of a successor to him and has, I think, with almost unanimity settled upon Lieut. Col. Lomax who now commands, and with but little interruption has since its formation commanded the Regiment and has won golden opinions among officers and men. He will, no doubt, be the next colonel of the Third Alabama Regiment.

The trial of Hunt, of the Mobile Gulf City Guards, the unfortunate sentry who shot Lieut. Storrs, came off yesterday and ended in his acquittal. There is but one opinion as to the dignity and fairness with which the trial was conducted. It has left on every mind a most favorable impression of the Virginia courts of justice and has convinced the most skeptical of the innocence of the accused. The principal testimony and that which saved Hunt's life, or at least his liberty, was the testimony of Mr. Harry Deas of the Mobile Cadets, who proved by conclusive experiment against numerous assertations to the contrary that guns such as the accused had, and his in particular, would, under certain circumstances, such as those in the case before the court, go off at half cock. Although the worst that could be charged on the unfortunate man was carelessness in the use of his weapon, or imperfect knowledge of his duties as a sentinel, the misfortune that befell him would make his stay in the Regiment almost impossible, and for this reason I understand that Capt. Hartwell has procured his free discharge.

Just as I mail my letter, the particulars of the engagement at Pig's Point reach me. The vessel is the *Water Witch,* not the *Harriet Lane,* as first reported. She fired seventy-six shots and was replied to by twenty-seven, three of which inflicted serious injury to her hull, and compelled her retreat. The Louisiana Regiment have received orders to hold themselves in readiness to march to Pig's Point at the first signal. Pig's Point is nearly opposite to Newport News, where the enemy is forming an entrenched camp.

CADET

NORFOLK, VA.

June 17, 1861[51]

Probably before this reaches you, the news of the great battle will have spread over the wires. Such at least is the general expectation here, based upon the evacuation of Harper's Ferry, a movement which public opinion explains with singular unanimity, and I hope correctly. It is thought that the whole of our troops lately concentrated there will be thrown upon the Western division of the Federal army which has to assail us in the flank and rear, and thus a force which might have been too powerful for us to cope with, will be annihilated in detail. I have heard military men say that Scott committed a fatal blunder in dividing his forces where a concentrated attack alone could have afforded a chance of success, and that he has fallen into a trap set for him by President Jefferson Davis and his Generals.[52]

While we thus confidently expect to hear of a brilliant and decisive victory in the Northwest, we have almost abandoned the hope of having a showing ourselves. As every setting sun beholds our position stronger than the day before, we feel more and more like that Mississippian at Fort Morgan who expressed his disgust at guard mounting, "because," said he, "I came here to fight Yankees, and here you are putting sentinels to keep them off." We begin to think that we have taken so much trouble "to keep them off" that they have lost the notion of coming at all. Certainly, our field and harbor defenses present a most formidable appearance and, to my inexperienced eye, look impregnable if held by even a small body of resolute men. Our entrenched camp, which protects the land approach to Norfolk, is one of the most magnificent sights I have ever beheld. The redans and lunettes, the high parapet and the deep broad ditch seem designed rather as a permanent fortification than as a temporary work of defense. Many hundred negro laborers are still daily employed in further strengthening and improving it. In addition, two companies of the Alabama Regiment each day take their turn in making fascines. These fascines are bundles ten feet long and eight inches in diameter, made of thin twigs and branches and tightly compressed bands of tarred rope or twine, and sawed off even at the ends. To make the fascines, the twigs (none of which must be more than an inch thick at the most) are laid on wood sawyer's "horses" placed in a row. When the proper quantity for a fascine is thus laid, they are compressed to the requisite size by a single application of lever power. The tying process is not unlike that of cotton bales in a cotton press. Our Cadets, being company A of the regiment, had of course the first trial at faggot-making,[53] and though they spent the greater part of the first day in learning how and in preparing needful appliances, they turned out forty-five that day, and a full hundred (with a few thrown in for good measure) on the next. Since then, the different companies have not probably averaged less than one fascine a day to each man. So, you see, the "boys" know how to work. Indeed, it would have delighted the hearts of many a Mobile father, or mother, or sister to see their sons and brothers, reared in wealth and ease, how zealously and cheerfully and handily they set themselves to their rougher duties of a soldier's life. Combining the ready intelligence of educated men with the strength and endurance of laborers, our volunteers are surely the most remarkable body of soldiers the world has ever seen, easily lured to hardship, self reliant, cheerful, and ever efficient in whatever duty may devolve upon them.

The general health of our regiment still continues surprisingly good. The number of deaths since the formation (only three, none of which are of Mobilians), is not much greater than might be expected of the number of men engaged in their peaceful pursuits at home. It is a noticeable fact, that to the regimental sick list the city companies contribute greatly less than the country companies, and this has been the invariable rule during the campaign thus far. My company has been peculiarly fortunate in this particular, the Cadets having invariably presented the smallest number of sick, though the largest company in the regiment. The Rifles have been equally fortunate. The Guards and the Infantry have at times suffered a little more, but never seriously nor to the extent of most of the companies of the country. I believe similar observations as to the relative health of volunteers from cities or from rural districts have been made in the Mexican War. If the fact is generally established, I should like to see it explained.

Since the beginning of this letter I am informed that Private Drisch of the Washington Light Infantry was discovered this morning in the wood near the camp, seriously though not dangerously wounded in both thighs by a pistol ball. A duel is supposed to be the cause, but the wounded man, in a spirit of chivalrous honor that all true men will appreciate, has refused to give any explanation whatsoever, which might possibly implicate someone else in a violation of the articles of war, and the whole matter will probably remain in impenetrable secrecy. No fears are entertained of his recovery and all who attend him speak with admiration of the heroic fortitude and patience with which he endures his suffering.

Last Sunday several shells were thrown near the Georgia camp at Sewell's Point, from Port Calhoun or "Rip Raps," a little over three miles off. Nobody was hurt and the shells scarcely excited attention, so completely have our men learned to despise the amazingly ineffectual fire of the Federals. The gun from which so long a range is obtained, and as appears with tolerable precision, is the "Sawyer Gun," an intricate and complicated invention which had been previously tested and condemned by a U.S. Board of Ordinance of which Brig. Gen. (then Colonel) Huger, who commands the forces in Norfolk Harbor, was president.[54] He laughs at the idea of this long ranged gun doing us any harm, though he thinks it admirably suited to the courage of those that use it. It can be fired only once in fifteen minutes, gets out of order after a very few fires, and is so intricate that none but the inventor can manage it at all. I have seen one of the shells which differs not greatly from the conical shell (with leaden coat and percussion caps) used by us in our rifled cannon.

I am still enjoying the treat of reading Northern accounts of the Bethel Church battle. My historical information is insufficient to supply me with a parallel to such a disgraceful defeat. Think of one regiment firing at another (their own friends) nine rounds, making nine thousand shots, besides artillery, at 150 yards, and killing with all this shooting but one man and wounding five—six shots telling out of nine thousand. Then think of Regiment

No. 2 running away in fright, having one man killed and five wounded! Yet such was the great victory of the Dutch over the Albanians. Think, also, how completely these Northerners show the leaders to have lost their heads, and with what terror-stricken exaggeration they speak of our strength and our fire. I know positively that we had but six pieces of artillery, five of which could not come into play until after the battle had been some time in progress, and but twelve hundred men all told, one-third of whom were disappointed in having a shot at the enemy. Since the world began I do not believe that such monstrous inaptitude on the part of commanders, and such cowardice on the part of the men, has ever scandalized a nation. The official reports of the Bombastes Furioso Butler himself, shows that he had five regiments and a reserve of two more, making between five and seven thousand men he sent against twelve hundred.[55] But the richest of the whole of this abortive attempt to gloss over the disgrace is the consolatory remark with which it was concluded, that "the engagement has proved that the rebels dare not meet us (the Yankees) on the open field." Their papers say that he, this hero of Bethel Church, "the right man for the right place," as the New York *Herald* most felicitously calls him—speaking the truth for once, though unintentionally—is preparing a grand expedition against Norfolk, in which he hopes to recover a reputation which he never had. I pray to Heaven, and wish from my inmost heart, that he will make such an attempt, but it is too good to hope for. So thoroughly have we frightened him, that his men sleep under arms even behind the walls of Fortress Monroe. So say correspondents of the United States papers.

Miss Evans of Mobile is still here, and so are most of the Mobilians whose presence here I have announced. Today, Hon. Howell Cobb pays us a visit, going to Sewell's Point and other parts of the Harbor. Jonce Hooper, the Secretary of the [Confederate] Congress, was also here on a flying visit a few days ago.[56]

For the first time among our troops was there such expectation of speedy peace as now prevails, and visitors from other places inform us that the same impression prevails elsewhere. It is thought that at least one great battle will be fought before the end of the month, and that this will suffice to convince the United States Congress, which meets on the 4th prox., of the hopelessness of the war. So may it be, if only the Third Alabama Regiment has a chance of proving their mettle before the peace is made.

CADET

NORFOLK, VA.

June 25, 1861[57]

Never since we left Alabama, has our camp been so devoid of incident of excitement as at the present moment. Dullness has reigned with undisputed sway for the last week or ten days. When I last wrote you we were in confident expectation of soon hearing of the destruction of McClellan's command by Gen. Johnson. It seems, however, that the Federals received timely notice of the trap set for them, and modified their plans accordingly. Certain it is that orders from Washington countermanding the advance, already commenced, were issued the same day that Harper's Ferry was evacuated, and several regiments which had already crossed the [Potomac] River, were at once recalled. We are still in hopes that a decisive blow may be struck before the meeting of the Washington Congress, so as to give strength to the peace party which, it is now ascertained, is likely to be more numerous than was at first expected. Monster petitions are being signed in the cities of the East which were lately so pugnacious in their temper, in favor of a speedy termination of the war, and the Representatives of these localities, always quick to catch the popular breeze, will not likely be untrue to their weathercock tactics in this instance. A similar healthy reaction, a partial return to common sense, is also manifested among the rural populations of the West. Newspapers, pretty good indices of public opinion, are declaring one after another, against the war. Resolutions have been introduced and in two cases adopted by State Legislatures, in favor of peace. This is as I expected. The Northern people are too calculating, too practical and money loving to spend their blood and substance in a useless war for a mere idea of sentiment. So long as the prospect of an easy contest deluded them, their martial ardor might rise to a white heat, but when it becomes clear that the certain consequences to the nation will be long years of heavy taxation, and the promised lands to their volunteers, the scanty allowance of six feet by four, the pomp and circumstances of war will lose their charm. Yet it is currently reported that Lincoln's message will be furiously warlike, and call for levies of men and appropriations of millions of dollars that would appall Louis Napoleon and startle the Czar of Russia. So be it. The more exorbitant Lincoln's demands are, the less likely they are to be granted.

To make the dullness here still more dull, the Yankees have stopped firing from their long range guns at "Rip Raps." Their innocuous shells amused our boys and supplied them with mementos of the war for their sweethearts at home. It is currently believed that that gun is "bursted." At least, at the last discharge the report was unusually loud, and the telescope betrayed a tremendous scattering among the enemy. Would it not be singularly appropriate if this vaunted invention, by which Sewell's Point was to be reduced from the safe and convenient distance of three and a half miles, had hurt only those that used it? One of the last exploits of the great gun was to fire at a party of ladies walking over the beach! Afterwards, it was announced in the Northern papers that a flag of truce had been hoisted near our batteries. Of course, nobody ever saw or heard of that flag, but it is known that one of the ladies (I believe Miss Augusta Evans, of our city, the gifted authoress of *Beulah*) immediately after the shot passed over the heads of the party waved a white handkerchief in triumph and derision at the cowardly foe.[58]

A few days since, two men deserted from Major Hardeman's battalion of Georgia Volunteers, now stationed near Sewell's Point Battery. They had received leave to go fishing in a little row boat, and after getting some distance from shore, they compelled the negro who rowed them to take them over to the [USS] *Cumberland.* The commander of that vessel sent back the negro and the boat with a note stating that the negro had acted under compulsion, and that the two white men, having expressed a desire to go North, he could not but accommodate them. The names of the renegades are A. C. Kimball and one Hemstead, both Northerners, and who had held at their last place of residence sufficiently respectable positions to gain admission to the Macon Volunteers, one of the finest companies in the Confederate service, and one in which two sons of Hon. Howell Cobb serve as privates. Neither of them had lived more than a few months in the South, but by their profession of excessive zeal they imposed upon the credulity of a trusting community. One was a clerk, the other the agent of a roof-slate company. I forbear comment, as the lesson which the incident teaches must be patent to all. It is needless to say that the places of the two scoundrels were filled the same day by two good and true Southern soldiers.

Besides the mortification felt by a body of chivalrous gentlemen, it having unwittingly harbored two such traitors in their midst, it was feared at one time that the desertions might have serious consequence. The camp to which they belonged has been moved so that the enemy could not discover the precise location, and therefore out of harm of the shells from "Rip Raps." The deserters either had not sense enough to betray a valuable secret, or the enemy was slow to act upon it, at all events such dispositions have since been made that their discoveries will be utterly useless. But look out for lies when they get among the newspaper men of the sensational Northern press.

A few days ago the Express brought me a mysterious package which, on being opened, was found to contain five boxes of choice cigars of the "Southern Confederacy" brand, manufactured and imported for Bagur Brothers of Mobile.[59] I and my friends remained ignorant until yesterday, to whom we were indebted for this most liberal and acceptable present, especially as it is but a short time since that I had to acknowledge a similar favor from Mr. Theo. Guesnard. Yesterday, however, I learned through a belated letter that my thanks were due to my clever friends on the corner of Royal and Dauphin, whose names I have already mentioned as the importers of this new and excellent brand. Some of the sharers of the gift advised me to send one box of the "Southern Confederacy" to *B*ethel *F*ailure Butler (for that is what his initials stand for) as a particularly appropriate and suggestive courtesy, but good cigars are too scarce here to indulge in such pastimes. In fact, we are wholly dependent for our smoking (except that of pipes) on our friends in Mobile, thanks to whom most of us manage, at least, to keep up the recollections of the flavor of a "Havana."

Later.—The big gun is alive again. Just as I was going to close, the report reached me that they have fired fifteen shots from "Rip Raps" at Sewell's Point Battery. All but two fell short, one shell bursting either in the muzzle or immediately on leaving it, the others fell without bursting, at distances varying from one and a half to three miles into the water. Of the two that reached the shore, one fell without bursting; the other buried itself three feet in the ground and then exploded, tearing up a large amount of earth. As before, nobody was hurt. The firing was at intervals of about twenty minutes. Our men look upon it as glorious fun, and curse the Yankees when a day passes by without one of these pyrotechnic exhibitions to which they have got to think themselves entitled as a slight compensation for the dullness of camp life.

CADET

ENTRENCHED CAMP, NEAR NORFOLK,

July 1, 1861[60]

After a dead calm of several weeks we are again thankful for a breath of excitement to ripple the surface of that ocean of dullness in which we have been submerged. There are weather signs of a gathering storm which we hail with indescribable delight, but whether, as in so many similar instances, the signs will once more disappoint us, is not my ken to say. Foremost among these signs is the fact that the Third Alabama Regiment is to be moved within the present week to a place some eight or nine miles from our present camp. As the order has not yet been issued and may not before this letter reaches you, I deem it imprudent to make public anything concerning our next destination, although everybody here is perfectly informed of it. Suffice it to say that our friends may write to us as heretofore with the certainty that their letters, in due course of mail, will reach us. The headquarters of the division to which we belong, hitherto located in the city, was today moved within the lines of our Entrenched Camp, behind which the various regiments composing the defense have now taken position.

Mrs. [Charles] Forsyth, the wife of our popular Adjutant, who for several weeks has graced the Alabama Camp with her presence, has returned to the city, and several other ladies, wives of officers of various regiments, who were residing in neighboring farm houses, have been or are about to follow her example. These things and others which I cannot detail, are construed, whether rightly or not, into indications that General Huger and Colonel Withers have received important information from the enemy, and that something or other is on foot. I devoutly hope it may be so, for we are literally in the Irishman's predicament—"*spoiling* for a fight."

Yesterday was the first periodical muster for the payment of the forces here. The disbursement will not be made for several days, and according to my calculations, the amount provided for the purpose will hardly suffice for more than two thirds of the pay due us. I do not of course set up my own calculations against those of the Confederate Treasury and the War Department, but mention the matter simply to introduce an idea which I have often revolved in my mind, and which has been well received wherever I have mentioned it. Our volunteer armies have that exceptional feature from nearly all other armies ever raised, that they are largely composed of those who represent not only the intelligence but the wealth of the country. There are thousands in the ranks who neither need nor desire the small pittance to which they are entitled as private soldiers, and there is not a man in our armies who, if he can afford it, would not take a special pride to fight for his country without pay. Now my idea is, that on each pay day every man should be allowed the choice to receive the amount due him in cash or to let it stand to his credit. Whoever might prefer the latter alternative should receive when discharged, or in the case of death his assignees for him, a bond or warrant of the Confederate States for the whole amount due him, made in his own name, and stating the nature of the service for which such amount is due. Not only would a large proportion prefer their pay in this form, but few of these "soldiers" bonds would ever be tendered for redemption, but they would be handed down as precious heirlooms and mementos of the great Revolution of '61 to the remotest generations.[61] It would require special legislation, and occasion some trouble in the Treasury Department to issue bonds or warrants of this character, but it would save millions of dollars without injustice or even inconvenience to individuals. Bonds of ordinary character would not effect the object I have in view, they should be payable only to the person named therein, or his lawful representatives, and they should specify the date of his entering into service, and the date of his discharge, as well as the capacity in which he served.

It is my melancholy duty to record the first death of a Mobilian since we all left home. Mr. A. Hooks of the Gulf City Guards, after a lingering illness, died yesterday of typhoid fever at the Hospital of the Sisters of Charity. He was a young man greatly beloved and esteemed, not only in his company, but in the whole Regiment, and his death is deeply regretted. It may be some consolation to his friends at home to know that during his illness he received every attention and had every comfort that home itself could have given him.

CADET

ENTRENCHED CAMP, NEAR NORFOLK

July 13, 1861[62]

Yesterday, Colonel Jones M. Withers received his commission as Brigadier General in the Confederate Army. The appointment has been long expected by everybody, and gives general satisfaction. Colonel Withers, as you know, has been here almost since our arrival here, in command of a whole division of the troops stationed on the Norfolk side of the Elizabeth River.

Almost simultaneously with his appointment, the official designation of the command, heretofore styled the First Division of Virginia Volunteer Forces, has been changed to the Second Brigade of Virginia Volunteers. As no other change but that of name is made, I am inclined to think that General Withers will be continued in his command, perhaps with the addition of another Alabama regiment. The appointment may be looked upon as a somewhat tardy recognition, not only of individual claims (General Withers being the highest in rank in the Mexican War of all the officers now in the service of the Confederate States), but also of the State of Alabama, which now has nine full regiments in the field outside of her own limits, without heretofore a single general officer.

It gives me sincere gratification to announce at the same time the promotion of two other Mobilians, Dan E. Huger, Esq., as Major in the Army of Virginia (now turned over to the Confederate States) and D. J. Withers as Aide-de-camp to the Governor of Virginia, with the rank of Lieutenant of Cavalry. Major Huger, as you know, was educated at a military school, entered the present army as Orderly Sergeant of the Mobile Cadets, was appointed Aide and more recently Acting Assistant Adjutant General to Colonel Withers when the latter took command of a Division, and in all these capacities he has proved himself an efficient, able and popular officer. He will at once be assigned to active duty with one of the Virginia Regiments.

The appointment of General Withers leaves the colonelcy of the Third Alabama Regiment vacant. We are uncertain whether the act giving to the President the appointment of field officers of Volunteer Regiments applies to Regiments formed before the passage, and therefore whether there will be an election or an executive appointment. In either case, however, Lieut. Col. [Tennent] Lomax will have no competitor. He is entitled to it according to the line of promotion and by the unanimous vote of the Regiment, which without but little interruption he has commanded since its formation. Amid many difficulties inseparable from an acting or temporary command he has succeeded in winning the hearts of those who in Montgomery were the most opposed to him. As I remarked in a previous letter, he is certain to be the next Colonel of the Third Alabama Regiment.

An unfortunate display occurred yesterday in the main street of Norfolk. Some members of our Regiment became involved in a brawl with some Virginia volunteers, in which, so far as I now know, the latter were mostly if not wholly the blame. Two of the Virginians were severely cut, and one shot, probably fatally, and the row threatened to become general, Virginians and Alabamians rallying from all directions to their respective comrades, when fortunately Major Battle rode up to the scene of action.[63] His order—"All men of the Third Alabama Regiment repair instantly to their camp"—was obeyed without a moment's delay, and as if by magic the strife was quelled.

A more remarkable example of perfection discipline it would be difficult to find.

I must close in haste, having to snatch a few minutes from other duties to write even this much. The health of our regiment, latterly not so good, is again improving. The intention of moving the regiment seems to have been abandoned for the present. Dr. J. C. Nott, accompanied by his family, paid us a visit of a few days, and then left for the Virginia Springs, where he will be ready within a few hours to reach the scene of the first general engagement with the enemy.[64]

CADET

ENTRENCHED CAMP NEAR NORFOLK

August 19, 1861[65]

Your correspondent could not find a better opportunity for breaking his long absence—due to various causes, among which absence and want of leisure are the principle—than by announcing the deserved success of our young and popular Adjutant, Lieut. Charles Forsyth of the Mobile Cadets, who last Saturday was elected Major of the Third Regiment Alabama Volunteers by a large majority. The vote of the first balloting stood: Lieut. Forsyth, 321; Capt. Ready, 138; Capt. Hunter, 131. You have doubtless been informed that at the former election of officers, when Colonel Lomax and Lieut. Col. Battle were chosen, none of the candidates for major, after repeated balloting, received a majority of the votes cast. The contest at that time promised to be warm and protracted, owing to the number of candidates which the declension of Capt. Sands of the Cadets, the senior Captain, had called into the field. (Captain Sands, to the repeated entreaties of his friends to accept the promotion, which he could have done without opposition, is said to have replied that he would rather return as Captain of his company than as Brigadier General.) I was then absent from Norfolk and know little of the workings of regimental politics during that period; but I believe that if Lieutenant Forsyth had himself been present, he being on a visit to his family, he would have been elected at the first election. As it is, the result gives universal satisfaction and leaves neither disappointment nor bitter feelings behind.

While on the subject of promotions, it gives me great pleasure to mention that two other Mobilians Messrs Robert B. Armistead and Henry H. Sengstak, both of the Cadets, have been placed on the staff of Brigadier General Withers as aides-de-camp. Since then, however, Mr. Armistead has received authority from the Secretary of War to raise a Regiment in conjunction with Zack C. Deas, Esq., of which the latter will be Colonel and Mr. Armistead Major. The Lieutenant Colonelcy is said to be destined for an officer of the regular army. As Alabama, despite the honorable sacrifice she has already made, still abounds in good men and true, these gentlemen will have little difficulty in collecting the requisite number of companies. Indeed, several companies are already recruiting for the purpose.

Another Mobilian, well known to the friends of our great road, John W. Goodwin, the talented Assistant Engineer of the Mobile & Ohio Railroad, has just received a commission as Brigade Quartermaster, with the rank and pay of Major. Major Goodwin left Mobile as a Sergeant in the Mobile Rifles, but for several months past has acted on the staff of General Withers in the capacity which is now confirmed by his commission, with a rare zeal and capacity. To him, principally, are we indebted for the admirable location of our splendid entrenchments which have so far kept, and I fear will always keep, the enemy at a safe distance beyond our guns.

I cannot conclude this hasty letter without expressing my surprise that so little—in comparison with other regiments which were not more brave nor more exposed—has been said about our gallant Fourth Alabama Regiment which stood the brunt of the Battle of Manassas and contributed so much to that glorious day. The Fourth Alabama was stationed at the extreme left where the enemy's overwhelming numbers made the attack, and of the four or five regiments which repulsed and delayed for hours that terrible tide, it suffered the most. Losing all its field officers early in the action, and doubly decimated (having twenty-five percent in killed and wounded), not a man left the battlefield, but when regimental and company organization had ceased to exist, continued the right in the ranks of the nearest company and regiment at hand. History has but few parallels to such heroism, and even in the ever memorable Battle of Manassas, but few of the innumerable accounts I have heard from eyewitnesses equaled, and none excelled the deeds of the Alabamians there. When I was in Richmond a few days after the battle, with exceptional facilities for gathering details of every description and from every point of view, the praise of the Fourth Alabama was in every mouth. It was thought the first among its peers of brave men, but the papers, always ready to magnify small things and to nurse small fames, seem to me to have been comparatively silent where there was no room left either to magnify or to exaggerate.

Here in Norfolk, we Alabamians are proud and a little envious of our brethren at Manassas. Envious, if this be the word, because we have despaired of an occasion to emulate them, and to prove that what was expected of us we lack but the opportunity to perform.

CADET

ENTRENCHED CAMP NEAR NORFOLK

August 27, 1861[66]

Of all things that try human patience, to be condemned for months to lie inactively under arms within sight of an enemy and within hearing of his guns, is the worst. It would be intolerable but for the occasional excitement of an alarm which revives the drooping spirits and renews for a time, at least, the hope that had almost died out. Such a godsend we had yesterday. A little before sunset a dispatch from the commander of one of the cavalry companies, stationed on the coast, arrived at General Withers' headquarters, announcing that two large frigates and two Baltimore boats, with barges in tow, were making slowly "at half stroke" towards Pleasure House Beach. The bearer of the dispatch added verbally, as he was leaving the camp, that six more vessels, probably transports, hove in sight.

Instantly the order was sent as fast as horses could carry them to the various regiments, to prepare for a march at a moment's notice, with two days rations and an ample supply of ammunition. The shouts which rose from camp after camp, and which could be heard an astonishing distance off, told when the orders were received. All night the men were on the *qui vive*,[67] expecting every moment to hear the welcome command, and to a late hour the camp fires were kept burning for the cooking of provisions. Meanwhile, however, a second dispatch arrived at headquarters, to the effect that the Yankee fleet had gone to sea again, standing to the south of Cape Henry.

The fact that the fleet was too large for a mere demonstration or a foraging expedition, and the reasonable supposition that the threatened landing was probably a feint to divert our forces from the real point of intended attack, still gives us a pleasant state of expectancy. A fleet such as that signaled off the Pleasure House Beach could carry, considering the short distance from Fortress Monroe, between 8,000 or 10,000 men and several batteries of artillery. You will remember that Wool has taken command at Old Point and he may be deluded with the hope of avenging himself on Scott by contrasting a brilliant descent on Norfolk Navy Yard with the disgraced defeat at Manassas.[68] At least, so we like to believe.

Several circumstances tend to confirm this belief. At Richmond it has been lately the general opinion that an attack would be attempted upon Norfolk. The troops at Old Point have been again considerably reinforced. There are other suspicious indications which have attracted the vigilant attention of our military authorities.

I must now close abruptly to save the mail. If anything occurs, I shall keep you advised as promptly as my opportunities will permit.

CADET

Part Two

"What Prevents the Recognition of the Confederate States?"

THE INDEX

A WEEKLY JOURNAL OF POLITICS, LITERATURE, AND NEWS.

OFFICE:—102, FLEET STREET.

Vol. I.—No. 5.]   LONDON—THURSDAY EVENING, MAY 29, 1862.   [Price 6d.

CONTENTS.

NOTES ON EVENTS OF THE WEEK.

The surrender of Norfolk, the blowing up of the Virginia, the destruction of the Gosport navy yard, and all public property, are events which will not surprise those who understand the Confederate policy of not sacrificing a single patriot by defending untenable positions, and of destroying that which might fall into the hands of the enemy. On the 10th, General Wool, with 5000 men, landed at Willoughby Point. When the Federals had marched to within three miles of the city, they were saluted with a few shotted guns and forthwith fell back, made a long detour, and arrived at the entrenchments at five p.m. The Mayor and Civic Council of Norfolk proposed terms of surrender, to which General Wool assented. Satisfied with this victory, General Wool and his troops watched the destruction of the Virginia, and the Gosport Navy-yard. On the 11th, after ascertaining that the Confederates were really gone, a powerful Federal fleet steamed to Craney Island; and General Wool's troops gallantly took possession of the city. The operations were directed by President Lincoln, assisted by Mr. Secretary Chase. Mr. Stanton was also present, and had a long consultation with General Wool and General Viele—perhaps as to the disposition of the spiked guns. The Mayor avowed the loyalty of the citizens to the Confederate Government. The Federal soldiers could not restrain cheers for President Davis, and groans for President Lincoln. There are graphic accounts of the disgust showed by the women at the sight of the Yankees.

Speculations are rife as to why the Virginia was destroyed without fighting another battle. The destruction of the famous ironsides was imperative, since she could not be moved out of the reach of the enemy. The explanation of her inactivity is, perhaps, that she had no opportunity of punishing the enemy, and the Confederates do not bark unless they have a fair chance of biting.

The Confederates, by latest accounts, were still falling back on Richmond, having destroyed the railroad at West Point. The operations are conducted with the greatest order and success. The Northern telegram says:—" The Confederate retreat is reported to be admirably accomplished; they carry their waggons and provisions in the daytime, and their troops by night, covering their retreat by a line of skirmishers stretched across the country, and driving in their stragglers at the point of the bayonet."

The reports as to the position of M'Clellan's army are rather contradictory. On May 13th, we are told " General M'Clellan's forces have advanced beyond New Kent Courthouse, within twenty-two miles of Richmond." On the 15th, we are informed that "in the night of the 13th a skirmish occurred with the Confederates, who were in their immediate front," and that "General M'Clellan's forces were at Cumberland, Pamunky River, twenty-six miles from Richmond." Are we to assume that the report of the 13th, as to M'Clellan's being within twenty-two miles of Richmond was false, or that, in consequence of the skirmish in the night of the 13th, the Federals had to fall back? By the latest received accounts we learn nothing of M'Clellan's whereabouts, but that "the Confederate and Federal outposts are only 100 rods distant from each other."

The assertion that the Confederates will make a stand at Bottom's Bridge, is a Yankee "guess;" but of this we may be sure, that M'Clellan will not be able to alter the plans of the Confederate leaders, or induce them to give battle at an unnecessary disadvantage.

The Confederates can afford to wait, but not so the Federals. Richmond is not an enemy's country, and the summer is at hand. Already, and as early as the 10th May, 800 invalided and wounded soldiers arrived at New York from Yorktown, by one steamer. Indeed, the invalids are coming in daily, and from all quarters.

Governor Sprague reports the Federal loss at Williamsburg at not less than 2000; but the loss is supposed to have been much heavier. The New Jersey Brigade alone had 563 killed and wounded. The Battle at West Point was a most unmistakable Federal defeat. The Northerners confess to a loss of 500 prisoners, and that the arrival of the gunboats "saved Franklin from suffering severe disaster." The plain English of this is, that Franklin did "suffer severe disaster," was defeated, and but for the arrival of the gunboats, the whole of his troops would have been cut to pieces, or made prisoners. There has been an engagement at Farmington, five miles north-west of Corinth. The Federal brigade, under General Pope, was attacked "by a Confederate corps, and after considerable resistance defeated and driven back. We have not received accounts of the losses on either side, but Mr. Stanton condescends to inform Europe that "the loss of the Federals was considerable." When the truth comes out, we shall find that Pope's brigade was roughly handled and completely routed. According to General Halleck's estimate, General Beauregard has under his command from 120,000 to 170,000 men. We quite understand the nervousness of the Federal Secretary of War in reference to the anticipated battle of Corinth, and give him credit for prudence and foresight, in ordering "that newspaper correspondents shall not be permitted to telegraph any account of the approaching battle at Corinth after it has taken place until the report is first revised by the military censor at Cairo."

On the 14th, General Halleck announced that he "would on that day move his camp four miles to the front. The Federal forces are at an average distance of two and-a-half to three miles from the Confederate entrenchments at Corinth." We presume, if the Federals are within three miles of the Confederate entrenchments, they cannot advance four miles without taking the said entrenchments. It would seem that the Federals think the only use of writing despatches is to produce a jumble and conceal truth. General Pope's defeated troops have been joined to the division under General Mitchell.

The Federals complain, and, we doubt not, with sufficient cause, of the badness of their ground. They cannot advance without meeting corduroy roads and bridges. The ground being in such a state not only impedes the progress of the forces, but is sure to engender a great deal of sickness.

The Charleston Mercury of May 5th, says:—

There is a feeling of perfect certainty of defeating Buell and Halleck in a signal manner. Corinth is far enough from the gunboats to give opportunity for capturing or destroying them. Hence, it has been selected as the battle-field. General and troops are alike confident.

There was a naval engagement on the 10th, above Fort Pillow, on the Mississippi. The first report was from Captain Davis, and stated, "that eight Confederate iron-clad gunboats attacked the Federal flotilla under Commander—.&c. The action lasted one hour. Six Federal vessels were engaged. Two Confederate gunboats were blown up, and one sunk. The Confederates then retreated under the guns of Foote. One Federal vessel was injured." Two days later, we are informed that "Captain Pennock officially reports that, in a naval engagement near Fort Pillow, one Federal gunboat was sunk, and one disabled." It is not impossible, that as Captain Davis ignored the Federal losses, he exaggerated the Confederate losses; and there is every reason to suppose that the Confederates gained the day.

General Butler, despite the "Union sentiment," and the enthusiastic "Union meetings," finds it necessary to rule New Orleans with military despotism. The Mayor and Aldermen have been sent to prison for refusing to take the oath of allegiance. General Butler has proclaimed that :—

The violation of property or persons protected by the Federal army will be punishable with death.

All persons must treat the Federal flag with the utmost deference and respect, under penalty of severe punishment.

The keepers of all public property, whether State, national, or Confederate, must make a return to General Butler's headquarters.

All shops and places of amusement are to be kept open in the accustomed manner, and service is to be held in the churches as in times of profound peace.

The circulation of Confederate notes among the poorer classes will be permitted so long as inconsiderate persons will receive them.

Federal officers will be appointed to examine all editorial newspaper comments and correspondence before its publication will be allowed.

All assemblages in the streets, by day or by night, are forbidden.

An "Apology" to the Tribune[1]

MOBILE DAILY REGISTER

8 May 1860

The *Mobile Tribune* accuses one of the editorial corps of the *Register* of being nothing but a foreigner and therefore having no business with American
politics—not exactly in these words but unmistakably with that meaning.
The offending party humbly pleads guilty to that crime, and deprecating the
Tribune's rigor suggests as extenuating circumstance that even he, in the hot-
test days of Know Nothingism, his great offence was overlooked, in view of
his reprieving his fault as early as practicable after he was born, by coming to
the South, he believes, at a much more youthful age than the *Tribune*'s editor.[2]
Further he suggests that at the age at which the South became his cherished
home, boys are expected to know but little of political science, so that perhaps he did not lose much by not coming earlier, but that he is deeply conscious of his shortcomings and from early boyhood to this moment has devoted the best part of his time and intellect to supply the deficiencies which
the *Tribune* ascribes to his birth. He also pleads that the country of his birth
has a system of confederated government similar, if not identical, to that of
the United States, and if there be any mystic influences in such things, States
Rights and Federal powers were discussed over his cradle as much as that of
the editor. Before the *Tribune* taught him better, he felt it no disability to have
been born of a race that never knew king nor feudal ruler, in the oldest republic in the world, the asylum of the fugitives of all creeds and all ranks on
the Eastern Continent, and the country which has given to the United States
a Gallatin and an Agassiz.[3] If the *Tribune* will pardon him this once, he will
try and never more be guilty of the assumption that has drawn upon his head

this deserved and dignified rebuke; but the Mobile *Register* sends its compliments to the Mobile *Tribune,* and begs to say that a newspaper is an impersonality and that it is neither true dignity nor good policy to penetrate behind that screen to assail or sneer at individuals, especially when no better case can be made out than in the present instance. The *Register* would also remark that in its intercourse with its neighbor and contemporary, it has never indulged in personal allusions, nor, as this temperate reply will prove, exceeded the bounds of editorial decorum; and further, that there are some intimations in the *Tribune*'s article to which the *Register* cannot condescend to reply.

Henry Hotze's Commission

R. M. T. HUNTER[4] TO HOTZE

Richmond, 14 November 1861

SIR: Having appointed you commercial agent of the Confederate States at London, I herewith enclose your commission. You will, with as little delay as possible, proceed to your post, and immediately after your arrival report yourself to our commissioner, the Hon. James M. Mason,[5] to whom you will exhibit your credentials and explain the general purposes of your agency.

You will avail yourself of every opportunity to communicate with this Department, and keep it advised of the tone of the English press and the current of public sentiment with regard to the struggle in which the Confederate States is now engaged; transmitting with appropriate comments such printed extracts from the public journals as you may deem to have an important bearing upon the question. You will be diligent and earnest in your efforts to impress upon the public mind abroad the ability of the Confederate States to maintain their independence, and to this end you will publish whatever information you possess calculated to convey a just idea of their ample resources and vast military strength and to raise their character and Government in general estimation. You will zealously strive to remove any fears that may be entertained abroad as to the reconstruction of the Union, from which we have separated, by showing that such a reconstruction is now impossible, and that it is the universal sentiment of the people of the Confederate States to prosecute the war until their independence shall no longer be assailed. You will keep constantly before the public view in Great Britain, the tyranny of the Lincoln Government, its utter disregard of the personal rights of its citizens, and its other notorious violations of law.

Contrasted with this you can justly and forcibly dwell upon the fact that peace and order have reigned everywhere in the Confederate States and that the laws have been constantly and impartially administered. You will also impress upon the people of Great Britain the importance of the trade which may be established between our respective countries, and assure them of the almost universal opinion in the Confederate States that as few restrictions as possible should be imposed upon that trade and those only for revenue purposes. If you should find it to be expedient, after leaving England you may visit Paris and report yourself to Mr. Slidell,[6] show him your commission and acquaint him with the objects to be accomplished by your agency. So far as these instructions may be found applicable you will, while in France, be governed by them. Much discretion, however, is left to you, and the Department relies for success upon your address and ability. You will herewith receive $750 on account of your salary, which is fixed at $1.500 a year, and $750 to be expended in carrying out these instructions.

I am, sir, etc.,

R. M. T. Hunter

Secretary of State

The "Washington's Birthday" Leader

HOTZE TO R. M. T. HUNTER. NO. 3

London, 23 February 1862.

SIR: I have the honor to enclose my first contribution to the English press, the leading editorial in yesterday's issue of Lord Palmerston's organ, the *Morning Post*.[7] In reading it, you will make due allowances for the necessity under which I felt myself of studiously maintaining an English point of view, and not advancing too far beyond recognized public opinion; and also a little for the timidity of a first step on untried ground. My object was to present that the inauguration of our permanent government should be passed wholly unnoticed by the London press (which otherwise would have been the case), to seize that occasion for a brief recital of the most impressive evidences of the unanimity of our resistance, and especially to point out the novelty and injustice of the theory apparently devised for our special case and unthinkingly repeated by many friendly to us, that a nation must be able to defend itself against all odds before it has a right to call itself a nation; in other words, my object was to forcibly suggest rather than positively assert conclusions in our favor. That I have succeeded satisfactorily in this object is proved by the fact that the article was published without any material alterations, only one or two expressions being somewhat enfeebled.

The result has greatly exceeded my expectations. The fact that the subject was not alluded to by any other journal besides the premier's recognized organ, and the prominence given to the article, rendered even more conspicuous by the simultaneous appearance of another editorial on American affairs, have lent it a significance which it certainly did not derive from any intrinsic merit. I have already learned from various sources that it has produced "a deep impression" in the clubs which are the principal foci of public opinion in the metropolis, and have been amused by having my attention called to it as unmistakably an emanation from Lord Palmerston.

Although this success is due to an accidental combination of fortunate circumstances which I could not have concerted, and of which I was not fully aware even while taking advantage of it, it has nevertheless greatly encouraged me; I confess that the nearer I approached the scene of my labors the more the difficulties of my position loomed up before me, and on arriving here as the advocate of our case through the most fastidious press in the world, a stranger with barely a few friends or introductory letters, with no extensive political or literary reputation to precede me and smooth my way, I felt almost disheartened. Now the most formidable obstacles are overcome. The columns of the journals to which I most desired access are open to me, and with this I have acquired the secret of the "open sesame" of the others I may need. I shall use the privilege moderately, neglecting no opportunity nor seeking to create artificial ones. As a rule I shall abstain from newspaper controversies, which only weary and prejudice the reading public, and shall be sparing of communications, which I find have generally few readers and carry little weight.[8] As an exceptional case I am now preparing, at Mr. Mason's suggestion, a review of the celebration of Washington's Birthday by the Federal sympathizers here, and especially of Mr. Adams's speech on that occasion, in the latter form. As the first-class English journals never accept an editorial without paying for it, usually a fee of from 2 to 10 guineas, I adhere to the plan which I had the honor to communicate to you orally, and which I find quite feasible, of presenting my articles to professional "leader writers," thus conciliating friendly good will where otherwise annoying jealousies might arise.

I remain, with great respect, your obedient servant,
Henry Hotze

MORNING POST [LONDON]

22 February 1862

The 22nd of February is the most revered of American anniversaries, and the only one which continues to be honored by both fragments of the dissevered Union. It is the birthday of Washington, whom Americans still love to call "the Father of his country," though they have long since forgotten the lessons of his example and the spirit of his teachings. This day, thus consecrated to the memory of the founder of the Republic, man's devices have made also the anniversary of the Republic's greatest trial, if not of its total destruction. It is now a little over twelve months since the world heard with some surprise, but more indifference, that representatives from seven of the States of the late American Union had met at an obscure inland town for the purpose of forming a new Union, the old one having been repudiated and solely abjured, through conventions assuming to embody and wield the supreme will and sovereignty of the people of those States. These States were speedily joined by others with the same motive, until the revolution thus initiated extended over nearly one-half of the territory of the United States and thirteen out of the fifteen States which in the vocabulary of American politics, have always been collectively styled "the South." The first step of the Southern delegates was to form a "Provisional Government" under a provisional constitution, which was to remain in force for one year. Their second step, while yet the revolution was an untried experiment—and but few of the States had ventured upon the perilous way—was to frame a "permanent" Government upon the solid basis of a constitution designed to excel the repudiated one in durability, as it did in many other essential features. It is this so-called permanent constitution of the States confederated against the United States that comes into operation this day, according to the program laid down a year ago, and which has so far been carried out in the minutest details despite the exhaustive strain and the fearful uncertainties of a war for existence.[9]

When we consider that this constitution depended for its validity on the ratification of each separate State, many of which States were still loyal to the old Union when it was first proposed; that before coming into effect it had to submit to the crucial test of a multitude of local and general elections, in which universal suffrage might express the prevailing sentiment of the remote rural district as well as of the populous central town; that those ratifications were promptly and unanimously given by the States, and these elections peacefully held with all the formalities of law—when we consider these indisputable facts, it becomes apparent that with the inauguration of the "permanent" Government the Southern revolution acquires an air of solidity and stability of which its leaders will not be slow to avail themselves at home and abroad.

We have before adverted to the extreme difficulty, not to say impossibility, of subduing a people so numerous, and occupying so vast a territory as the Confederates, if such a people is really united in a desperate resistance. That they are so united the whole course of events tends strongly to prove. The revolution seems to have been effected without internal commotion, and the old Government, which was supposed to have so strong a hold upon the affections of the masses, seems to have been shaken off with as much ease and unconcern as a worn-out garment would be by its wearer. Few, if any, of the officers and employees, from the judge of a Federal Circuit to the pettiest village postmaster, seem to have been displaced—a peculiarly significant fact in America, where every change of incumbents of the Presidential chair vacates all offices, great and small. Among the leading men of the new order of things we find few new names, and among these names the adept in the mazes of American politics readily recognizes a fair representation of all former political parties. In consequence, we have heard but little of political arrests or passport annoyances, and nothing of State prisons. So far as we can judge at this distance, the press, usually the first object of revolutionary surveillance, is under fewer restrictions, and more outspoken, than that of the "loyal" States. The numerous levies which the revolution required must necessarily have been drawn mainly from districts most densely peopled with whites, and where, by inference, the slaveholding interest might be supposed to be least deeply rooted. Yet there appears to have been little resort to conscriptions or impressments, and the militia have been called out in a few denuded and suddenly threatened localities. The slaves themselves, upon whom the Federal Government relied as an important element of success, have remained quiescent producers of food for the armies, and in frequent instances accompany their masters to the field, or render useful service as spies on the movements of the enemy. Considering the small accumulated wealth of the South, the voluntary contributions to the revolutionary treasury have been astonishingly large, independent of the fact that the troops of the Confederation have in a great measure been raised, clothed, and even fed by individual patriotism. If these evidences fail to convince the impartial spectator of the unison of feeling with which all classes are said to support the revolution, its leaders may point with some show of force to the additional evidence afforded by the Government this day inaugurated.

It must not be forgotten, also, that a revolutionary Government which has once reached this point possesses many of the advantages, without some of the disadvantages, of an old-established Government. It rallies around it the mass of the timid and hesitating, whose timidity and hesitation are the best pledge of their allegiance. A year is a long period in the history of a people like the Americans, and the Southerners, having maintained their independence for that period, deem it conclusive evidence that they will always be able to maintain it. In the eyes of its citizens, therefore, the new Republic is no longer an experiment, but an established fact. Besides, the Confederates find in the very desperateness of their struggle resources which perhaps they would have sought in vain in a well-filled treasury and amply-stocked arsenals. Such is the nature of this war, that every man's fortune and the solvency of every corporation depend more or less directly on the permanency of the incoming Government, which may thus rely upon more ignoble but less evanescent motives than the popular enthusiasm which sustained its provisional predecessor. What Earl Russell said in the House of Lords a few days since—that "the Government of the United States are engaged in a civil war perhaps one of the most serious and formidable in which any country was ever engaged"—is certainly not less true today, when, with the anniversary of Washington's birth, commences the first regular six years Presidential term of Mr. Jefferson Davis.

It is true that few nations have ever succeeded in creating an independent existence when altogether left to their own resources. Infancy, both of a nation and an individual, needs the fostering care of others to ripen into vigorous life; and in either case the new born Hercules, crushing the serpents in his cradle, finds few analogies. This fostering care in the shape of timely assistance has usually been supplied to nascent nations by the self-interest, the policy, or the ambition of older sisters; and it has seldom been required of the newcomer, as a proof of her right to exist, that she should exhibit the strength of full maturity and be able to defend herself against all assailants. Judged by this test, many would lose the right to live which is now unanimously accorded to them. Had so rigid a rule been applied, the two most memorable national contests of modern times might have had a very different issue. Despite their heroic resolves and deeds, the Netherlands would not probably have triumphed over the then gigantic power of Spain without the moral support of all Protestant Europe, and the "material aid" of men and money from England and Germany.[10] The United States would scarcely date their independence from 1776 had not France and her allies endorsed the declaration of that independence, at first by surreptitious but valuable favors, and ultimately by the whole power of their armies and navies. In each of these cases the help was granted when the cause which asked it seemed most desperate, and therefore most in need of help. In like manner, most men will admit that Italy has not regained her long-lost nationality without incurring a heavy debt of obligations.

The Confederate States have not the benefit of any of those adventitious circumstances by the aid of which other nations have struggled into existence; and if, as does not now appear probable, the unequal conflict ends in their re-conquest by the United States, it will be for that reason. Geographically so situated, that where not blockaded by the enemy's cruisers or confronted by his armies, they are hemmed in by boundless deserts, or by a neighbor poorer than themselves, they are almost wholly excluded from the moral and commercial communication with the rest of the world which their opponents enjoy to the fullest extent, and which a nation at war so imperatively needs. The sympathies of civilized mankind, when not absolutely opposed to them, have at best been but passive in their behalf. Actual assistance, either in money or otherwise, they have wisely forborne even to solicit. Yet, with all these disadvantages, if the Government of the United States should succeed in re-annexing them to its still extensive dominions, Democracy will have achieved its grandest triumph since the world began. It will have demonstrated to the ample satisfaction of its present and future proselytes that it is even more puissant in war than in peace; that it can navigate not only the smooth seas of un-endangered prosperity, but can ride safely through the fiercest tempests that would engulf every other craft laden with human destinies; that it can descend to the darkest depths of adversity, and rise from them all the stronger for the descent. All that for fifty years its worshippers have declaimed and sung would be but dull prose to the paeans which would thenceforth ascend in its praise. It would be said, and not unjustly said, that it had not only reared an empire as if by magic, but when that empire was riven in twain, when an enemy numbering his hosts by hundreds of thousands was in sight of its capital, it was a question only of a little time, less bloodshed, and some money, to rebuild that empire by conquering nine millions of a united people and a country of a million of square miles! And who can doubt that Democracy would be more arrogant, more aggressive, more leveling and vulgarizing, if that be possible, than it ever had been before?[11]

"The Question of Recognition of the Confederate States"

MODERATOR LETTERS TO THE *MORNING POST*

17 March 1862

Sir,

Every British heart re-echoed the hopeful wish expressed by Earl Russell on Monday last in the House of Lords, that "within three months, perhaps even less, we may see the close of the civil war in America."[12] But many joined in the noble earl's wish who did not share his hope. The contest, all men know, can close in but one of two manners, either by the admission of the Confederate States into the family of nations, or by their subjugation or voluntary submission. The latter event Earl Russell does not contemplate, for with the hope he expressed is coupled the further hope that the contest may so end as to open to each of the contestants a course of happiness and freedom. And that there might be no doubt left in what manner this course of happiness and freedom is to be opened to both, he emphatically declares his belief that the old relations between the two States cannot be renewed, and that they are indeed "two States inhabited by men of very different education and perhaps very different natures." The only end of the contest, then, which a statesman who surveys so vast a field as the Foreign Secretary of the British Empire deems possible, and that which he considers as near at hand, is, "that the North, whatever may be their military successes, whatever may be their naval victories, whatever positions they may capture, will at last consent to a peaceable separation of two States which might both be mighty."

The vast majority of the British public have long since arrived at the conclusion that this is the only possible termination of an otherwise interminable war; the vast majority, also, will unite with Earl Russell in the wish that such may be the termination, there being no other consistent with the peace and happiness of either North or South; but unless her Majesty's Secretary for Foreign Affairs is in possession of facts of which the public cannot even conjecture the existence, it will be difficult for any large portion of that public to see so near and short a road to a goal to which the only apparent way is through long years of bloodshed, of individual suffering, of mutual exhaustion and ruin.

Amazing as is the versatility of American character, and sudden as have been the gyrations of public opinion, which have so often rendered it hopeless to account rationally for events in that country, it is scarcely within the limits of possibility that so great a change in the determination of a whole people should take place, not only without any newly-risen cause, but despite many powerful incentives to perseverance. Is it conceivable that a nation which has patiently endured the most humiliating disappointments, and gathered new hope from each successive defeat, will of its own accord relinquish the prize for which it has made such fearful sacrifices at the very moment when it believes that this prize is within its grasp, and those sacrifices about to be repaid? Is it probable that a people which could not see the hopelessness of attempting impossibilities when its very capital was threatened by a victorious foe will see that hopelessness now when its own flag waves over a hostile capital?[13] Those overgrown armies—which, under the most favorable circumstances, would be a serious obstacle to peace—will they be content to stop short in the very high tide of victory, and in the very sight of that Promised Land whose fertile fields and sunny skies were to be their reward?

The versatility of the Northern mind is due to a feverish excitability of temper, of which perhaps no people—not even the proverbial Parisians— have afforded a parallel. The history of the North for the last thirty years, in its finances, its politics, its social development, may be described as an oscillation between the extremes of hope and fear, of joy and despondency. In probably no other national characteristic is the difference between North and South more marked. In the present war the pendulum still obeys the original impetus with accelerating velocity; and though no one can doubt that its returning vibration will be equally violent, who can decide at what point of the arc it will stop before it does return? Surely not at that point where it receives a new impetus in the same direction, and, if possible, even more violent than the first. Will a ship, driven headlong against the breakers by a furious tempest, change its course and seek a harbor while the blast redoubles its violence, and the reckless crew set all sail.

A versatile nation is not one which calmly reviews its past course, which, in the moment of triumph, recognizes the hollowness of delusive successes and at the brink of the abyss braces itself against the torrent that would sweep it over. Versatility means such a susceptibility to extraneous or adventitious impressions as produces in the possessor effects seemingly incommensurate to the cause, and impel him heedlessly in any direction until that direction is again changed from without. Whence shall come that shock which alone can stop the North in its mad career, and divert that freshet of popular passions into a more natural, or at least less devastating channel? The great defeat which in the ordinary progress of events we foresee will not of itself produce this shock, for what defeat could be more disastrous and more bitterly humiliating than that at Bull Run?

There is one way, and one way only, in which the Northern mind can be shaken from its dream of fondly-hugged illusions. Among these illusions the one most generally prevailing, the parent of all the others, the most disastrous in its effects, is that which leads the masses of that people to believe that they are engaged in a holy and necessary war of self-defense and self-preservation. Were this a war of boundaries, of adjustment of debts, of redress of grievances, a war for any imaginable motive between two foreign nations, we might hope that the opportune moment for an honorable peace would be seized. But none of these ordinary motives obtain in the American war. The Northern people have so long been taught by every demagogue from every stump, that they are the greatest, the freest, mightiest, most enlightened, most moral, most prosperous, and the bravest people on the earth; that, indeed, they are a chosen people; that the Continent is theirs by manifest destiny, and the other inhabitants thereof are but tenants at will; that the world trembles before them while it admires and envies them. So thoroughly has this belief penetrated the Northern mind and grown with the growth of that people that they cannot understand how any part of so magnificent an empire can seriously desire to forego such present and prospective glories, such might, such happiness, and so many blessings. They deem it their right and their duty, in the fulfillment of the mission with which they believe themselves charged, to propagate these blessings, though it be with fire and sword, and to exterminate, in the name of religion and civilization, those who by "wicked rebellion" place obstacles in their path. Were the Governments of the world to declare, what the public opinion of the world has long since declared, that they are engaged, not in a civil, but in a foreign war; not in preserving the integrity of their own territory, but in taking by force the territory of others; not in sustaining a lawful Government, but in seeking to subvert one as lawful as their own—if the Governments of the world were to declare this by recognition of the Confederate States as an independent nation, the Northern people would for the first time be startled to a sense of the true position they occupy. Their first feeling would be that of surprise that the world had dared to do this. The next, to measure for once the real proportions of the enterprise which they must then abandon or prosecute against the moral convictions of all mankind. Then, and then only, would come the recollection, strongly urged by those whose voices are now drowned amid the roar of the hurricane, that a country need not necessarily extend from the Atlantic to the Pacific, to be a great and a powerful country; that they still had a territory vast enough to satisfy the most exorbitant ambition for empire—a territory twenty times larger than the most puissant monarchy of Europe; that they still had a population equal to that of half a dozen kingdoms joined together, and room five times their number. The more calculating classes would reflect that they still have an advantage over the European competitor, by closer proximity, prior connections, and more intimate acquaintance of its wants in that most profitable of all markets, the vast agricultural regions of the South. Once the tide [begins] setting in that direction, the world would again have to exclaim at the versatility of American character on witnessing the ease, the rapidity, nay, the zeal, with which the Northern mind would adapt itself to, and even congratulate itself on, the new state of things.

In the earlier stage of the war the North tried and condemned to death as pirates the privateers—men it had captured, acting in this in strict accordance with its theory that the war was only the suppression of an insurrection, in which the belligerent rights belonged exclusively to itself. But the world refused to consider as pirates men who acted under the forms and sanctions of the law of an established, albeit only *de facto,* Government, and to treat as a mere riot or *émeute* a revolution which extended over half a continent, and armed nearly half a million men. The world refused to admit in its full extent the Northern theory, and the North was forced to abandon, at least in practice, what the world refused to admit.[14] Similarly it must abandon the whole theory, if the world, tired of a senseless and causeless war, refuse to admit it any longer in any part. By the recognition of the Confederate States the war becomes one of boundaries, of adjustment of debts, of future commercial and other relations—objects that neither side would now go to extremes in contending for, and which are capable of being settled, or at least arbitrated.

Whether such recognition would be consistent with the logic of facts, with a sound policy, and more especially with the dictates of impartial justice, I will demonstrate in another letter.

I am, sir, your obedient servant,

MODERATOR

20 March 1862

Sir:

Earl Russell's prediction of a speedy culmination to the American war is based upon the hope—expressed with all the emphasis pertaining to the words of a statesman who wields so vast an influence and commands so extensive a range of vision—that the character of the war will be changed by the abandonment of the theory upon which it is now conducted by one of the belligerents. This theory is, on the part of the North, that the war is one of self-preservation—a war in support of the authority of a lawful Government against the treasonable designs of a "wicked rebellion"—a war to maintain a nation's identity and the integrity of its territory—a war, in brief, necessary in itself, and just as holy in its motives. That this theory is false, the British public need not be informed at this late day. No one of equal authority has ever so pointedly expressed its fallacy as did Earl Russell when, to the assembled peers of Great Britain, he declared that the only hope for either belligerent of happiness and freedom lay in their peaceable separation into two States which might both be prosperous and mighty.

In my letter of Monday last I endeavored to convince you that the character of the Northern people afforded no reason for expecting a voluntary abandonment of this theory on their part. Were their Government, based on a firmer foundation than the troubled waters of popular passions, or even less exposed than is to be swayed by every fitful gust of public opinion, we might, indeed, expect from the calm wisdom and far-sighted sagacity of the statesman that which it were vain to expect from an excitable and infuriated multitude. But every one the least acquainted with the political theories of America knows that in the Northern States the direction of public affairs comes from below, and not from above. If those large inflammable masses, who Mr. Lincoln calls "his masters," are to be taught their error, it must be long training in the school of afflictions and disappointments, and even those stern teachings will scarcely be listened to by ears still ringing with shouts of triumph, and by minds buoyed with dazzling visions of conquest. I endeavored to convince you that this false theory, without which the North would never have undertaken the war, will not be abandoned so long as all the Governments on earth admitted its correctness by placing the victims of the theory under the world's ban as insurgents. That the Governments of the world must formally express this almost unanimous verdict of the world's public opinion before the North can be expected to understand, or understanding, to admit, that the war is waged for the subjugation of a people who only ask to be let alone to manage their own affairs in their own way, and who have as clear a right to do so as the North itself.

I proposed in my last the query whither this forcing the North to a sense of its true position by admitting the Confederate States into the family of nations, would be consistent with the logic of facts. I might have spared myself the trouble of answering this query by the reflection that no argument I can adduce will put the logic of the facts in so clear a light as the conclusion at which Earl Russell arrived, that the best interests of both parties required separation into independent States. There are, however, some considerations which, though not new, may be worth repeating. Whether we consider the late American Union as a Confederation of States as it was in theory, or as *ab inillo,* a league between the two great rival Powers of the North and the South, as its whole history proves it to have been in practice, the logic of the facts is equally irresistible. If we take the theoretical view of a Confederation of States, we must admit that foreign dealings with those States have been with them as States, and never as a consolidated nation. When Great Britain acknowledged the independence of those States, she did so of each separately, and that independence was acknowledged quite as formally and solemnly for Virginia, North and South Carolina, and Georgia, as for Massachusetts Bay, New York, and Pennsylvania.[15] Indeed, the South comprises a greater proportion of States whose individual independence Great Britain recognized than does the North. If, on the other hand, we chose the more practical division of the late American Union between the "North" and the "South," we find the latter determined as one man to break up the league which bound it to the former, and it would be difficult to show why one partner should have the rights which are not admissible in the other. The South occupies more than three-fifths of the territory which was inhabited when Great Britain recognized the several colonies as States. Its present Government bases its legitimacy upon precisely the same political theories and political facts as the Governments of the North—precisely the same combination of popular and States representation. It is not necessary to fall back upon American theories of government to show the absurdity of a claim of jurisdiction of the part of twenty-two States over eleven other States, unless we suppose the eleven States to be subjects or provinces of the twenty-two, or unless we admit, to its fullest extent, that might gives right, and that any stronger Power may lawfully rule a weaker. If we look upon the belligerents as two different peoples—different, as Earl Russell pronounces them, in education and in perhaps in their natures—the South need not fear comparison. In unanimity of resolve, in the magnitude of individual sacrifices, in the reliance of its Government on the loyalty and devotion of its citizens, an impartial judge would not, perhaps give the advantage to the North. If a claim can be rightfully established on British sympathies in favor of either on the ground of kindred and blood relationship, it must tell fearfully against the aggressive party in this conflict. Both originally settled by the same race, what has given the North, once the weaker of the two, the daring to threaten the South, once its superior in numbers and dominion, with subjugation? Is it not that for half a century the North has absorbed the surplus population of all Europe; while the South, from circumstances as well as policy, relied on the natural increase of the parent stock? Where are those great cities which are rightly called the third and fourth largest German cities in the world, and where those vast States in which the English tongue is the legal, but not the spoken language? Are they in the North, or in the South? Which of the two, in soberness of judgment, deliberateness of resolve, and heroic self-devotion, gives evidence of closer affinity to British blood?

These questions are answered by facts, and these facts tell their own logic. A people, in which every man is a soldier, and every woman a seamstress for the army, cannot be said to lack the compactness which entitles it to be treated as a nation. A people which arms nearly half a million men in its defense, while its ports are blockaded, and the commerce and sympathies of the world shut out, which for twelve months kept an enemy, superior in numbers as in equipment, at bay on the extreme outposts of its furthest frontiers, and during that time tranquilly organized a complicated Government based on universal suffrage, cannot be said to lack either the ability or the determination to maintain its independence.

I rely upon the authority of Earl Russell for the logic of the facts. The same authority will not fail me when, in my next letter, I shall endeavor to show that the recognition of the Confederate States of America is equally consistent with sound policy and the dictates of impartial justice.

I am, sir, your very obedient servant.

MODERATOR

24 March 1862

Sir:

Self-interest may be called the conscience of nations, and if the perception of self-interest is enlightened and comprehensive there is perhaps no safer guide to justice and fairness in their dealings with each other. Great Britain, Europe, Civilization, have important, and I believe the same, interests at stake in the present war in America. Whither do those interests point? Each daily page of contemporary history obtrudes this question so loudly that no thoughtful mind can refuse to hear it. Is it the interest of Great Britain, of Europe, or of Civilization, that the greater, and by far the wealthier, portion of the North American continent should again be the dominion of a single haughty, overgrown, defiant power? That democracy, in its exaggerated American form, should be reinstated as the lawless arbiter of the destinies of one hemisphere, and the standing menace of the other? That the region of the globe which furnishes the most important staple of the world's commerce should be the tributary of any one country, and especially one which treats all the world as enemies?

One of the chief causes of the rapid advance of Europe in all polite and useful arts has been its division into independent societies, allowing the development of many phases of national character, each influencing and correcting the other, and by their mutual friction promoting the intellectual development of all. England lavished her blood and treasure to resist the formation of one despot Power extending its sway over all Europe. Is it more desirable or less injurious to the healthy growth of civilization that one despot Power should sway America? England, the seminary of liberty and the champion of free institutions the world over, has ever for herself and others repudiated democracy, or the rule of mere numbers substituted for the rule of intelligence and virtue. Has this rule of numbers instead of virtue and intelligence proved less fatal to true liberty in America than in Europe, or have its fruits been more wholesome than the Sodom's apples it has borne elsewhere? For years England has striven to unfetter commerce, and to open every portion of the globe to its fertilizing irrigation. The whole of mankind has profited with her by this beneficent policy, which has made the desert verdant, and peopled the wilderness with thrifty inhabitants. Can she consent to see the cotton and tobacco fields of the world walled in by a Chinese policy imposed by fire and sword on the lawful proprietors?

I say Chinese policy, because legislation like the Morrill tariff resembles in its causes, even more than in its effects, the favorite legislation of the Chinese empire.[16] Of the latter it has been justly observed that in a material sense it required no foreign intercourse, because it was a world in itself, and by its gigantic internal traffic supplied the place of foreign trade. Much of the same holds good in a reconstructed American Republic holding the South as a conquered province. With an empire embracing every climate and production, with gold from California, cotton, sugar, rice, and tobacco from the South, what should the North care for foreign commerce? When it can buy in a close market all it needs, and sell in a close market all it produces, what need is there for reciprocal treaties with foreign nations? Would not the products of its own provinces be sufficient to supply every want, to employ every loom and anvil, to load every ship, and to pay the monopoly price of everything it chooses to give in return? Grant that New York and Boston will suffer in their trade by sharpened Morrill tariffs, what matters it when they are more than compensated by the more effectual exclusion of the foreign trade from the Southern market? Every European merchantman the less at their wharves would be replaced by more than one of their own, and their sails would all the oftener half circumnavigate the globe in so-called "coasting voyages" from the Atlantic to the Pacific. And having none to compete with it in the market where it buys, what should prevent this favored nation from competing with all others in the markets where it may choose to sell? Who can undersell a dealer who buys his goods at his own prices, and who needs never fear a surplus on hand? That the picture is not overdrawn it is not now necessary to prove by statistics. The fabulous capacity of production and consumption which the South possesses has been demonstrated by such "figures" as cannot "lie," and were these figures less eloquent, the enormous efforts of the North to retain them on the credit side of its ledger would make them so. Of the commercial policy of the North we have a fair example already; what that policy would be were the South reduced to a helpless dependency, it is not difficult to conjecture, nor how and by what means it is expected to pay the cost of the conquest.

But it may be said that because another has a good thing this is no reason why we should envy and seek to take it from him. Very true. But if another seeks to take by force a thing which is not more his than ours, there is no reason why we should not step in to prevent it. What right has the North to invade and conquer the South? To impose military governors over the States which were once its equals and allies? What right has it to legislate for people who have and who desire no voice in its government? To pay its soldiery by the confiscation of the lands of men whose only crime is that they defend their own homes, and obey the authority of the State which has the first claim to their allegiance? To hold a country inhabited by eight million freemen, as it alone can expect to hold it, as an insurgent province? Surely this right is not derived from the fact that the South once consented to live under a common government with the North. Surely by this consent to a common government could not have been meant a government of the North over the South. It was a government, too, based upon the empirically-proclaimed principle that "all just government depended on the consent of the governed;" a government voluntarily framed by free and independent States as such, not for purposes of internal administration which each retained for itself, but for the management of common and external concerns; and therefore recognized by other Governments not as the government of a national unit, but as that of united States. Of these States, united for special purposes, each was to be the equal of every other. What has occurred since to make some of the States subjects of the others, and what clause is there in the compact expressly entered into for the common good to make that compact irrevocable for the sole good of one party and the lasting injury of the others? Suppose it was the South which invaded the North, which would retain the latter for its own selfish advantage in a union that had become hateful and drained it of its life blood; suppose Southern armies occupied Northern towns, and Mr. Davis's governors ruled over conquered Northern States. Would not the aggrieved North appeal to the aid and sympathy of all the civilized world, and would that aid and sympathy be wanting?

We hear things of justice, of international obligations, of the sanctity of constitutional government. What bitter mockery when these terms are used to defend an unholy attempt on a nation's liberties! Is it justice to let a weaker people, straining every nerve in defense of its dearest rights, be crushed and trampled under foot by another people simply because the other is the stronger? Because a confederation of free and equal States has been recognized by foreign Governments, do international obligations require these Governments to permit two-thirds of those States to reduce the remaining third into subject provinces? Have any international obligations been incurred towards the North which are not equally incurred towards the South? Great Britain long since disclaimed the odious principle that her own colonies, grown up under her fostering care, should be held and governed only with a view to her own profit and selfish advantage. Yet in the name of international obligations she is asked to sanction the attempt of the North to hold its equals and former allies in a state of dependency to which the colonial condition was independence. The sanctity of constituted Governments! Is it intended to proclaim that the democratic Governments have a sanctity that does not pertain to the Governments of monarchs; that no matter how unjust and tyrannical they may become, the consent expressly given cannot be withdrawn, though it may be justly withdrawn when it is only implied; that though a king may not rule over injured and unwilling subjects, yet one people may rightfully rule over another people whom it has the power to subdue by arms. The Czar of Russia may not wrest Constantinople from the scepter of the Turk, but the northern democracy may lawfully conquer New Orleans because eight millions of people are less than twenty-two.

So far, I believe, few will dispute the justice of my views. That the facts—sound policy and justice to all parties—require the separation of the late American Union into two independent States, public opinion has long since proclaimed with singular emphasis and unanimity. Whether the recognition of the Confederate States as an independent nation would of itself bring about this result and terminate the war, is less universally admitted, and to this consideration I shall, with your permission, devote my next and last letter.

I am, sir, very respectfully, your obedient servant,
MODERATOR

31 March 1862

Sir:

Few, I believe, will dispute that the time and manner of solving this question depends mainly, if not wholly, upon Great Britain. When her Government took the first important step toward recognition by acknowledging the belligerent rights of the "insurgent Power," all the Governments of Europe promptly followed her example.[17] It would be somewhat difficult to allege any good reason why they should be more slow to follow the same example in taking the final step. Indeed, the supposition seems well grounded that some at least of these Powers await the setting of that example with impatience. But the initiative can be taken by no other than England. Her close relationship with both parties to the contest, her more intimate knowledge of their character and resources, and the direct interest she has in the issue, point to her as the natural arbiter of the merits of the quarrel, and make her verdict that of the European nations in council assembled.

Assuming, then, that the recognition of the Confederate States by England would be tantamount to recognition by all the Powers of Europe, it remains to be shown whether her voice is less potent on the other hemisphere. No one denies that such recognition would greatly encourage and strengthen the party on the defensive, and correspondingly depress and weaken the stronger and aggressive. Yet fears are often expressed that the opportune moment is past, and that even recognition would now fail to effect its object, the termination of the war. Those who entertain these fears forget how powerful an agent non-recognition is in the continuance of the war. When Mr. Lincoln, with a rather novel construction of his constitutional right to call out the militia to suppress insurrection, passed a *posse comitatus* of 75,000 three months' volunteers to enforce the reading of the riot act to the seceded States, neither he nor the people who applauded his violation of the constitution were conscious that they were engaging in a war perhaps the most formidable in the dimensions of modern times.[18] Congress, which alone has the power to declare war, was not convened until months afterward, not until the eve of the Battle of Bull Run, when "treason" was to be crushed at one fell blow. Secession was looked upon as a political demonstration for the purpose of threatening the North into compliance of more advantageous terms of federation; and this demonstration was to be met by a demonstration of force on the part of the North. Many of Mr. Lincoln's most sagacious advisors, Commander General Scott himself, thought the number of 75,000 men unnecessarily large for the purpose then intended. When the demonstration, instead of frightening the South, only increased its strength by giving it the vast and populous Border States, and when Bull Run succeeded Bethel; and Washington, not Richmond, had become the endangered capital, opinion indeed changed, but did not for the better. Each successive disappointment was easily explained by the inadequacy of the demonstration, and each successive disaster only proved that greater efforts were needed, but not that success was impossible. Thus it happens that the North, by degrees, one might almost say, unconsciously became involved in a war from which the greatest military Power would have recoiled, and which, had the North itself foreseen and understood its true character, it would have never undertaken. The Governments of Europe, by delaying the recognition of the Confederate States beyond all possible precedents, tacitly admit the feasibility of the enterprise, in which the North has already made such fearful sacrifices that it cannot be abandoned so long as the faintest hope remains of regaining by still further sacrifices what is already lost. The North is in the position of a man who sits to a gaming table to make a moderate venture, and who, stung by repeated losses, and encouraged by the bystanders, doubles his stake until he has spent the last farthing of his substance.

I have previously pointed to the obvious fact that the admission of the Confederate States into the family of nations would change the whole character of the contest, making it a foreign instead of a civil war, and that it would startle the people of the North to a sense of their true position. It would do more. Besides being of a necessity accompanied by a recommendation of peace, couched in polite but firm language, it would of itself be the most emphatic and significant remonstrance against the further continuance of the war. Such a remonstrance by the united commonwealth of civilized nations no Government of Europe in this age could long withstand, and America has no immunity from the pressure of the public opinion of Europe. The Northern people, on the contrary, are notoriously sensitive to European opinion; and in proportion as their self-love is now buoyed and flattered by the very magnitude of the war, and of the efforts it requires, the reaction will be when, instead of the world's fancied admiration and awe, that war and those efforts shall have provoked the world's unqualified condemnation. But this same self-love, the intensity of which has long been so striking a feature of the national character, would find consolation for all disappointment in the reflection that the remonstrance of all the world was necessary to make them abandon an impracticable undertaking. Any nation may honorably decline a conflict in which all the world is its antagonist. It is necessary to refer to the Trent affair as an illustration of my meaning!

Again there must surely be among the Northern people men of sober judgment who see the hopelessness of the contest, and deprecate its continuance. To express their views and tender their counsels would now be punished as treason. Symptoms are not wanting that even among the politicians who have so recklessly hurried their nation into ruin, many are beginning to perceive that they have gone too far, and would gladly retrace their steps could they do so without danger of their political fortunes. To all such men the recognition of the Confederate States by European Powers would be at once the welcome pretext and the safe occasion. In a people so impressible and impulsive the moral effect of such recognition would gather volume and power as it descended and diffused itself among the lower strata of society, like a sound reverberating through fathomless caves. What to the Cabinet Minister would be an untoward, but not altogether unforeseen, diplomatic *contretemps,* to the volunteer of the camps would appear as the unalterable decree of fate, for in it he would see, not the diplomacy of Europe, but its armies and navies.

In my former letters I have endeavored to show that the war will not end for many years, not even by the mere exhaustion of the belligerents, so long as Europe remains a listless spectator. I have endeavored to show that justice, humanity, the best interests of Governments and of civilization, require Europe to act, not by exertion of its material force, but by its equally irresistible moral power. If I have failed now in convincing your readers that the exertion of that moral power alone would terminate the war, it will not have been for want of convincing reasons, but for the lack of ability to forcibly array them.

I remain sir, very respectfully, your obedient servant,

MODERATOR

The Index *on Recognition*

"OUR OBJECT"[19]

The *Index,* 1 May 1862

It has been thought advisable to issue this Journal for the following reasons: In the first place, there are many millions of people, kinsmen of the people of this country, who have now been for some time shut off from all communication with the rest of the civilized world. To any statement of the loss and suffering they endure, it will be replied, that these are the consequences brought upon themselves by their own act; but the blockade which stifles them is also, in one most important direction, a blockade of the industry of Europe. Great interests are affected by it, entirely innocent of offence. If the Southern States formed a country like Japan or Madagascar, it might be of little concern here what the destruction of property or life with which they are visited, simply because they desire that self-government which Englishmen practice themselves, and usually commend to others. But, instead of isolation of this kind, they are more peculiarly and closely connected with the largest industrial class of Europe than any other country whatever. When interests so great as these are thus interwoven, nothing that affects one can be a matter of indifference to the other.

In the next place, it is notorious that the Government of Washington exercises now another rigid blockade—that of the intelligence of the Northern people; permitting only that to pass which has first obtained its approval. The system of passports and the employment of spies have indeed been abandoned; but its control of the telegraph and censorship of the press have become more and more rigid. In many countries, freedom of the press is restrained by law, and infractions of such law are visited with the penalties provided for them. In the United States the perfect freedom of the press is an absolute provision of the Federal Constitution, which declares, "Congress shall make no law abridging the freedom of speech or of the press." Hence it is altogether beyond the power of the Supreme Legislature of the country to enact any law interfering with the liberty of the press, which stands upon the same foundation, and is sanctioned by the same authority as the Congress or the President, for all came into existence under the provision of the same instrument. And if there be any one of them which was held more sacred than the others by those who framed that Constitution, that one is the freedom of the press.[20] Thus, when the State of Virginia ratified the Constitution, she passed a Declaratory Act, bearing date 26th June, 1788, in which are these words: "The liberty of conscience and *of the press* cannot be cancelled, abridged, restrained, or modified by *any* authority of the United States." But what the law cannot do, and what the Constitution absolutely prohibits, is now in full operation by those who are urging this war in the name of that Constitution; who vindicate their reverence for it by treating its enactments with contempt, and, with a logic happily unknown in Europe, break it to keep it intact.

Three great political principles were especially cherished by the founders of the Republic—freedom of person, of speech, of the press. The whole of these have been violated, not in some special instance, under peculiar circumstances, with hesitation or regret, but openly, throughout the whole of the North, on the most trivial occasions, and without the slightest affection of concern. Apologists plead as an excuse, that the national safety is in jeopardy. Is, then, a Constitution intended as a guide in days of tranquility and ease alone? Freedom of person or of speech will not be endangered in times of prosperity and peace, but in those of turmoil and excitement; and thus at the only time when these safeguards of the Constitution come into vitality, they are spurned. This is as if a shelter should be carefully preserved so long as there be sunshine, to be leveled with the ground when it begins to rain.

And where is this national safety endangered? The Federal Union consists of an indefinite number of distinct states, each separately organized. At what particular cipher of an indeterminate number does the national safety reside? That number is now 34 states, but the national safety was not a matter of apprehension when there were but 20. It may be answered, that there has been a principle of constant growth, entirely free from danger. But the Union has safely existed under a reduced number. Of the 13 original states only 11 were in the Union for a period of two years. Where was the national safety then? Texas was an independent sovereign state, acknowledged as such by several powers. The safety of no one was endangered by this, and if there was security at that period, why this alarm because Texas reverts to the position she held before? Further, the Constitution expressly provides for a condition of affairs in which one-third of the states then existing might be apart from and foreign to the rest. This is all that Secession amounts to—that a third of the states desired to occupy that position, in relation to the rest for which the Constitution expressly provided in the first instance.

But whatever the hollowness or the validity of the excuses for the existing state of affairs, there can exist no doubt as to the fact that all the intelligence permitted to the public in the Northern States, and transmitted to Europe, is confined to such statements as meet the views of the Washington Government. The ear of Europe is condemned on the one side to silence, and on the other to listen only to that which has passed through a bureau, and has been approved by a censor. If this be so, it cannot but be desirable that some means should be provided through which the public may be enabled to hear both sides. None will dispute the old adage that "one tale's good until the other's told." The only manner in which intelligence can be obtained from the South, at the present time, is by the letters arriving, many of them from Englishmen and from writers whose standing in the community is well known. Of these not a few are colored with strong personal feeling, but the majority contain information of much value. We shall be enabled largely to avail ourselves of these sources of information, and it is believed that, by a continuous and careful selection from them, much truth may be elicited. We propose to give weekly all intelligence of interest received from the North, and to accompany it with a commentary, in which we shall endeavor to point out what may appear to us entirely fictitious and what exaggerated. In this task we have reason to expect the assistance of those who, from long residence in the country, will be able to bring to the investigation the best of all implements—knowledge.

Of the importance of arriving at the truth in the present conjuncture few can entertain a doubt. There is, indeed, no problem of which the correct solution is so essential to Europe at the present moment as that which involves the question, whether a new Power is really added to the family of nations—whether a great outlet for the industry, and a vast field for the enterprise of the Old World, are cleared from artificial obstructions; or whether this great movement is to prove but any abortive effort, to be crushed by greater power, and swell still further the magniloquence of the 4th of July orations? It may be said that time will assuredly answer the questions. But the steed starves whilst the grass is growing. Tens of thousands are pining in want this day, and their number must increase week by week; these cannot bid their hunger wait for years. The day will assuredly arrive when it must become the imperative duty of the European Governments to decide the question for themselves. Here, over the dominion the size of twenty kingdoms, there exists a Government now in the second year of its existence, appointed by the formal action of the Legislature of each of the Confederate States, and in each of them sanctioned by a vote of the people—maintaining in the field an army of more than 300,000 men—upheld by many millions of people, with a self-sacrifice, a devotion, and a unanimity rarely equaled in modern history, and sustaining law, order, freedom of speech and freedom of the press throughout its wide domain. As a question of fact, is this a Government or is it not? Once admitted to be such, it is then the bounden duty of other Powers to acknowledge and recognize the fact. If disputed, and held to be only an effort to form a Government, the Powers will, in that view, await the development of events. When and how finally to decide is an anxious consideration very rapidly approaching, critical in its consequences both to the Old and New World. What effort can be idle whose aim is to bring forward evidence and throw light upon the subject?

But when we state that the leading object of this journal will be to advocate the cause of the Southern Union, let it not be assumed that this will be done in the spirit of heated partisans. We believe it to be the cause of justice and of truth, and hold that it cannot be served by suppressing truth or distorting it. Our columns will be open to any writer of ability on the other side. The defects and shortcomings of the Southern States we shall make no attempt to conceal; on the contrary, we propose to call an error an error, and a defect a defect; taking as a guide the last message of the Southern President to its Congress, in which facts grievously depressing are stated in simple English, with that manly candor which is above the fear of shrinking from the truth. There are those who thought the tone of that message, contrasting so directly as it did with the Northern style, was proof of debility, if not of abandoned hope. Let those who thus judged study the events that have since occurred; the endurance of that little island, the vigor displayed in the battle in Tennessee, the judgment in the defense of Yorktown, the skill in the construction of the *Merrimac;* and they will find that these qualities may exist, and do exist, without Mr. Lincoln's policy of concealment, or the boastful arrogance of the North.

"THE INGREDIENTS OF THE CONTENDING ARMIES"

The *Index,* 3 July 1862

When men speak of money as being the sinews of war, they assert that which is only partially true. No doubt large resources often conduce to victory, though they do not insure it, and it is certain that nations have often carried on war successfully with very limited means. Notwithstanding all the modern and costly improvements in the art of warfare, notwithstanding the arrogant boast of the United States during the Crimean War that the taking of Sebastopol was merely a commercial question, it is a fact that the reliable sinews of war are the men that compose the army. For parade purposes, any people—Mexican or Chinese—can be converted by drill into good soldiers, but it requires inherent fighting qualities to make good fighting soldiers. Besides the more physical pluck and endurance, much depends on the spirit that animates an army. Mercenary troops have often displayed great bravery and determination on the fields of battle; but the endurance that is not daunted by privations or discouraged by all but overwhelming odds, or dispirited by reverses, is the offspring of a nobler motive than the hope of pay and plunder. In the memorable contest that issued in the independence of the Netherlands, the Spaniards, animated by the hope of booty, displayed wonderful resolution and devotion. Notwithstanding this, the enormous power of Spain could not crush the determination of the Netherlands to maintain those liberties and rights that were dearer than life and property.[21] Hence it is that history does not record a single instance of the permanent subjugation of a people determined to vindicate their independence. Remembering this, if we glance at the ingredients of the contending armies that are now waging war in America, we discover another assurance of the invincibility of the South.

The change of Government, engendered by secession, was effected in the most peaceable, orderly, and constitutional manner, without noisy demonstration, and without one thought of the deadly hostilities that have ensued. Not only were the Confederates unprovided with the munitions of war, but the possibility of the North trampling on the Constitution which it professed to serve, and warring against the independence of sovereign States with whom it had been in federation, was not even entertained. The call to arms found the citizens of the Confederacy busied with peaceful pursuits; but at that call to defend country and home against the lawless design of the North to attempt the conquest of the fair and rich domains of the South, every citizen evinced his patriotism by offering his services as a soldier. No wonder, despite the unpreparedness, it was an easy matter to organize the Southern army. The regiments that sprang up, as if by magic, were manned by the scions of the noblest and richest families. Lawyers forsook their clients—physicians, their patients—planters, their broad estates—to become private soldiers, and to submit to discipline as rigorous and uncompromising as the discipline of any army in the world. There was no clamoring for commissions; the only demand was to be enrolled in the army destined for the defense of the country. In the diary we have been publishing entitled "Three Months in the Confederate Army," the organization of a company is described that was composed of young men whose birth, education, and wealth entitled them to mingle with the highest circles of society. The social standing of the members of that company was not exceptional. In the sacred cause of national independence, it was thought that no sacrifice could be too precious; the higher a man stood, the more he felt bound to offer his life on the altar of patriotism. Of course, citizens of inferior social grades rallied around the Confederate standard; but in the Confederate army there was not a foreign regiment—not one mercenary soldier. Those who had the means furnished their own equipments, found their own rations, and expected no pay. Those who had not the means accepted cheerfully such equipment, rations, and pay, as the Government could offer. In short, the army of the South was, and is, an army of patriots. No marvel that, though cut off from warlike supplies, the Confederates have held their own against their enemy, superior in numbers and having the advantage of unlimited access to the stores of Europe. No marvel such an army is not disheartened by the loss of frontier cities, and feels confident that the sacred cause for which it contends must triumph, even though that triumph may be preceded by great tribulation.

We have looked at the composition of the patriotic army of the South; let us briefly notice the ingredients of the marauding army of the North.

At the outbreak of the war, or rather, in the excitement before the outbreak of the war, unquestionably many citizens of the United States enrolled themselves as "Three Months' Men." How did they act? On the eve of the memorable Battle of Bull Run, at the sound of the Confederate artillery, these "Three Months' Men" found all their martial ardor had evaporated; pleaded that their terms of service had expired, and made from the field and the roar of the enemy's artillery. We say, advisedly, that from that time few, very few, natives of the United States, always excepting the levies made in some of the Western States, have been found enrolled in the Northern armies. When there is a panic about the safety of Washington, the 7th New York Regiment marches down Broadway, with flying colors, amidst the cheers of the mob, and proceeds to Washington, feeling confident, if there is any actual danger, they will scent it afar, and be able to make a prudential return to New York with whole skins. Whether there is such a thing as bravery amongst the natives of the North, as well as the braggadocio, we know not; but we do know that the natives of the North have not shared the perils of the wicked war waged against the South. They are like a well-known Italian Revolutionist, whom is a physical and moral coward as well as a cunning knave, and who hires assassins to do the bloody and treacherous work that he himself is afraid to attempt.

One of the last regiments raised by the Federals was Wilson's Fire Zouaves, composed of the jail birds of New York. Well, perhaps it is as honorable to carry on an aggressive war with convicts as with foreign mercenaries; and the army of the North is mainly composed of foreigners, the majority of whom are Germans, who only fight for present pay and plunder, and the hope of sharing the spoils of the conquered South. Not only is there a large German element in almost every regiment, but some divisions are wholly composed of Germans; for example, General Siegel [*sic*], who, in the revolution of '48, was the leader of the Baden insurgents, and is now entrusted with a high command in the Federal army, is not a naturalized citizen of the United States. So important does the Federal Government consider it to maintain and increase their influence over the Germans, that Mr. Schurtz [*sic*], who has lived only six years in America, was appointed United States' Ambassador to Spain, as the reward of political harangues to his countrymen. Let anyone take up the muster-roll of the Northern army, and he will perceive that we do not unjustly designate it as an army of foreign mercenaries. Sometimes the scourings of the Northern cities are attracted by the bounty to enter, or are pressed into the service—of such men was composed the division of General Casey, that imitated the cowardly conduct of the "Three Months' Men" at Bull Run, by running away at sight of the enemy, and leaving their braver companions to bear the brunt of the battle.[22] Convicts, a pusillanimous mob, a sprinkling of native Americans, but mainly mercenaries, compose the army that, in the name of humanity, endeavors to trample on the rights of humanity; that, under the plea of defending the Constitution of the United States, violates that Constitution; that is, in fact, the instrument of the dollar-worshipping people of the North to steal the liberties of the South; not that the Northerners care for their own or any other nation's liberty, but they crave for the conquest of the South, because they lust for the riches of the South. Happily, they must kill before they can take possession, and the spirit of Southern liberty is invulnerable, and the North cannot hire a sufficient number of foreign mercenaries to exterminate 8,000,000 of a superior race.

To those who are astonished, and perhaps grieved, at the terrible bitterness evoked in the South by the ruthless invasion of the North, we commend the calm consideration of the ingredients of the contending armies, confident that then they will no longer wonder at or condemn the loathing and deadly animosity so universally manifested.

"WHAT PREVENTS THE RECOGNITION OF THE CONFEDERATE STATES?"

The *Index*, 22 January 1863

Does anyone doubt that if Government were to meet Parliament with a proposal to end the American war by the recognition of the Confederate States, the proposal would be received with acclamation? Does anyone doubt that if the leaders of the Opposition were to give the signal, either Government would offer no resistance, or the triumphant majority would be swelled even from the Ministerial benches? These are admitted facts, which have become elementary maxims in all considerations of the American question, from whatever point of view. The members in either House who desire the success of the North, or would oppose the recognition of the South, if proposed by competent authority, can be counted on one's fingers. On this question men are not divided into hostile camps by party lines. There is no public sentiment arrayed against it; on the contrary, nine-tenths of every great party and of every really influential class are sincere well-wishers of the South, and anxious for the termination of a useless contest. Other measures, of less imperative urgency and less momentous in their consequences, have, within our time, convulsed the country with agitation and roused the bitterest and most relentless enmity. This measure, the most important of the day, and the most necessary, would scarcely raise a ripple on the surface of public opinion, would surprise no one, and would encounter serious opposition nowhere. What, then, prevents the recognition of the Confederate States?

Arguments in favor of this most simple and only effective mode of ending a disastrous war suggest themselves to every mind, are in everybody's mouth, and are naturally and logically deduced from obvious principles of policy, humanity, and justice. It exhausts the skill of ingenious causists to show any reasons, approaching to the dignity of arguments, why the Confederate States should not be recognized as a nation. Is it because these States lack the population, the territorial extent, or even in historical character, which entitle them to be considered as a nation? They have a population one-third as large as that of Great Britain, they occupy a territory many times greater than that of the most powerful Continental monarchy, they have for nearly two years maintained vast armies in the field and made the world ring with brilliant deeds by land and by sea. Is it that the stability of their Government, its hold upon the loyalty of its citizens, or its ability to defend itself against all attacks, have not yet been exposed to a sufficient test? Few Governments have ever had to call upon a people for similar sacrifices of blood and treasure; few have ever met with so unanimous and devoted a response; loyalty has been unshaken even in the conquered cities, and resisted alike the influence of bribes and threats; a million of armed men have been hurled against this Government, hundreds of millions of money have been expended to overthrow it, and today it is stronger, morally and physically, than when the attempt was first made. Is it because the Confederate States have municipal institutions repugnant to us that we should not recognize them as a nation? We treat as diplomatic equals Spain and Brazil, who both maintain the same institutions in a far more repugnant form; Russia, which but yesterday had forty millions of white serfs; we are close allies of Turkey, whose manners and religion are crimes in our eyes; we even hold official intercourse with the savages of Dahomey and Ashantee. The admission of a political fact is a very different thing from the admission of a moral principle, or the approval of a governmental theory. As well might we refuse to recognize the political existence of France because trial by jury is not administered according to our ideas of justice, or that of Russia because the use of the knot and the *pléte* prevails with undiminished cruelty, as to make the civil status of a portion of its population the cause of our refusal to recognize the political existence of a Transatlantic Confederation. By an exact parity of reasoning we should refuse to recognize or hold converse with the United States even at the present day. Is it because the war in America has not lasted long enough, has not brought evil and misery sufficient in its train, that we should not exercise the power we have of ending it? The most fanatical champion of the North cannot deny that the patience of England heretofore has been at a cost less only than that incurred by the combatants themselves.

It is seldom that now, in the second year of the war, any such objections as these we have recited are seriously advanced against the recognition of the Confederate States, at least by men who value a reputation for common sense. More usually the admissions are freely made that the new Confederation has exhibited all the conditions of a vigorous and self-sustaining nationality; that its overthrow by any efforts its adversaries can bring against it is no longer within the range of probability; even Mr. John Bright admits that the question of slavery does not enter into the political relations of Governments;[23] it is further admitted on all hands, that in remaining a passive spectator of the war, this country resists the promptings of the most powerful motives of self-interest—yet, when all these admissions are made, we stop short of the irresistible logical conclusion. To escape this conclusion the opponents of recognition take refuge in certain vague and contradictory assertions. Thus it is said that recognition is dangerous, that it is useless, and sometimes even, that it is unnecessary. It does not appear to occur to these special-pleaders that the first duty of a great nation is to be just, that an act of justice can never be unnecessary or useless, and that it is weakness or cowardice to delay it because it is dangerous. To this plea of danger, a strange one to set up for the acceptance of the English people, we have, however, already replied more at length elsewhere. Suffice it here to say that it would surpass all precedents of human folly, were a man, whose left arm is palsied, to cut off voluntarily his right arm as well—were the North, having failed in its enterprises by land, to shut itself out from the high seas. The pleas of uselessness, is with characteristic inconsistency, always made by those who are most forward in threatening the British empire with the wrath and vengeance of the Yankees. If those threats be well founded, recognition must, in the opinion of those who make them, result in an instantaneous abandonment of all attempts upon the South, for the most bigoted of worshippers of the "Model Republic" will not believe it capable of making war at the same time in the South and against Canada, against the armies of Jefferson Davis and the fleets of Great Britain. Recognition cannot be at once dangerous and useless; but it may and will be neither. If it was useless the South would not so earnestly desire, nor the North so zealously deprecate it. We need not here recapitulate the arguments with which our readers are familiar, which show that recognition by foreign powers must be the inevitable preliminary to any proposals of peace from either of the belligerents. An able writer has aptly paraphrased and compressed them by saying, "Recognition is the cut which severs the mortified limb from the suffering body. The patient will resist the operation so long as he can, and must not be expected to perform it himself, but when it is over he thanks God for it."

The last plea, that recognition is unnecessary, deserves special examination, since it is intended to impose upon many whose sympathies are active in behalf of the South. It is argued that recognition is unnecessary, because the independence is already secured beyond all hazard, and the object of British policy is therefore attained without the necessity or risk of further action. But why should the independence of the South be a British object? Primarily, because the consummation of that independence opens to British industry and commerce the most lucrative and necessary market of the inhabited globe. So long as the Southern ports are sealed, the plantations wasted and abandoned, what matters it to the British interests whether the authority of Jefferson Davis is spontaneously obeyed, or that of Abraham Lincoln enforced in Nashville or New Orleans? Secondly, it should be a British object, in the adjustment of the balance of power in the New World, to secure a sincere friend and a powerful ally. Can we expect to find the friend in the people of the South if we alienate their affections by pertinaciously withholding, and causing others to withhold, in this great crisis, a simple act of justice? And further, if this war smolders on, as unquestionably it will if not extinguished by Europe, until it shall have consumed the vitals of the South as well as the prosperity of the North, shall we find in a pauperized country either a powerful ally or a profitable customer? The cotton fields of America have yielded to England a richer harvest than they have to their owners. If England can forgo the wealth these fields have brought to her, can at the same time be deaf to the appeals of justice, humanity, and kindred blood, and abdicate her proud position among the powers of the earth, then indeed is it unnecessary to recognize the Confederate States of America.

History will ask what prevented the natural termination of so cruel a war, and the statesmen of England will find it difficult to answer the question. They cannot plead that they lacked the power. They cannot plead that party necessities frustrated its exercise, or that a great outside pressure of public opinion overawed them their superior wisdom and foresight. They cannot even plead that grave reasons of foreign policy fettered their free agency. With Europe at peace, with all the other powers, ready to follow their lead, public opinion ripe for the step, free to act, and all the world waiting for their action, the Statesmen of England can only say to posterity that in 1863 they deemed it dangerous, useless, and unnecessary to stop the American war.

The Ebb and Flow of Recognition: Diplomatic and Personal Correspondence

London, 11 March 1862

SIR: I am able, today, to write in a much more cheerful spirit than in my last of February 28. The fall of Fort Donelson, paradoxical as the assertion may appear, has been useful in its effects upon the public opinion.[24] It has proved to our friends here the necessity of greater energy of action, and it has furnished food for serious reflection to that vast majority of the British public who, counting upon the financial exhaustion of the North and the heretofore uniform success of the South, hoped that the much desired separation would be permanently secured without the expense and responsibility of interference on their part. Our recent misfortunes presage to them a protracted war, checkered with alternate successes and reverses, leading to no decisive results, and hence many are now anxious to do something to strengthen us who but a few days ago professed themselves indifferent spectators of the contest. The enclosed extracts from leading papers will show you the spirit in which the fall of Fort Donelson is commented upon, and, I believe, give a fair impression of public opinion. No journal of any influence, not even the *Telegraph,* which is now in the Northern interest, has represented that event as the harbinger of conquest by the North.

I am in a measure responsible for the tone of some of the enclosed extracts. With persons controlling organs of public opinion, whom I met for that express purpose, I thought it our obvious policy to somewhat underrate the importance of the "Border States." "Our constitution," I said to them, "was framed and our Government organized for the States comprised in the cotton region proper. The vast territory which now forms the theater of the war was acquired by us after that war was declared, and our present provisional capital lies a thousand miles to the north of our original and natural capital. Even should the North succeed in overrunning the great States of Virginia, North Carolina, Missouri, Kentucky, and Tennessee, the Southern Confederacy would be precisely what Mr. Lincoln found it on the day of his inauguration. The blood and treasure of the North would have been exhausted in gaining temporary possession of its outer ramparts, and the citadel would still remain untouched." In one, at least, of the *Times* articles, almost my very words are reproduced. Whatever from your point of view may be your judgment of the policy of this line of argument, you will, I think, not fail to perceive that the English press has of late evinced a clear understanding of the practical impossibility of reconquest and of the unalterable determination of our people never to submit. In this respect, then, our recent disasters have not injured us.

On Friday last the debate on the blockade was opened in the Commons by Mr. Gregory, and yesterday in the Lords by Lord Campbell (Stratheden). I have not the honor of a personal acquaintance with Mr. Gregory, else I should have endeavored to convince him that New Orleans was not more effectively blockaded than any other port. I was present at the delivery of his speech and much gratified at the rapt attention and unexpectedly hearty applause with which it was received. There was no intention in either house to push the question to a vote, nor to initiate open hostility against the present Government. It was simply a "demonstration" intended for our benefit, and has fulfilled that expectation. The speech of Lord Campbell, himself one of the ministerial peers, has at least had the good effect of eliciting from Earl Russell the reluctant admission, in substance, that a reconstruction of the American Union was not possible.[25]

Simultaneously with Lord Campbell's speech I made the attempt to commit the *Morning Herald,* Lord Derby's organ, to an open attack, in the spirit of that speech, upon Earl Russell.[26] I should have produced no small political effect, had I succeeded. The editor however, instead of publishing my article as an editorial, altered it into a communication, which, although an unusually conspicuous place was given it, could not have the significance I wished it to have.

I may remark in this connection that the *Trent* affair has done us incalculable injury, insomuch as it enabled the Government to make political capital, which renders it hopeless to attack them in their management of foreign relations. Their internal policy is indeed vulnerable, as you will see from an article in the *Herald,* also enclosed, but I am unable to conjecture now how far this may serve to effect the much-desired result, the displacement of Earl Russell by someone who, if not a friend, shall at least not be an avowed enemy of our nationality.

On the same sheet which contains the debate in the Commons on the blockade you will find an editorial to which I must caution you not to ascribe undue importance. The *Times* does not in this instance express prevailing opinions, nor even the views of its editors. It is perfectly understood that this paper, although independent, never refuses its services to the Government when required in any special emergency, such as snubbing some speaker in either house whose topic is inconvenient or embarrassing. If the article proves anything, therefore, it proves that Earl Russell was not altogether easy at the turn the blockade question might take in Parliament.

I can not too strongly impress upon the extreme importance of providing me with information. Even the value of a few newspapers can scarcely be exaggerated. So far I have received nothing either from our Department or from the correspondent I had employed previous to my departure for Europe. If I had Southern intelligence, though ever so sparingly or irregularly, I should wield a real power in journalism here, which even my unremitting labor and hitherto singularly good fortune will not give me. May I hope that you will interest yourself in my efficiency as your agent to the extent of sending me, by whatever opportunity may present, files of papers or such other intelligence as you may think proper, and in the judicious use of which you will rely on my discretion?

I have the honor to remain, very respectfully, your obedient servant,

Henry Hotze

HOTZE TO CONFEDERATE SECRETARY OF STATE. NO. 7

London, 25 April 1862

SIR: The enclosed extracts will sufficiently indicate to you that the cotton famine, so long predicted and so unaccountably delayed, has at last overtaken the land, with all its train of destitution and ruin. Articles like those in the *Economist* and *Times* require no comment. If I had £100 at my disposal at this moment I feel confident that I could initiate an agitation, without compromising your Department, which should be scarcely less in extent and effect than the corn-law agitation. In fact, I have already received various direct and indirect propositions of this nature and I dare say Mr. Mason still more. But, without resorting to such questionable means, I am confident that the Government will soon be forced to act. Parliament has almost literally nothing to do. And but for American affairs would certainly have to be prorogued[27] a month or six weeks earlier than usual. This may also hasten events.

From France come faint rumors of diplomatic developments favorable to us, upon which it is not my province to speculate. This much, however, I may say, that I have little hope of the initiative, either in raising the blockade or in recognition being taken by the Emperor. The French public are either wholly indifferent to the events in America or sympathize faintly with the North, partly from sentimental considerations and partly because they see in the power of the United States a counterpoise to that of Great Britain. Besides, the Emperor has grave difficulties at home. During a recent brief visit to Paris, I attended, thanks to a London acquaintance of mine, a breakfast at which I met several prominent men of the Orleans party. Mr. Slidell was also present. Making all due allowance for the medium by which I was surrounded, I came away with the conviction that a temporary alliance had been effected between all the parties opposed to the imperial regime, and that the social extremes had met, the proletarian and the Legitimist, for a common object, which they considered almost within their reach. For the first time in his reign, Louis Napoleon has retracted from a defiantly assumed position in the Mountaban affair, and this is regarded even by many thinking men in England as the beginning of the end. A few days ago the telegraph informed us of the acquittal, amid the cheers of the multitude, of Mires, against whom the Emperor had for 18 months waged a personal feud. It would not surprise me to hear at any moment of a revolution in France, but it would surprise me if the year ended without such a catastrophe.

In Germany the suffering arising from the stoppage of the American market is beginning to be felt almost as severely as in England. The annulling of the enormous contracts of the Federal Government in Europe by the new Secretary of War has added to the distress, and involved in it many of the wealthier classes. I regret that we have not at this time a skillful diplomatic representative in Germany. If he was a German by birth, it would be all the better, for the Federal appointment of Swartz [sic] to Spain, so detestable in every other, has contributed much toward enlisting the warm sympathies of Germany, which by reaction has done us infinite harm in the Western States. Such a representative, however, should be not only a man of great intelligence and knowledge of the people, but a man of vast wealth and disposed to spend it freely. The news of the victory at Corinth (for, despite the distorted accounts of the North, no friend of the South doubts a brilliant and decisive victory) has had an admirable effect, and but that it is in a measure counter balanced by the evacuation of Island No. 10, would probably be sufficient to cause our recognition. The latter has now become, in my opinion, only a question of the opportune moment. The brilliant achievements of the *Virginia* are still in everybody's mouth and one of the staples for newspaper leaders. I sent you some of the earlier specimens via Havana, through Mr. Helm. Two days after the news arrived, Lord Paget, the secretary of the Admiralty, announced in Parliament that no more wooden ships would be built.

Two more newspapers, the *Herald,* Lord Derby's organ, and the *Standard* (same proprietors and, excepting the leaders, one and the same paper, though each with its own circulation), have voluntarily placed themselves at my disposal. The editor in chief of both called on me and offered me the use of the columns, including the editorial columns, of both, of which offer I have, though guardedly, availed myself. A similar arrangement has been effected with the *Money Market Review,* a weekly of small circulation but great authority among capitalists.

I have now, after mature deliberation, concluded to establish a newspaper wholly devoted to our interests, and which will be exclusively under my control, though my connection with it is known only to a few initiated and will not be suspected by the public at large.[28] On this subject I shall write you more at length in my next. Meanwhile you will perceive from the prospectus which I enclose, my plan for making the paper a machine for collecting, comparing, and bringing before the public with proper comments the vast amount of important information which is received in Europe through private channels. This was most difficult to accomplish, and I did not seriously contemplate the new publication until I had assured a reasonable success. The assistance of two personal friends, Mr. H. O. Brewer, of Mobile, and Mr. A. P. Wetter, of Savannah, together with my private resources, enabled me to overcome the pecuniary difficulties of the enterprise and to place its publication, for at least three months, in a manner worthy of the cause, beyond the possibility of failure, even if every copy of the paper had to be given away during that time. Mr. Spence is warmly enlisted in its support, and will contribute regularly and largely with his eloquent pen. What there is of Southern literary talent I may, I think, confidently rely upon, and I hope to cause you an agreeable surprise with the first number of the Index.

Mr. Spence's valuable book is still on its career of usefulness.[29] It is now being translated into French by Mr. George Begonin of Mobile, and into German by Mr. A. P. Wetter, of Savannah. If the translations have but a little of the success which the original has justly achieved, the Southern Confederacy, when it formally takes its place among the nations of the earth, will not come as a stranger among them.

I have the honor to remain, very respectfully, your obedient servant,

Henry Hotze

HOTZE TO J. P. BENJAMIN. NO. 11

London, 26 September 1862

SIR: It is difficult to exaggerate the profound impression produced in this country by the brilliant successes of our arms.[30] The sympathies of the intelligent classes are now intensified into a feeling of sincere admiration to which even the few presses that continue hostile to us can not altogether withhold utterance. If it can not be said that this feeling is generally shared by the lower classes, it is at least certain that they also are swayed by that British instinct which hurrahs for the combatant who deals the hardest blows. There is only one class which as a class continues inimical to us—the Lancashire operatives. With them the unreasoning, it would perhaps be more accurate to say instinctive, aversion to our institutions is as firmly rooted as in any portion of New England, to the population of which they, indeed, bear a striking resemblance. They look upon us, and by a strange confusion of ideas upon slavery, as the author and source of their present miseries, and I am convinced that the astonishing fortitude and patience with which they endure these miseries is mainly due to a consciousness that by any other course they would promote our interests, a feeling which certain supposed emissaries of the Federal Government have worked zealously to confirm. Some good might have been effected by scattering among this population the recent letter of the Federal President to Horace Greeley, but this required a more elaborate and expensive machinery than my means enabled me to organize.[31] Besides, extreme caution is required in everything pertaining to Lancashire, as the accusation has more than once been made against the agents of the Confederate Government of planning an agitation in that district, an accusation, I need not add, which never had any foundation in fact except the ease with which it was known such an agitation could be set in motion.

The message of the President at the reassembling of Congress has been received with unqualified praise by the press of London. The enclosed extracts contain the tributes paid by some of the leading organs of public opinion to the dignity, moderation, and statesmanship which have marked all our official documents. There never was a period so favorable as the present for the discharge of the duties with which you have entrusted me. All information concerning the South and especially the material and organization of our armies is eagerly sought by the leader writers who find a profitable market for it in the journals and magazines with which they are connected. One writer usually writes for several publications, and I have thus the opportunity of multiplying myself, so to speak, to an almost unlimited extent. Every detail of the plan which I laid before the Department previous to my departure for my post has been successfully carried out, only on a much larger scale and in a far vaster field than I anticipated. The establishment of the *Index* enabled me on occasion to assume the position of employer of the pens of some of these gentlemen. Thus, at least half the articles in the *Index* are written by Englishmen, who, only a few months ago, had but imperfect knowledge of and little active sympathy with the South. It is my object and hope, by this means, to found a school of writers whose services in the moral battles we still have to fight will, from their positions, be more valuable than those of the ablest pens of our own country. Some time is yet required for my complete success in this respect and above all, larger pecuniary means. It is true that before you could have received my request for additional funds you nearly doubled the amount which I thought sufficient when appointed to my duties, yet with the vista opening before me I feel that I could advantageously expend twice and even three times the sums I am authorized to expend. What I have been able to accomplish has been done by allying others with me in bearing the expenses, and even this would have been impossible had I not been able to rely on private resources and personal influence.

Thus I have in a very limited degree subsidized newspapers by procuring them subscribers among friends, my contingent allowance coming in for but a small contribution. I have similarly aided various useful publications, the principal burden of expense being borne by others. Again, in maintaining the *Index* at an expense of £40 a week, I have thus far used much more of my own money and that of friends than of the funds intrusted to me by the Government. Many useful enterprises I have been reluctantly forced to forego altogether for lack of means.

Among the most important effects upon public opinion produced by our great successes is the fear that, by the triumphs of the South, that reconstruction of the Union might be accomplished, which could never have been expected from the triumph of the North. An extract which I enclose from the *Daily Telegraph,* the paper of largest circulation in London, is a fair expression of this fear. While I would not lend myself to propagate or confirm an impression which I know to be erroneous, I yet do not deem it politic for the present to make myself active in dispelling it. I have long been persuaded that reconstruction by the triumph of either party over the other is what the Government and people of Great Britain would make every sacrifice to prevent, and that one of the chief causes of the inaction of the former has been the conviction that the efforts of the North were futile. To whatever extent, therefore, the impression may gain ground that the Union can be erected anew upon the prostration of the North instead of the South, to that extent it operates in favor of our objects. In fact the suggestion has already been made in quarters hostile to us that the Confederate States should be recognized now lest they might have to be recognized with a territorial dominion larger than it was prudent to allow them.

I feel it my duty to inform you that since the prorogation of Parliament I was absent from London for several weeks during the month of August, keeping however in such constant communication that I could at any time have returned to my post within thirty-six hours. My primary object was to consult oculists of eminence about my eyes, the condition of which from overexertion had become alarming. I endeavored to connect my journey with my duties by procuring the publication of a German translation of Mr. Spence's celebrated book, performed by Mr. A. P. Wetter, of Savannah. I was less successful in this than I expected, finding none of the great publishers willing to affix their names to the book, owing to the universal prejudice against our cause and country. This prejudice, I have been informed, has much abated within the past few weeks. A cheap edition of the book, to the cost of which I shall contribute about £20, is now in course of publication. Should the war be much longer prolonged, it might be worthy of your consideration whether a competent agent might not be of service in Berlin or some other large German city. He should be thoroughly conversant with the manners and the language of the country; if possible a native, and a man of wealth willing to spend it. Considerable reflective influence might be exerted by such a man over the Germans of the Northern and Western States.

I take pride in saying that the *Index* though I could but imperfectly guide it during my absence, in nowise discredited the high rank among weekly periodicals which, despite its brief existence, it has already assumed. This is a proof that it is established on a firm and permanent foundation, and not dependent on the chances that may befall a single man. I am indebted for this gratifying result to my manager and assistant, J. B. Hopkins, esq., whose excellent judgment has been strikingly attested whilst representing me in the *Index*. Mr. Hopkins is an Englishman who has zealously and successfully applied himself to the study of the great question involved in the independence of the South. He is the author of an admirable paper read before the Social Science Congress at its last session and which attracted much attention; also of a well-filled introduction to the *South Vindicated*, just published by General Williams, late U.S. minister at Constantinople, under Mr. Hopkins' editorship. I am further under obligations to Percy Greg, esq., one of the most talented leader writers of London, who besides being a valuable contributor to the *Index* is one of our most efficient supporters in the columns of the *Saturday Review* and other literary and political periodicals of high standing. In thus particularizing to you some of our English allies, I am influenced by the importance of courting and retaining such support. These gentlemen are not citizens of the Confederate States and expect no favors of any kind, but some of those opportunities may arise which you know so well how to use, of making them aware, by a single word, perhaps that their efforts are noticed and appreciated.

As I write, the *North American* brings news of a defeat of our armies and their retreat into Virginia.[32] The public will attach little importance to this report unless abundantly confirmed. But should it turn out to be true, it can not now affect public opinion materially. That public opinion is decidedly averse to the North, and considers our formal admission into the family of nations as a foregone conclusion.

I have the honor to remain, sir, very respectfully, your obedient servant,
Henry Hotze

HOTZE TO J. P. BENJAMIN. NO. 26

London, 23 July 1863

SIR: The news of the check sustained by our forces at Gettysburg, coupled with the reported fall of Vicksburg, was so unexpected as to spread very general dismay not only among the active sympathizers with our cause, but even among those who take merely a selfish interest in the great struggle. The disappointment was proportionate to the confidence which had come to be generally entertained that our arms were about to achieve the crowning triumph of peace. Under this sense of disappointment the public mind was in danger of exaggerating the magnitude and real significance of the events. The news received last night has somewhat reassured the shaken confidence in our ultimate success, but all is still perplexity, surprise, and alarm. The current into which public opinion will finally settle depends on the attitude of our people, and as I know that this will be as resolute and unwavering as during the dark period of last summer, I do not fear that we shall lose ground here. If they enforce the conviction that the war will be indefinitely protracted so long as England encourages the North to assail our independence by ignoring it, our recent misfortunes may not be without some compensating effects. I send you files of all the principal dailies, which, however, will indicate very little beyond the painful surprise with which the news was received. The *Times,* always throwing its weight on the side either of the North or South according as either seems losing, makes this morning a strong effort to rally the sinking spirits of our English friends. The tonic effect will be excellent, whatever motive may actuate the *Times* policy.

It is unfortunate for us that at this very moment Europe feels itself on the verge of a general war. Russia has rejected, with but slight attempts at conciliation, the joint proposals of England, France, and Prussia on the subject of Poland.[33] In France public opinion is in a state of unprecedented ferment; all parties and all classes uniting in a clamor for war which must drown the soberer counsels, if such there are, in the imperial cabinet. I doubt whether this feeling is less strong in England, though its expression is subdued by the more sedate temper of the people and their instinctive aversion to war. Austria has of late entered into a career of liberalism, very commendable in itself, but which may have committed it too far on this question to make retreat safe or possible. There is, therefore, a substantial danger of a European war, in the turmoil of which we should be wholly lost sight of.

The situation calls for extreme exertion as well here as at home. While it is politic to accept the facts in their stern reality, without attempting to disguise them under forced constructions or flattering hypotheses, it is necessary by acts even more than words to sustain the courage of our friends and supporters. A more than ordinary moral fortitude is demanded of the representatives of Southern views. The merest quaver of nerve on their part would be deemed a symptom of despair. You will not therefore be surprised that I am giving to my operations an extension which only the urgencies of the crisis could warrant, and I shall feel it my duty to neglect no opportunity for impressing upon the public the undiminished vitality of our cause. One of the means which I had commenced to adopt while I still thought that the hour of peace was approaching is on so large a scale that I should somewhat doubt your approval had not the turn in our affairs proved it so unexpectedly opportune. Finding that the "Address of the Southern Clergy to Christians Throughout the World" had produced excellent effects wherever it could be brought under public notice, I have not contented myself with merely publishing a pamphlet edition, but have arranged that a copy shall be stitched up under the same cover with this or the next month's number of every respectable religious publication, as also the two leading political reviews, the Quarterly and the Edinburgh, just out. A quarter of a million of copies of the address are by this means brought under the eyes of between one and two millions of readers in every part of the world where the English language is spoken.[34]

For the suggestion of this original, and in its magnitude, unprecedented mode of giving universal publicity to a document, I am indebted to the Presbyterian publishing house of Messrs. Nisbet & Co., who have undertaken to carry it out without compensation for the very considerable trouble it involves. The expenses, small in proportion to the work, will yet not fall short of £250. As I had arranged to disburse through the *Index* very nearly, if not quite the amount of my contingent allowance, this sum would make a serious reduction in my means. Mr. de Leon, however, to whom I have just communicated my plan, and who heartily approves of it, as do all whom I have consulted, has offered to share half the expense, which I have gratefully accepted. These and other heavy outlays, outside of my permanent scheme for action, have induced me to defer the dissemination of the commercial circular, of which I spoke in my No. 22, in order to spread my disbursements over a larger period of time. But this consideration is overruled by the conviction that now is the proper time for striking all the blows in quick succession and I shall therefore forthwith carry this plan also into execution. As I dare not reduce any of my other expenses, it is certain that I shall for the first nine months of the present year exceed the very liberal allowance which the President has made me out of the secret service fund, and this I do with unfeigned reluctance, and with a deep sense of the responsibility which I assume. I can only hope that the events of the future will enable me to make such reductions as to restore the proportions fixed by you.

I learn with much regret that Colonel Lamar is about to return home.

During his short stay here a very cordial friendship has sprung up between us, and I have found his society a great assistance to me in the discharge of my duties. My own mind is impoverished by constant writing without sufficient opportunity to replenish with reading and reflection, and the suggestions of his fruitful intellect were an invaluable advantage to me. I am endeavoring to persuade him to stay, if only until this great crisis in our affairs is passed safely.

I remain, with great respect, your obedient servant,
Henry Hotze

HOTZE TO J. P. BENJAMIN. NO. 48

London, 6 August 1864

SIR: A review of the political situation, although it is some time since I wrote you on general affairs, need occupy no great space. Now that the session is over the ministers are enjoying their triumph at small adulatory gatherings and select banquets and showing how little they deserve success by complacently, and even boastfully, ascribing to themselves what is really due to accident and the public apathy. Thus Lord Russell had the assurance to say at the lord mayor's dinner given to her Majesty's ministers that the position of England had never been prouder nor her influence greater than at this moment, an announcement which, to the honor of the audience be it said, was received in silence, succeeded, as soon as the first sudden effect of astonishment had worn off, by a buzz of general conversation. Lord Palmerston has betrayed, by exhibitions of ill-temper and the gratification of little personal spites and revenges in the closing days of the session, how thoroughly he must have been scared and how narrow he considers the escape to have been. Meanwhile the country has given another evidence of the steady growth of the Conservative, or at least opposition feeling, in the defeat for the first time in this generation of the Liberal candidate in the populous constituency of Exeter. Unfortunately, as the last Parliamentary battle has proved, the strength of the latent protest against the ministerial policy is wasted by want of tact and want of principles or courage on the part of the leaders of the opposition, and thus the weakness of the administration only serves as a pretext and excuse for its inaction.

Abroad everything is now as quiet as the most imbecile of "*après moi le deluge*" statesmen could desire.[35] No great danger has been averted, no great question solved but everything has been put off for the moment, and procrastination has gained at least four or five months of ease, at what cost the future alone can show. Denmark has been forced into a peace so ignominious that the Legislative Assembly, on hearing the terms announced, was as silent as Earl Russell's auditors at the lord mayor's banquet, but afterwards passed a resolution to the effect that this silence was not to be construed into approval. A few months will, of course, be spent in negotiations of details, but the basis is accepted and is such an one as even the Germans themselves a year ago would have thought preposterous. In Poland the last act of the tragedy is played out and the curtain falls, probably forever, on the execution of the principal chiefs of the National Government, the transportation of the others to Siberian fortresses, and the expropriation of nearly the whole body of landed proprietors. A sort of earthquake has passed over the Mussulman populations, beginning in Algeria, shaking the Government of Tunis, and largely manifesting itself in a revival, or rather outbreak, of Mohammedanism in the Ottoman Empire. These are the impotent protests against the proselytism of Western Europe, but either they have no longer or not yet any serious importance.

There is, therefore, absolutely no excuse left in the present state of Europe for inattention to American affairs. Yet you will have seen, better than I could tell you, how absolutely hopeless it still is to expect anything in our favor for some time to come, or until we shall no longer need it. In this respect there seems little to choose between the English and French Governments, except that the former has at least been consistent in its coldness, while the latter has raised expectations apparently only to disappoint them the more cruelly. As Mr. Mason has been sojourning for several weeks past in England, he has probably advised you of our prospects here, as Mr. Slidell will have done from France, and I need therefore do nothing more than report the conclusions at which I believe every Confederate sympathizer in Europe has now arrived, that any present hope of recognition is a delusion.

The military events are watched with all the more anxious eagerness and it is noticeable that the public, sympathetic to us, invariably receives with evident uneasiness the news of every offensive movement on our part beyond our own territory. Bright as the prospects of General Early's invasion into Maryland were admitted to be, the first intelligence of it affected the loan unfavorably.[36] I doubt whether even the capture of Baltimore or Washington would so much reassure public anxiety as a decisive victory over Sherman.

Financial difficulties, perhaps even a crisis, are foreseen in the course of next autumn, due partly to over speculation, but accelerated by the reports of bad harvests in America and in southern Russia, and above all the enormous amounts of specie required for the purchase of cotton. Our own financial condition abroad appears to be excellent. We have gradually got rid of the adventurers and leeches that throve upon the public purse and affected to be considered patriotic, or devoted friends, and have formed new connections at once more advantageous and more respectable. Despite the serious doubts of the fate of Atlanta the loan has kept at a quotation of 75 to 77 which proves inherent strength. The new commercial system, though scarcely yet in its infancy, has thus far worked so beneficially as to promise when fully developed to fulfill literally and even to exceed my own glowing anticipations. I can only hope that no amount, of Pressure brought to bear upon the Government, from any quarter whatever, may induce it to swerve from the policy which dictated these salutary measures.

The first rumor of peace negotiations caused considerable sensation both in England and France, but when the details of the Niagara Falls correspondence became known, the public seemed disposed to avenge their disappointment by pitilessly ridiculing both parties. I have done my best, under an urgent necessity which you will appreciate, to disconnect the Government and its trusted agents from time eccentricities of persons whose notoriety in Europe is much greater than the esteem in which they are held.

I have the honor to remain, very respectfully, your obedient servant,
Henry Hotze

A Primer on Southern Society

HOTZE TO FELIX DUCAIGNE

London, 23 August 1863

DEAR Sir: As the political director, if not nominal editor, of the *Index* I beg to acknowledge your favor of yesterday, correcting certain errors into which the Paris correspondent of that paper has fallen in referring to your biweekly letters to *La Patrie* from Providence, R.I. I am uncertain whether your letter was intended for publication or only for private information, but until I hear from you to the contrary, shall regard it as the latter. In either case I shall direct that no unfair or disrespectful references to you shall in future appear in the Paris correspondence.

I thank you cordially for the friendly sentiments you profess for my country and its cause, and I am far from wishing to take issue with you on the opinions which you hold with regard to our institution of slavery. As, however, you do me the honor to ask me for "indications which I may think calculated to give you a right idea of the social condition of the South," being about to prepare an article on that subject for the *Revue Contemporaine,* you will perhaps pardon me if, deeply interested as I am, that so influential a journal should not undersignedly misrepresent us, I caution you against a few of the most essential errors into which a European is likely to fall.

It is customary to represent the class of slave owners as a small and tyrannical oligarchy, and to produce this impression a most disingenuous treatment of statistics has been resorted to. You will please, therefore, remember that the 345,239 holders of slaves enumerated in the United States census of 1850 are families, not individuals, and according to ascertained laws this number must be multiplied by five to produce the number of persons directly interested in slave property; in other words, nearly 2,000,000, or about one-fourth of the estimated white population. Moreover, even this figure does not include the very large numbers who hire, not own slaves as domestic servants; nor does it include the vast majority of the professional classes, merchants, physicians, lawyers, etc., who, without either owning or hiring slaves, have an indirect but none the less strong interest in slave property, since they are by family and business ties intimately connected with the planting interest. These considerations will convince you that slavery has far deeper roots in the social system than is generally supposed.[37]

Secondly, a classification according to the census of the slave-owning families gives very different results from what is generally supposed. Only 9 families in the South hold between 500 and 1,000 slaves; only 2 hold over that number, while largely more than one-fourth of them hold less than 5 slaves. Thus the holding of a small number of slaves in close contact with their masters is the general rule; the accumulation of large numbers of slaves under one proprietor who can bestow but little personal attention to them, is the exception. I shall by tomorrow's post send you valuable statistics on this as on other subjects.

A third and widespread error is that the mass of the Southern white population is in a state of poverty and degradation. The events of the war have sufficiently refuted this calumny, but it may be of service to you to know that according to the census one-half of the white male population is engaged in agriculture and that 563,138 out of the entire 840,929, or five-eighths of those so engaged, owned their farms.

You will see from these indisputable official figures that the Southern people are not divided into those two classes of fabulously wealthy and luxurious aristocrats on the one hand and miserable vagabonds on the other, which the popular idea represents them to be, but that property is distributed with an equality which has no parallel in any other country except perhaps France.

On the subject of education, religion, etc., the census will inform you that the South is but little behind the North, making allowance for its more scattered population. It has fully as many churches and schools as either England or France. About one-third of the white population are communicants of some Christian church. Although mostly Protestants, divorces are of less frequent occurrence than at the North; in some States, as in South Carolina, they are not granted at all. The statistics of crime are remarkably small; prostitution is almost unknown, except in the larger cities, and pauperism does not exist at all. You will please also remember in spite of your hostility to slavery that slavery is less a question of property than it is a form of civil government over an inferior race only a few generations removed from barbarism and equal in numbers to one-third of the master race. The Yankees, as you will see by a very fair exposition of their plantation management in [the] last *Index,* do not propose, while nominally freeing the slaves, to give them civil and political rights. They will none the less make the Negro work for the benefit of the white man under compulsion, and instead of the patriarchal form, which had many extenuating features, they would substitute a "workhouse system" which retains all the worst characteristics without any of the compensations or advantages of slavery.

Of books and reviews I can indicate to you but few. The South has hitherto had no literature of its own. Travelers have usually visited it with strong prejudices and written either to subserve political and party purposes or with a view to pleasing biased readers rather than investigating the truth. Many have only allowed themselves to be the vehicles of repeating slanderous or ridiculous fictions. The two books that will give you the best view of the social manners of the South are the book of travels by Miss Murray (a maid of honor to the Queen) and Miss Frederica Bremer's, *Homes in the New World.* Statistics are the best study of the social condition of the South, and of these I will send you tomorrow all I can collect in so short a period and far away from home.

With the enormous productiveness of the country you are doubtless already quite familiar. The cotton culture alone produces annually about 1,000 million francs' worth of exportable staple. I [had] almost forgotten to remind you, in treating your prolific subject, that whatever the theoretical evils of the slave system are, they are in practice modified by many restraining influences. Practically the master's power over the slave is not greater than that which he has over his wife and children. The instinct of self-preservation in society at large, and the public opinion of a Christian community, protect the slave far more effectually than mere laws, though I am not prepared to deny that many improvements are required and will certainly be made in the laws when the South, resting from her struggle, has time and leisure for self-examination.

Very sincerely, yours,
Henry Hotze

The Genius of the Editor[38]

The cherished ambition of my life is to make the *Index* a worthy representative in journalism of the highest ideal of that Southern civilization which is as yet only in its infancy. This ideal is as far removed from a blind idolatry of the past as from the conceited contempt of the past, which characterizes our age. It is but faintly expressed in the hackneyed phrase of "liberal conservatism." It means progress without subversion, liberty with order, fraternity without equality, love and good will to all men without professional philanthropy; it is trust in the wisdom of Providence rather than in human ingenuity. It is the opposite of Yankeeism of whichever hemisphere and whatever tongue or nationality, not even excepting Southern Yankeeism—for there is such a thing. It is the protest against the heresies and fallacies peculiar to our century, which in its inmost heart exalts the steam engine and the electric telegraph above God. I have spoken seriously because whenever I touch upon this subject, I am always thoroughly in earnest.

A journal which should adhere to such a creed, subordinating to it all other considerations of pecuniary or political success, will not, to be sure, reform the world, nor pretend to attempt it, because it will not be conducted by either lunatics or fanatics; but such a journal must in time acquire influence and authority, and be a great accession of strength to the party, or sect, or country it represents. The more universal it becomes, that is to say, the more branches of human thought and the more topics of interest it can embrace, the more widely, provided the central idea be never lost sight of, will its influence and authority be felt.

In this lies the genius of the editor. To be cosmopolitan and yet to have a country, to be miscellaneous and yet to have an object; to be tolerant and yet not indifferent; to be moderate and yet to have strong convictions; to be instructive and yet not dull; to be entertaining and yet not frivolous; this is the unattainable editorial perfection which should be aimed at. He should see with the eyes of the public, and hear with the ears of the public, and yet have eyes and ears of his own. The fault most men commit, and which I constantly commit, is to fancy that what does not interest me does not interest the public, and to act as if a distasteful subject was disposed of by being passed in silence. Try, as far as possible, to avoid this fault. Try to make the *Index* more and more a newspaper, an epitome of the world, where each thing has its appropriate place, and where none occupies too much. With the American question we cannot do this, but in time we may approach nearer to symmetry even in that.

It is easier to make rules than to keep them, and to preach than to practice. But I have you by the button-hole now, and may not find another so good opportunity for a lecture on the theory and philosophy of journalism. Be patient therefore, while I give you yet a few more details, rather of my experience than of my practice.

English journalism as a rule sacrifices too much to the "leader." American journalism is too careless of it. The *"leader"* gives body, tone, flavor, character, to a newspaper; but it is not the newspaper itself. Without its other departments symmetrically proportioned, a newspaper would only be a magazine, or a leaf out of a volume of essays. A paper is always judged by its *"leaders"* (because they are to it what the face is to the human body) but it is scarcely ever bought or read *for* its leaders.

What people buy a newspaper for is, as the name implies, the *news.* Not necessarily or exclusively the current events of the day, but *information* on something they desire to know. I have told you above in what an editor's *genius* consists. It is to know what his readers desire to know and to find it out for them. But there is something practically even more important than *genius;* it is *skill.* Now an editor's *skill* consists in dressing the information he has to give in the most attractive manner; and to display it in the most accessible way. It is *pièce de résistance* which give éclat to a dinner, but it is the uniform excellence of all of the dishes and of the service, which puts the guests in good humor and keeps them in good digestion. Just so it is with the editorial gastronomy. Pay, therefore, if you wish to succeed as an editor, the most scrupulous attention to the *details* of the paper. These are very generally neglected, and in the *Index* peculiarly so. Nor must you think such work on details beneath editorial dignity. There is practically more influence to be exerted by a casual comment in a note or a paragraph, or by a mere turn of the phrase in which a bit of intelligence is given, than by the leader column, properly so called. The latter is the heavy artillery of a newspaper, which though it makes more noise, kills fewer than well-directed and well sustained fire of small arms.

I have spoken of the genius of the editor and of his skill. Let me say a word about the editor's *art*. As of other things, so here, of course, the *ars celare artem*[39] is the highest. But the special art of the editor is to always have something in his *bill of fare* which tempts the appetite of the public, and to display it conspicuously without descending to the vulgar catch-penny tricks of the trade. It is not possible to command that something at will and it is therefore often good policy, in seasons of abundance, to lay by for the season of scarcity. Still, that species of economy can be carried too far as newspapers' tit bits are apt to get stale, and it is better on the whole to have occasionally a dull paper, than by straining too hard after uniformity, arriving at—uniform dullness.

In a weekly paper, more particularly one which addresses itself to a distant public, there is always an unfailing resource, to which, before concluding, I should not omit to direct your attention. It is "selections." I know scarcely a department of a paper in which the genius, the skill, and the art of the editor is so thoroughly tested. He there requires that little of each which in the aggregate is called *tact*. The best advice I can give you in this respect is to cut or copy whatever in your reading, serious or miscellaneous, strikes you as curious, interesting or otherwise worthy of preservation—a brilliant thought, a bit of quaint statistics, a felicitous expression, strays and waifs and odds and ends of all sorts. Depend upon it they will be welcome to your readers and oblige those you can quote from. The way to use such matter is to throw it into a drawer or a box and draw upon this reserve funds as occasion may serve.

In this matter you avoid the greatest dangers of editorial life, that of padding and stuffing, and hastily finding "copy" only to fill up space, becoming thus the slave of the mechanical exigencies of the paper. The danger is even greater than that of "over-setting," having too much "copy," by which the foreman of the printing office becomes your colleague. A model paper has always a little over, but never too much.

And so I end my epistle, which, commenced long since and resumed at different periods, has grown to an intolerable length. I can only promise (and with safety too) that in future I will spare you such inflictions, and I remain

> With kindest and most cordial feeling
> Sincerely your friend
> Henry Hotze

A *Plan to take the* Index *to America*

Hotze to Joel Cook, 22 April 1865

My Dear Sir:[40]
My present object in writing to you is to consult you regarding the feasibility of an idea which the suddenly altered aspect of affairs and the possibly impending political revolution in America, have of late caused me to take into serious consideration. If, what I do not believe, but what has now entered into the province of possible contingencies, the armed resistance of the South, east of the Mississippi, should be overcome, the most difficult problem of statesmanship would arise that has ever perplexed the counsels of any nation. I am of opinion that when the passions of the war have subsided, the practical sense of the American people will again come into the ascendant, and sternly decide against the party in power the question whether the "reconstructed" Union should be Africanized or a white man's government. This question may or may not be peacefully settled in the North, but it certainly contains the seeds of civil war, and in any event journalism will have an important play in it.

I have therefore thought of publishing a special cheap American edition of the *Index,* which—bringing down the latest European news to Saturday evening and embodying greater variety of miscellaneous matter—I could without great additional expense make a most attractive weekly paper. The English edition, published at 6^d, and sold (I believe) in New York at 50 cents, now circulates in America between 300 and 400 copies, that is to say more than any other English newspaper except the *Illustrated News* and perhaps the *Times.* A special edition on cheap paper, if not less than 3000 copies, could be reprinted here at a rate to allow of its being sold at 10 or 12 cents. This would of course leave us no margin of profit, but that is not my object.

What I wish to trouble you with is, first, your personal views on the practicality of the plan, and more particularly: Whether a sale of 3000 within the range of the U.S. Post Office could be reasonably expected at the price indicated? What amount of publicity and credit the paper now enjoys and may hope to enjoy under the supposed new regime? To what extent advertising it might be advisable or necessary?

What modifications, to ensure success, the paper would require over and above those I have indicated, viz. the news brought down to Saturday evening, and the addition of literary, theatrical, and eclectic miscellanies? Any suggestions upon these or other points connected with the plan, which your experience in journalism may enable you to make, would be extremely valuable to me, and deemed a favor which I should take great pleasure in reciprocating. Apologizing for troubling you so often and so much,

I remain, very cordially your friend,
Henry Hotze

Part Three

"The Natural History of Man"

Dr. Josiah Clark Nott. (Mobile Medical Museum)

Excerpt from "Analytical Introduction and Copious Historical Notes"

Written as an introduction to *The Moral and Intellectual Diversity of the Races*

Whether we contemplate the human family from the point of view of the naturalist or of the philosopher, we are struck with the marked dissimilarity of the various groups. The obvious physical characteristics, by which we distinguish what are termed different races, are not more clearly defined than the psychical diversities observable among them. "If a person," says the learned vindicator of the unity of the human species, "after surveying some brilliant ceremony or court pageant in one of the splendid cities of Europe, were suddenly carried into a hamlet in Negro-land, at the hour when the sable tribes recreate themselves with dancing or music; or if he were transplanted to the saline plains over which bald and tawny Mongolians roam, differing but little in hue from the yellow soil of their steppes, brightened by the saffron flowers of the iris and tulip; if he were placed near the solitary dens of the Bushman, where the lean and hungry savage crouches in silence, like a beast of prey, watching with fixed eyes the birds which enter his pitfall or greedily devouring the insects and reptiles which chance may bring within his grasp; if he were carried into the midst of an Australian forest, where the squalid companions of kangaroos may be seen crawling in procession, in imitation of quadrupeds, would the spectator of such phenomena imagine the different groups which he had surveyed to be the offspring of one family? And if he were led to adopt that opinion, how would he attempt to account for the striking diversities in their aspect and manner of existence?"[1]

These diversities, so graphically described by Mr. Prichard, present a problem, the solution of which has occupied the most ingenious minds, especially of our times. The question of unity or plurality of the human species has of late excited much animated discussion; great names and weighty authorities are enlisted on either side, and a unanimous decision appears not likely to be soon agreed upon. But it is not my purpose, nor that of the author to whose writings these pages are introductory, to enter into a contest which to me seems rather a dispute about words than essentials. The distinguishing physical characteristics of what we term races of man are recognized by all parties, and whether these races are *distinct species* or *permanent varieties* only of the same, cannot affect the subject under investigation. In whatever manner the diversities among the various branches of the human family may have originated, whether they are primordial or were produced by external causes, their permanency is now generally admitted. "The Ethiopian cannot change his skin." If there are, or ever have been, external agencies that could change a white man into a negro, or *vice versa,* it is obvious that such causes have either ceased to operate, or operate only in a lapse of time so incommensurable as to be imponderable to our perceptions, for the races which now exist can be traced up to the dawn of history, and no well-authenticated instance of a transformation under any circumstances is on record. In human reasoning it is certainly legitimate to judge the future by the experiences of the past, and we are, therefore, warranted to conclude that if races have preserved their identity for the last two thousand years, they will not lose it in the next two thousand.

It is somewhat singular, however, that while most writers have ceased to explain the physical diversities of races by external causes, such as climate, food, etc., yet many still persist in maintaining the absolute equality of all in other respects, referring such differences in character as undeniable, solely to circumstances, education, mode of life, etc. These writers consider all races as merely in different stages of development, and pretend that the lowest savage, or at least his offspring, may, by judicious training, and in course of time, be rendered equal to the civilized man. Before mentioning any facts in opposition to this doctrine, let us examine the reasoning upon which it is based.

"Man is the creature of circumstances," is an adage extended from individuals to races, and repeated by many without considering its bearing. The celebrated author of *Wealth of Nations* says "that the difference between the most dissimilar characters, between a philosopher and a common street porter, for example, arises, not so much from nature, but from habit and education."[2] That a mind, which, with proper nurture, might have graced a philosopher, should, under unfavorable circumstances, remain forever confined in a narrow and humble sphere, does not, indeed, seem at all improbable; but Dr. Smith certainly does not mean to deny the existence of natural talents, of innate peculiar capacities for the accomplishment of certain purposes. This is what they do who ascribe the mental inequality of the various branches of the human family to external circumstances only. "The intellectual qualities of man," they say, "are developed entirely by education. The mind is, at first, a perfect blank, fitted and ready to receive any kind of impressions. For these, we are dependent on the political, civil, and religious institutions under which we live, the persons with whom we are connected, and the circumstances in which we are placed in the different places of life. Wholly the creatures of association and habit, the characters of men are formed by the instruction, conversation, and example of those with whom they mix in society, or whose ideas they imbibe in the course of their reading and studies." Again: "As all men, in all nations, are of the same species, are endowed with the same senses and feelings, and receive their perceptions and ideas through similar organs, the difference, whether physical or moral, that is observed in comparing different races or assemblages of men, can arise only from external and adventitious circumstances." The last position is entirely dependent on the first; if we grant the first, relating to individuals, the other follows as a necessary consequence. For, if we assume that the infinite intellectual diversities of individuals are owing solely to external influences, it is self-evident that the same diversities in nations, which are but aggregations of individuals, must result from the same causes. But are we prepared to grant this first position—to assert that man is but an automation, whose wheelwork is entirely without—the mere buffet and plaything of accident and circumstances? Is not this the first step to gross materialism, the first argument laid down by that school, of which the great Locke has been stigmatized as the father, because he also asserts that the human mind is at first a blank tablet.[3] But Locke certainly would not mean that all these tablets were the same and of equal value. A tablet of wax receives an impression which one of marble will not; on the former is easily effaced what the other forever retains. We do not deny that circumstances have a great influence in molding both moral and intellectual character, but we do insist that there is a primary basis upon which the degree of that influence depends, and which is the work of God and not of man or chance. What agriculturalist could be made to believe that, with the same care, all plants would thrive equally well in all soils? To assert that the character of a man, whether good or wicked, noble or mean, is the aggregate result of influences over which he has no control, is to deny that man is a free agent; it is infinitely worse than the creed of the Buddhist, who believes that all animated beings possess a detached portion of an all-embracing intelligence, which acts according to the nature and capacity of the machine of clay that it, for the time, occupies, and when the machine is worn out or destroyed, returns, like a rivulet to the sea, to the vast ocean of intelligence whence it came, and in which again it is lost. In the name of common sense, daily observation, and above all, of revelation, we protest against a doctrine which paves the road to the most absurd as well as anti-religious conclusions. In it we recognize the fountain whence flow all the varied forms and names under which Atheism disguises itself. But it is useless to enter any further the refutation of an argument which few would be willing seriously to maintain. It is one of those plausible speculations which, once admitted, serve as the basis of so many brilliant, but airy, theories that dazzle and attract those who do not take the trouble of examining their solidity.

Once we admit that circumstances, though they may impede or favor the development of powers, cannot give them; in other words, that they can call into action, but cannot create, moral and intellectual resources; no argument can be drawn from the unity of species in favor of the mental equality of races.[4] If two men, the offspring of the same parents, can be the one a dunce, the other a genius, why cannot different races, though descended of the same stock, be different also in intellectual endowments? We should laugh at, or rather pity the man who would try to persuade us that there is no difference in color, etc., between the Scandinavian and the African, and yet it is by some considered little short of heresy to affirm, that there is an imparity in their minds as well as in their bodies.

We are told—and the objection seems indeed a grave one—that if we admit psychical as well as physical gradations in the scale of human races, the lowest must be so hopelessly inferior to the higher, their perceptions and intellectual capacities so dim, that even the light of the Gospel cannot illumine them. Were it so, we should at once abandon the argument as one above human comprehension, rather than suppose that God's mercy is confined to any particular race or races. But let us earnestly investigate the question. On so vital a point the sacred record cannot but be plain and explicit. To it let us turn. Man—even the lowest of the species—has a soul. However much defaced God's image, it is vivified by His breath. To save that soul, to release it from the bondage of evil, Christ descended upon earth and gave to mankind, not a complicated system of philosophy which none but the learned and intellectual could understand, but a few simple lessons and precepts, comprehensible to the meanest capacity. He did not address himself to the wise of this world, but bade them to be like children if they would come unto him. The learned Pharisees of Judea jeered and ridiculed him, but the poor woman of Canaan eagerly picked up the precious crumbs of that blest repast which they despised. His apostles were chosen from among the lowly and simple; his first followers belonged to that class. He himself had said: "I thank thee, O Father, Lord of heaven and earth, because thou hast hid these things from the wise and prudent and hast revealed them unto babes."[5] How then shall we judge of the degree of intellect necessary to be a follower of Jesus? Are the most intellectual, the best informed men generally the best Christians? Or does the word of God lead us to suppose that at the great final judgment the learned prelate or ingenious expositor of the faith will be preferred to the humble, illiterate savage of some almost unknown coast, who eagerly drinks of the living water whereof whosoever drinketh shall never thirst again?

This subject has met with the attention which its importance deserves, at the hands of Mr. Gobineau, and he also shows the fallacy of the idea that Christianity will remove the mental inequality of races. True religion, among all nations who are blessed with it and sincerely embrace it, will purify their morals and establish friendly relations between man and his fellow man. But it will not make an *intellectually* inferior race equal to a superior one, because it was not designed to bestow talents or to endow with genius those who are devoid of it. Civilization is essentially the result of man's intellectual gifts, and must vary in its character and degree like them. Of this we shall speak again in treating of the *specific differences of civilization,* when the term *Christian civilization* will also be examined.

One great reason why so many refuse to recognize mental as well as physical differences among races, is the common and favorite belief of our time in the infinite perfectibility of man. Under various forms, this development theory, so flattering to humanity, has gained an incredible number of adherents and defenders. We believe ourselves steadily marching towards some brilliant goal, to which every generation brings us nearer. We look with a pity, almost amounting to contempt, upon those who preceded us, and envy posterity, which we expect to surpass us in a ratio even greater than we believe ourselves to surpass our ancestors. It is indeed a beautiful and poetic idea that civilization is a vast and magnificent edifice of which the first generation laid the corner stone, and to which each succeeding age contributes new materials and new embellishments. It is our tower of Babel, by which we, like the first men after the flood, hope to reach heaven and escape the ills of life.[6] Some such idea has flattered all ages, but in ours, it has assumed a more definite form. We point with pride to our inventions, annihilating—

we say—time and distance; our labor saving machines refining the mechanic and indirectly diffusing information among all classes, and confidently look forward to a new era close at hand, a millennium to come. Let us, for a moment, divest ourselves of the conceit which belongs to every age, as well as to every country and individual; and let us ask ourselves seriously and candidly: In what are we superior to our predecessors? We have inventions that they had not, it is true, and these inventions increase in an astonishing ratio; we have clearer ideas of the laws which govern the material world, and better contrivances to apply these laws and to make the elements subservient to our comfort. But has the human mind really expanded since the days of Pythagoras and Plato? Has the thinker of the nineteenth century faculties and perceptions which they had not? Have we one virtue more or one vice less than former generations? Has human nature changed, or has it even modified its failings? Though we succeed in traversing the regions of air as easily and swifter than we now do broad continents and stormy seas; though we count all the worlds in the immensity of space; though we snatch from nature her most recondite secrets, shall we be aught but men? To the true philosopher these conquests over the material world will be but proofs of the greatness of God and man's littleness. It is the vanity and arrogance of the creature of clay that make him believe that by his own exertions he can arrive at God-like perfection. The insane research after the philosopher's stone and the elixir of life may be classed among the many other futile attempts of man to invade the immutable decree: "Thus far and no farther." To escape from the moral and intellectual imperfections of his nature, there is but one way; the creature must humbly and devoutly cast himself into the ever-open arms of the Creator and seek for knowledge where none knocketh in vain. The privilege he has enjoyed in all ages, and it is a question which I would hesitate to answer whether the progress of physical science has not, in many cases at least, rather the effect of making him self-sufficient and too confident in his own powers, than of bringing him nearer to the knowledge of the true God. It is one of the fatal errors of our age in particular, to confound the progress of physical science with a supposed moral progress of man. Were it so, the Bible would have been a revelation of science as well as of religion, and that it is not is now beginning to be conceded, though by no means so generally as true theology would require; for the law of God was intended for every age, for every country, for every individual, independent of the state of science or a peculiar stage of civilization, and not to be modified by any change which man might make in his material existence. With due deference, then, to those philosophers who assert that the moral nature of the human species has undergone a change at various periods of the world's history; and those enthusiasts who dream of an approaching millennium, we hold, that human nature has always been the same and always will be the same, and that no inventions or discoveries, however promotive of his material well-being, can effect a moral change or bring him any nearer to the Divine essence than he was in the beginning of his mundane existence. Science and knowledge may indeed illumine his earthly career, but they can shed no light upon the path he is to tread to reach a better world.

Christ himself has recognized the diversity of intellectual gifts in his parable of the talents, from which we borrow the very term to designate those gifts; and if, in a community of pure and faithful Christians, there still are many degrees and kinds of talents, is it reasonable to suppose that in that millennium—the only one I can imagine—when all nations shall call on His name with hope and praise, all mental imparities of races will be obliterated?[7] There are, at the present time, nations upon whom we look down as being inferior in civilization to ourselves, yet they are as good—if, indeed not better—Christians than we are as a people. The progress of physical science, by facilitating the intercourse between distant parts of the world, tends, indeed, to diffuse true religion, and in this manner—and this manner only—promotes the moral good of mankind. But here it is only an instrument, and not an agent, as the machines which the architect uses to raise his building materials do not erect the structure.

One more reason why the unity of the human species cannot be considered a proof of equal intellectual capability of races. It is a favorite method of naturalists to draw an analogy between man and the brute creation; and, so far as he belongs to the animal kingdom, this method is undoubtedly correct and legitimate. But, with regards to man's higher attributes, there is an impassable barrier between him and the brute, which, in the heat of the argument, contending parties have not always sufficiently respected. The great Prichard himself seems sometimes to have lost sight of it. Thus, he speaks of "psychological" diversities in varieties of the same undoubted species of animal, though it is obvious that animals can have no psychological attributes. But I am willing to concede to Mr. Prichard all the conclusions he derives from this analogy in favor of unity of the human species. All dogs, he believes, are derived from one pair; yet there are a number of varieties of dogs, and these varieties are different not only in external appearance, but in what Mr. Prichard would call psychological qualities. No shepherd expects

to train a common cur to be the intelligent guardian of the flock; no sports-
man to teach his hounds, or their unmixed progeny, to perform the office of
setters. That the characteristics of every variety of dogs are permanent so long
as the breed remains pure, every one knows, and that their distinctive type
remains the same in all countries and through all time, is proved by the mu-
ral paintings of Egypt, which show that, 2,000 years B.C., they were as well
known as in our day. If then, this permanency of "psychological" (to take
Mr. Prichard's ground) diversity is compatible with unity of origin in the dog,
why not in the case of man? I am far from desiring to call into question the
unity of our species, but I contend that the rule must work both ways, and
if "psychological" diversities can be permanent in the branches of the same
species of animals, they can be permanent also in the branches of the human
family.

"The Position and Treatment of Women among the Various Races of Men as Proof of Their Moral and Intellectual Diversity"[8]

The reader will pardon me if to Mr. Gobineau's scale of gradation in point of beauty and physical strength, I add another as accurate, I think, if not more so, and certainly as interesting.[9] I allude to the manner in which the weaker sex is regarded and treated among the various races of men.

In the words of Van Amringe, "From the brutal New Hollander, who secures his wife by knocking her down with a club and dragging the prize to his cave, to the polished European, who, fearfully, but respectfully and assiduously, spends a probation of months or years for his better half, the ascent may be traced with unfailing precision and accuracy."[10] The same writer correctly argues that if any principle could be inferred from the analogy to animals, it would certainly be a uniform treatment of the female sex among all races of men; for animals are remarkably uniform in the relations of the male and female in the same species. Yet among some races of men *polygamy has always prevailed, among others never.* Would not any naturalist consider as distinct species any animals of the same genus so distinguished? This subject has not yet met with due attention at the hands of ethnologists. "When we hear of a race of men," says the same author, "being subjected to the tyranny of another race, either by personal bondage or the more easy condition of tribute, our sympathies are enlisted in their favor, and our constant good wishes, if not our efforts, accompany them. But when we hear of hundreds of millions of the truest and most tender-hearted of human creatures being trodden down and trampled upon in everything that is dear to the human heart, our sympathies, which are so freely expended on slighter occasions or imaginary evils, are scarcely awakened to their crushing woes."

With the writer from whom I have already made copious extracts, I believe the *moral and intellectual diversity* of the races of men cannot be thor-

oughly and accurately investigated without taking into consideration the relations which most influence individual as well as national progress and development, and which result from the position occupied by women towards
man. The truth has not escaped former investigators—it would be singular
if it had—but they have contented themselves with asserting that the condition of the female sex was indicative of the degree of civilization. Had they
said, of the intrinsic worth of the various races, I should cheerfully assent.
But the elevation or degradation of women in the social scale is generally regarded as a *result,* not a *cause.* It is said that all barbarians treat their women
as slaves; but, as they progress in civilization, woman gradually rises to her
legitimate rank.

For the sake of the argument, I shall assume that all now civilized nations
at first treated their women as the actual barbarians treat theirs. That this is
not so, I hope to place beyond doubt; but, assuming it to be the case, might
not the fact that some left off that treatment, while others did not, be adduced
as proof of the inequality of races? "The law of the relation of the sexes," says
Van Amringe, "is more deeply engraven upon human nature than any other;
because, whatever theories may be adopted in regard to the origin of society,
language, etc., no doubt can be entertained that the *influence of woman must
have been anterior to any improvements of the original condition of man.* Consequently it was antecedent and superior to education and government. That
these relations were powerfully instrumental in the origin of development, to
give it a direction and character according to the natures operating and oper-
ated upon, cannot be doubted by anyone who has paid the slightest attention
to domestic influences, from and under which education, customs, and government commenced."

But I totally deny that all races, in their first state of development, treated
their women equally. There is not only no historical testimony to prove that
any of the white races were ever in such a state of barbarity and in such moral
debasement as most of the dark races are to this day, and have always been,
but there is positive evidence to show that our barbarous ancestors assigned to
woman the same position we assign her now: she is the companion, and not
the slave of man. I have already alluded to this in a previous note on the Teutonic races; I cannot, however, but revert to it again.

As I have not space for a lengthy discussion, I shall mention but one fact,
which I think conclusive, and which rests upon incontrovertible historical
testimony. "To a German mind," says Tacitus, "the idea of a woman led
into captivity is insupportable. In consequence of this prevailing sentiment,

the states which deliver as hostages the daughters of illustrious families are bound by the most effectual obligations." Did this assertion rest on the authority of Tacitus only, it might perhaps be called into question. But Caesar dealt with realities, not idealities; he was a shrewd, practical statesman, and an able general; yet Caesar *did* take females as hostages from the German tribes, in preference to men. Suppose Caesar had made war against the King of Ashantee, and taken away some of his three thousand three hundred and thirty-three wives, the mystical number being thus forcibly disturbed, might have alarmed the nation, whose welfare is supposed to depend on it; but the misfortune would soon have been remedied.

But it is possible to demonstrate not only that all races did not treat their women equally in their first stage of development, but also that no race which assigned to woman in the beginning an inferior position ever raised her from it in any subsequent stage of development. I select the Chinese for illustration, because they furnish us with an example of long-continued and regular intellectual progress which yet never resulted in an alteration of woman's position in the social structure. The decadent Chinese of our day look upon the female half of their nation as did the rapidly advancing Chinese of the seventh and eighth centuries; and the latter in precisely the same manner as their barbarous ancestors, the subjects of the Emperor Fou, more than twenty centuries before.

I repeat it, the relations of the sexes, in various races, are equally dissimilar in every stage of development. The state of society may change, the tendency of a race never. Faculties may be developed, but never lost.

As the mothers and wives of our Teutonic ancestors were near the battle-field, to administer refreshments to the wearied combatants, to stanch the bleeding of their wounds, and to inspire with renewed courage the despairing; so, in modern times, matrons and maidens of the highest rank—worthy daughters of a heroic ancestry—have been found by thousands ready to sacrifice the comforts and quiet of home for the horrors of a hospital. As the rude warrior of a former age won his beloved by deeds of valor, so, to his civilized descendant, the hand of his mistress is the prize and reward of exertion. The wives and mothers of the ancient Germans and Celts were the counselors of their sons and husbands in the most important affairs; our wives and mothers are our advisers in our more peaceful pursuits.

But the Arab, when he had arrived at the culminating point of his civilization, and when he had become the teacher of our forefathers of the Middle Ages in science and the arts, looked upon his many wives in the same light as his roaming brother in the desert had done before and does now. I do not ask of all these races that they should assign to their women the same rank that we do. If intellectual progress and social development among them showed the slightest tendency to produce ultimately an alteration in woman's position towards her lord, I might be content to submit to the opinion of those who regard that position as the effect of such a progress and such a development. But I cannot, in the history of those races, perceive the slightest indication of such a result, and all my observations lead me to the conclusion that the relations between the sexes are a cause, and not an effect.

The character of the women of different races differs in essential points. What a vast difference, for instance, between the females of the rude crusaders who took possession of Constantinople, and the more civilized Byzantine Greeks whom they so easily conquered; between the heroic matron of barbarous Germany and the highly civilized Chinese lady! These differences cannot be entirely the effect of education, else we are forced to consider the female sex as mere automatons. They must be the result of diversity of character. And why not, in the investigation of the moral and intellectual diversity of races and the natural history of man, take into consideration the peculiarities that characterize the female portion of each race, a portion—I am forced to make this trite observation, because so many investigators seem to forget it—which comprises at least one-half of the individuals to be described?

The Register *Reviews* Moral and Intellectual Diversity of Races

MOBILE REGISTER, 19 DECEMBER 1855

This is a bold, original, and learned work, which has created quite a sensation in Philadelphia, where it was published, and if we are not greatly deceived, is destined to take a much deeper hold upon readers of the South.

The question of *original* Unity or Diversity of Races is not one discussed by the author; but he takes the human family up where history first finds them, and treats the Races as they then existed, and have existed even since—he says it is needless to attempt to explain how Teutons, Jews, Mongols, Negroes, Arabs, Egyptians, Australians, &c., originated—it is a fixed fact that they have all existed for several thousand years in their present forms, and we have no reason to expect that the next two thousand years will produce on them either physical or moral effects which the last two thousand have not produced.

Treating the present diversity of Races then as a fixed fact, he goes on to show the history of each, what part it has played and is capable of playing in the great drama of civilization. Each form of civilization, he says, is but the instinct of a race—it works out the ideas which nature intended it to develop and could work out no other. The Anglo Saxon or Celt, could never have worked out the civilization of China or India and vice versa—no change of circumstances can ever make a negro look, think, or act like a white man. One of the most curious and ingenious ideas in this book is that which attributes the downfall of all ancient Empires to the mixture of races, and not vice, luxury, bad governments, &c., as generally supposed.

Altogether, this book is a very remarkable one, and calculated to excite thought—coming, too from a French Savan, it will not be charged with sectional prejudice, as many of our Southern books are.

Mr. Hotz[e] has translated the work admirably and has added copious and very valuable notes. Dr. Nott in the appendix has added the latest discoveries in natural history, calculated to illustrate the views of the author.

Letters to Gobineau

1 JANUARY 1856

Monsieur le Comte,

In virtue of my office as your interpreter before the American public, and having various matters to communicate which require a direct correspondence, I take the liberty of personally addressing you. Du reste, les amis de nos amis sont nos amis,[11] and I may safely refer you to Mr. Gliddon and Dr. Nott, the latter of whom is an intimate and valued friend of mine and who will both do me the honor of giving me an introduction. By way of preface, let me state (though to so accomplished a scholar as yourself, an apology of this kind is scarcely in its place) that I adopt the English language in writing to you, because—though familiar with the French—long habit has made the former more natural and easy to me, and because I know that while I spare myself difficulties, I am creating none for you.

A volume of the English version of *Inégalité des Races* is no doubt by this time in your hands. It was for the purpose of allowing you time previously to examine that work, that I have delayed this letter until the present time. I now proffer my explanations, for they are undoubtedly needed, as you must have been considerably surprised at the material alterations I have taken the liberty of making. I hope, however, that after learning my reasons you will not suspect me of presumption or rashness. Your work was written for an European circle of readers, that is to say, a class of savants and literati. Our reading public is a very different one—we are a nation of readers, but readers for the most part of limited—or—what is worse—of superficial education. With us, the press has an enormous influence; its verdict in the majority of cases decides the fate of a new book. That press, however, forms no exception in point of literary attainments to the mass of the nation. The editors, with few exceptions, are men who have no superior capacity or fitness for the task they assume, but who, nevertheless, pronounce ex cathedra on all subjects and upon all occasions. It follows from this that an argumentative subject like yours, must be treated here somewhat differently from what it can be in France; and this alone will serve to excuse at least a portion of the alterations I have thought it necessary to make. But if you further consider that readers of superficial education read superficially, and that we—proverbially the busiest, most hurried, nation of the world—seldom find much time to allot to any subject no matter how important and interesting, you will become convinced of the necessity of such alterations. Nor is this all. The subject you are treating—and treating with such boldness and ability—is the rock upon which the vessel of state will wreck one day, perhaps ere very long. It is even now again the cause of bloodshed in a newly formed territory, it is what has prevented our Congress from organizing, though assembled for many weeks; it is a subject which comes home to our very door; nay crosses our thresholds and penetrates the privacy of our domestic life. Of course I speak of slavery, and though your work never alludes to this "bone of contention among us," you well understand the intimate connection of the questions you agitate and those which make this so-called Union anything but what its name implies. I understand from a letter of Mr. Gliddon that you are yourself a native of this hemisphere, and further allusion to the bearings of your work on the slavery question would be useless.[12] I cannot, however, but add that beside that difficulty, there is another connected with such investigations, one too, which in France you feel but slightly. The united Protestant Churches, but especially the Presbyterian, are bitterly opposed to the slightest intimation of original diversity. The Calvinistic dogma of hereditary sin is thereby threatened, the authority of the Bible impugned. Now [in] spite of our innumerable isms, our spirit-rappings[13] and women's rights etc., we are a very religious people, and the pulpit, in some form or other, exerts a much more potent influence that it does in Europe. In short, we are here placed in absolutely the same circumstances as those classes in Athens and Rome whose relations to the masses of the people you so justly indicate in your first volume. The slightest suspicion of what is called infidelity—for this charge is often made against our very religious people—creates an alarm that operates like the cry of "Stop Thief" and frightens away precisely the class of readers whose ear I was most anxious to gain. You will understand, then, the exquisite caution I had to observe in order to accomplish my purpose—a purpose for which your work seemed to me to be excellently adapted—the propagation of the truth of "irradicable differences." So far there is every appearance of success. The anti-slavery press, in mentioning the book, has either tacitly or openly endorsed the great fact, a thing that they had never done before. They have uniformly recommended the work to their readers; no unfavorable notice from either North or South has at yet reached my eye, though I have now over a score from leading periodicals before me. This I might perhaps adduce as evidence that I had rightly understood the temper of our people. Briefly—to cut short apologies of which by this time you must be wearied— I thought your ideas grand and in the highest possible degree useful, but I thought that more good might be effected by bringing forward prominently these ideas, though at a slight detriment to your own personality—and I have paid more attention to the former than to the latter. I have aimed to make the book in every sense a popular one; and it is for that reason that I omitted the chapter on "Language" which—I am convinced—would have done more harm than good.[14] Your prominent idea of the degeneracy (etymologically speaking) of the whole human race, and their final extinction, would have precluded the book from the very slightest chance of success in the United States. I tried the experiment in intelligent private circles and was appalled at the result. I have therefore expunged every trace of it from the English version. When the book has once established its reputation on a firm basis, as it necessarily must, a more correct version may appear. Believe me, then, that I have honestly and to the best of my abilities consulted the spirit of the nation for whom I was writing; I have conscientiously sacrificed what appeared of doubtful utility to what was essential and of immense practical importance. Judge me not, therefore, rashly;—but wait the result, which I am not over-sanguine in saying will be that your well-deserved fame will spread over the western world—you recognized as the founder of a new school in the study of historical and political philosophy. If you will allow me the honor, I shall be your first disciple, and a zealous one you may be assured of ever finding me, for I have been several years in pursuit of the ray of light which your work afforded me. I have been long convinced of the irradicable differences, mental as well as physical, among races; all that I wanted was to have the specific differences of civilizations clearly brought before my mind. You have done that, my thanks, sincere and heartfelt thanks for it. Hence forwards my historical studies will be no longer "groping in impenetrable darkness," they will have a direction, an aim. Great names will have to be opposed: even Gibbon must be ranked among our opponents. But truth must prevail—as

Fichte says, there is in the mind of man an intuitive perception by which—though often deceived—he unconsciously recognizes a truth, even without demonstrations. Onward—and while you measure swords with worthier antagonists, the Guizots, Humboldts, Gibbons etc. of the old world; depute to me the minor task of meeting the Bancroffts and the most popular lecturers and writers of the new.[15]

Many minor details I should have wished to explain in regard to my English version of your great work, but reserve the discussion for a future occasion, if you do not consider this intrusion on your valuable time an offense not to be repeated. I should esteem it as not only a very great honor, but also an assistance which would be invaluable to me in preparing "a second edition," if you were to favor me with your opinion of my first. Any suggestions you might make shall be considered as commands, and whatever faults you may think I have committed in the first, shall be cheerfully and conscientiously emended in the second. If a tyro in science like myself may presume to offer his services in any manner, pray command me; and accept the expression, as sincere as it is humble, of my highest regard and respect.

Henry Hotze

11 JULY 1856

M le Comte de Gobineau

Dear Sir:

It is with the liveliest satisfaction that I acknowledge the receipt of your favors of 20 March and 20 April from Tehran, both of which reached me nearly at the same time. I had reasons to fear a less favorable judgment of my very imperfect though well intentioned performance. The friendly tone of your letter emboldens me now to add a few more explanatory remarks, which, I hope may perfect that thorough entente cordiale between us, I so ardently desire.

History has been my mistress from the earliest period of my self-thinking existence, and in my acceptation of the term, its study comprises all that is worth knowing. My situation in a country in which the footstep of the red man is scarcely yet erased and where there is not a white man's homestead that dates half a century back, the total absence of public libraries and the extreme rarity of the private, precluded me for the most part from resorting to original sources, and threw me almost entirely upon the assistance afforded by secondary authorities. Of course in this, describing you the disadvantages under which I have labored and still labor, I do not convey to you a faithful picture of the United States, but only that portion in which I live, where there is scarcely one white man of forty years of age a native of the soil. The longer-settled portions of this country and the large cities, though still far behind Europe in this respect, afford greater literary resources, of which, however, I can but temporarily avail myself. So much for my apology which you will please bear in mind whenever you find my will not seconded with commensurate power.

Your book reached me at a critical stage of my studies. I had become weary of winnowing contradictory opinions to no better result than gathering heaps of chaff. My frequent intercourse with Dr. Nott caused me to direct my attention in some degree to ethnology. But it afforded at first but a scanty glimmer of light. The discussion of original unity or diversity interested me but little, with you I think that, as you very epigrammatically express it: "*L'utilité c'est de démontrer qu'il est inutile*,"[16] and this I have sufficiently expressed in my introduction. I am neither Unitarian nor Polygenist, I regard the whole question as one of the mysteries of creative power, which it is neither necessary nor possible to probe.[17] I therefore demanded of ethnology to give me the moral and intellectual character of a race. But here I found myself again at sea without a compass. Nothing but vague generalities, for the most part either unmeaning or contradictory. On the other hand, I found almost the entire host of modern historians arranged in defense, if it were ever disputed, of the proposition that national character is the result of long continued series of circumstances and varies with them. This is the keynote of Gibbon's great historical epic; it is expressly stated by Hume: "it is vain, says he to argue of origin from national disposition. Nations change very quickly in these particulars, etc."[18] And so on through the whole catalog of respectable historians. I saw clearly the circular argument, but I had no better to substitute in its place. Imagine then the enthusiasm with which I devoured your book. Here was the light I had sought for so earnestly and perseveringly, which had so often given me a transient gleam and then left me more in the dark than ever. I was like the pilgrim in an old German lyric, who entering a chapel, grumbled at the blurred and blotted glass that admitted a scanty light into his place of devotion, when behold! The clouds were withdrawn from the sun and what to his ignorance had seemed an unsightly daub, proved a brilliant glass painting by a master-hand.

I did not agree with you throughout, I thought many of your arguments inconclusive to any who had not previously studied in the same direction and sought a like aim, I had not then your concluding volumes, and but dimly perceived the drift of many things in your second; but I saw three great ideas which permitted me to see nothing else. Your etymological definition of degeneracy which did away with most of my previous difficulties. The specific differences of civilizations which had never before been clearly recognized, and which had been a pet theory with me for years, which had caused me to devour every book on China I could lay hold of, and which had gradually developed itself from a careful perusal and annotation of Guizot, with whom I found myself differing at almost every step. Lastly there was an emphatic denial of the Schlegelian school of philosophy, of all the cant and thrash about boundless progress, of all the Elihu Burritt and Emerson nonsense that had always profoundly disgusted me. There had been much of this latter mania in the U.S. and in spite of the failures of numerous "phalansteries," etc., it was still gaining ground[19] Spirit-rapping was but a phase of it. Scarce a poet in the Northern states but is crazy in some one or other note of this same gamut. Grave senators on the floor of our highest legislative chamber have made themselves the mouth pieces of the same all-pervading notions. The fanaticism of two-thirds of the American people on the subject of the slavery institution in the South, this fanaticism which has grown in the last thirty years and which now more than threatens the dissolution of this Union, this and much more I have not space to mention, seemed to me but so many heads of the same unconquerable hydra. You were the first that calmly, philosophically, seemed to aim a shaft at the heart of the monster.

To present, then, these three great ideas in prominent relief to the American people in such a manner as to gain all ears, offend no prejudices, wound no religious tenderness, was the task I determined to attempt. Its execution, I frankly confess, was beyond my strength; but with the enthusiasm and sanguine hopes of a young man, I overlooked all difficulties. The glorious goal in view, I had no eyes for the pitfalls and mires, that obstructed my path nor for the utter inadequacy of my strength to safely reach my journey's end. Not the least of my difficulties was to reconcile your plan with mine. I wanted the book to be a popular one, and retrenchment in some places, expansion in others became unavoidable. Gradually, however, the alterations grew much more considerable than I had expected.

A few words about my introduction, the length of which must have struck you as disproportionate.[20] It is to be regarded as a sort of wholesale definition. The American mind is essentially averse to speculation, and to gain any large class of readers to the consideration of any thing that savors of this unpalatable ingredient, you must coax them by making the way as smooth and the ascent as gentle as possible. Besides many verbal definitions which I thought necessary, I considered it expedient to give a general outline of the ground to be investigated, a sort of chart which should prevent the dullest mind from going astray. More over I wished to advance the idea, so far as I know, peculiarly my own, that in the study of race we can have no other analogue but the individual of which the aggregates are composed. Do not misunderstand me: I do not mean that we must reason from isolated, individual instances, far from it; but that, what is sure of the individual must be sure of the aggregate. I am wrong in saying that this idea is peculiarly my own, but at least my application of it I believe to be. It is in fact nothing more than the obvious truth—that the science of ethnology requires a profound knowledge of that mystery of mysteries—the human mind. Man being distinguished from the most anthropomorphous of brutes infinitely more by mental attributes than by anatomical differences, he forms a genus apart in which zoology has but a subordinate right to classification, and must resign many of her pretensions into the hands of the metaphysician. The chief difficulty, it appears to me, in assigning to a race its specific moral and intellectual character is to define how far such character is modified or its manifestations controlled by extraneous circumstances; and this difficulty cannot, I believe, be overcome except by carefully inquiring how far individual character is affected by similar influences. In other words the race must be regarded as an individual whose biography is at present what we call history. This is the idea, which I attempted—I fear with but indifferent success—to advance and defend in my introduction.

There is yet one point upon which I must touch, and here, as upon all others, I shall be perfectly frank towards you. Gliddon and Nott have objected to a tinge of piety which they pretend to find in my style and treatment, and which, they aver, gives an undeserved nimbus to the writer. Being unwilling to arouse religious prejudices and moreover firmly convinced that the subject could be treated without doing so, I was anxious to steer a different course from Gliddon, and it is possible, that I may have erred on the opposite side. Claiming for myself perfect independency of thought in matters of religion as well as in all others, I grant the same to every one else; and every principle of courtesy and natural equity compels to have the same respect for the opinions of others I wish them to have for mine. As society in a more confined sense lays us under many restrictions in the use of language which yet are compatible with sincerity, so society of large has a certain conventional style and tone to which, I think, we are bound to conform when it does not imply a sacrifice of what we might imagine to be the truth. Did I feel within myself the capacity and vocation of a religious reformer, I should undoubtedly speak without fear or favor; but where such topics are collateral merely, if I happen to differ from the majority of my auditors or readers, have I a right unnecessarily to obtrude my opinions, knowing them to be offensive? I have thought it unnecessary to express publicly what in reality is my sincere opinion, that all religions not excluding the Christians, take their mould and features from the character of their professors. The Christian religion has repeatedly changed its features during the course of the ages and invariably borne the impress of the prevailing tendencies. It has varied also with the ethnical characteristics of its followers, whether they called themselves Calvinists, Lutherans, Greeks, or Catholics. It has been dogmatical or speculative, gentle and tolerant or bigoted and sanguinary, pure and philosophical or essentially polytheistic and idolatrous, in strict accordance with ethnical peculiarities. The human sacrifices of the Druids have been repeated by their descendants under different name whether orthodox or dissentient. The same Mexican races that slaughtered their fellow-citizens for the honor of the deity have clamored in latter periods for an *auto-da-fé* on the site itself of the ancient temples. The same sanguinary spirit in matter of religion in purely white races has caused heretics to be burnt in Catholic Spain and witches in Calvinic Scotland or Lutheran Sweden, and has brought Quakers to the gallows in Puritan, liberty-loving New England; has devoted thousands of wretched Jews to the most inhuman tortures in every part of Europe. I have said enough to show you that I am not bigoted in religion; but think me not bigoted in philosophical indifference. I have ever honored each man's belief, and in matters where all are so prone to err, I have never thought myself justified to scoff and scorn.

I greatly fear that I am too much taxing your patience by this very long epistle. But I thought it well to say so much that you might thoroughly understand the motives and manner in which you were introduced to the American public. With regard to this introduction, believe me that your introducer has since become conscious of many errors, for some of which he may plead youthful rashness and literary inexperience; but however great they may be, he has never been consciously wanting in the sincere and cordial respect he feels towards you. I reiterate the hope that you will frankly and without fear of wounding a man's vanity, state to me whatever objections you may find to the matter or manner of the book that is now in your hands. I flatter myself with being a sincere searcher of truth and always ready to be convinced even where it conflicts with cherished preconceptions.

I have written to my publishers to collect whatever the American press has said on the subject of the book, and shall forward you as soon as possible the principal articles. Personally, I have not kept a single one, having but a very indifferent opinion of the judgment of our press. Most of the notices that fell under my eye, contained nothing but stupid, commonplace praise. A few seized the occasion of contrasting the delicacy of the work on the subject of religion with the very different course adopted by Messrs. Nott and Gliddon, and said nothing further. Only one or two seem to have seized the true idea and adopted the just point of view from which it is to be regarded. The book is pronounced "suggestive, interesting," but nothing further. Real criticism it has elicited only from private sources, and has reached me in my correspondence. This is in the highest degree flattering and encouraging. Briefly, your book has not, whether from faults of mine or other causes, met with a very brilliant reception on this side of the Atlantic; it has not produced the sensation I had rashly expected for it, but it has had a success perhaps more really to be desired than ephemeral newspaper notoriety, it has been highly approved by the most intelligent, ergo the smallest, class of readers, and it is steadily, though slowly, progressing. It is in reality doing vastly better than any one, saving myself, had expected from a book of such a character in our eminently practical country.

Technically speaking, the first edition of 1000 copies is nearly exhausted and we shall probably soon want another.

I should have liked to say a few words on your objection to my idea about the Germanicity of Protestantism. I know well the difficulties of the position and appreciate your arguments, but I have still one or two in reserve which I would like very much to submit to you, though the already overgrown size of my letter precludes me from doing so at present. Will you permit me to do so in my next? In the meanwhile, permit me to assure you again of the sincere and cordial respects of

Yours very truly
Henry Hotze

The Index *on Racialism*

"A WORD FOR THE NEGRO"

The *Index,* 12 February 1863

The emancipation scheme of the North is condemned in advance by the insincerity of its motive, since its authors scarcely care to deny that they regard it purely as a military measure to "crush the rebellion"; and Mr. Lincoln has himself publicly declared, that if he could restore the Union by freeing none of the slaves, or by freeing some, and leaving the others in slavery, he would do so.[21] It is condemned by the interests of mankind and of civilization, since it aims at converting into a barren waste one of the most fertile and productive regions of the inhabited globe. It is condemned by the laws of God and man, since it is in open violation of that Constitution for which the North professes to wage war, and since it incites and employs servile insurrection, with the attendant horrors of rapine and murder, which are crimes alike against the laws of God and man. For these reasons the unanimous voice of the virtue and intelligence of this country has denounced the scheme, and the most active efforts to enlist or entrap respectable sympathies in its behalf have signally failed. But if men are found with whom these reasons are not sufficient, who would disregard divine and human laws in the blindness of fanaticism which does evil that good may come from it, and who would set the interests of four million blacks above those of eight million whites, of humanity at large, and of civilization; then, even in the views of such men—even in the interest of four million of negro slaves—must the Northern scheme of emancipation be condemned.

Within less than fifty years, unaided by immigration or importation from abroad, the African race in the slaveholding States of North America has grown from half a million souls to nearly four million. This unprecedented natural increase argues, according to the ascertained laws of population, not merely a high degree of physical well-being, but a much better moral status than is in this country usually assigned to the negro slaves. It is impossible to suppose, unless at the same time we suppose the divine ordinances to be suspected in this special case, that a race sunk in gross vices and living in habitual violation of natural and moral laws, could thus grow and multiply. Facts accessible to every painstaking inquirer leave us in no doubt or perplexity on this head. The religious statistics of the Confederate States inform us that the number of negro communicants of the various Christian denominations is largely over four hundred thousand, or considerably more than 10 percent. Of the entire slave population—religious statistics which compare favorably with those of the laboring classes in any other country, and can probably not be equaled in any other which has no established church. An important point regarding the moral condition of the slaves deserves attention. The precepts and terrors of religion—the imitative instincts of the negro race—the influence, nay, the self interests of the masters—all combine to ensure not only the universal and outward observance, but the sanctity of the marriage tie among the negroes. If men will reason on this subject as they do on others, they cannot fail to see how powerful is each of the agencies we have mentioned, and more particularly one which we have not mentioned— the intuition, as we shall term it, since there are those who will not admit that holier motives can actuate slaveholders—which makes the white women of the South the natural and most efficient protectors of the chastity of the female slaves. The hand can surely not have been an unfriendly one which has thus raised the negro from the turpitudes of the African savage, and which, in his upward progress, screens him from temptations to which the wants and cares of a precarious existence expose all men, and his race particularly. The criminal statistics of the negro are equally satisfactory, and prove him remarkably free as well from the greater crimes as from the lesser offences against law and order. Thus, in a half century has the fierce sanguinary African become a Christian laborer, contented with his lot, industrious, under a moral guidance rather than a system of rigorous coercion, and looking upon the white man as his friend, teacher, and protector. Well may the Southerner say that all the heroism and self-sacrifice of missionary efforts in heathen lands have not borne one tithe of these fruits. Now, let the conscientious philanthropist lay his hand on his heart, and ask himself whether during these fifty years of slavery, the negro has not made greater progress towards

freedom than he can ever make under such liberty of license as the North offers him—license to plunder, to burn, and to murder? Is the lesson which he
is yet to learn before he can take his place as a free laborer to be read by the
light of his master's burning dwelling? Will religion find him a more docile
pupil when his natural affections have been poisoned in their founts, and
he has embraced his hands in the blood of those whom from childhood he
has been wonted to honor and love? Will the negro rise or fall in the scale of
civilization by such a training; and is he the friend or the enemy of the black
race who desires for it such a future?

But it is obvious that, were it possible thus to rekindle in the negro the savage instincts of his African descent, the white man, being numerically, as well
as in every other respect, the stronger, must in very self-defense turn against
and exterminate him as he would a dangerous wild-beast. Assume however,
that the fratricidal hand of the Northern white man assisting the negro in
the cruel work, the white man of the South succumbs, will the condition of
the negro be then improved? Suppose the intelligence of the South banished,
its youth massacred, its lands divided among the Northern conquerors, what
then? The new proprietor will soon learn that without the negro's toil, his
cotton, and rice, and sugar fields, are of no value. Under one form of servitude or another he will compel the negro to toil. Universal experience proves
that the stranger makes a far more exacting, more mercenary, and less considerate, and less patient master than the man who was born to that condition,
between whom and the inferior race there is the lifelong acquaintance of
each other's virtues and faults, the natural confidence and ties of natural affection which inevitably must grow from these. The negro, under the care of
his former master, has given the most incontrovertible proofs of physical and
moral well-being, by his marvelous natural increase from half a million of
souls to four millions in fifty years, or at the rate of 16 per cent per annum, an
increase which has fully kept pace with the requirements for unskilled labor
in the slaveholding States, and has precluded even the temptation for the re-
opening of the African slave trade. In the North, as a free laborer, the negro,
although recruited by fugitive and emancipated slaves, has remained station-
ary as an item of population during the same period. A similar phenomenon
is noticed in regard to the negro population of the West Indies, where the
insufficiency of labor is a constant subject of complaint. It may be fairly assumed that, under his new Northern master, the negro would not multiply
so rapidly as he has heretofore done. The deficiency must in that case be supplied from abroad, and since neither the German, nor the Irish, nor the native

American, can withstand the semi-tropical sun in summer time, nor the miasmal exhalations of the cotton, rice, and sugar soils, this supply must come from Africa. It will then depend on circumstances alone whether the supply shall come under the old and proscribed name of the slave trade, or cloaked under the disguise of a more euphonious name.

"THE NATURAL HISTORY OF MAN"

The *Index,* 23 July 1863

The most dangerous dogma of modern times, and that which, unconsciously to the majority of those who accept it, underlies nearly every social, political, and religious heresy which mars our civilization, is the dogma of the equality of man. Our daily experience belies it, our instinctive convictions repudiate it, our constant practice ignores it; and yet we continue to assert it, and in its various forms build upon it elaborate structures of theory. The feeblest intellect recognizes a difference between self and fellowman, between one nation and another; a careless glance suffices to convince even the vulgar of the broad distinctions between the white man and the negro, or between them and the Chinaman or the Hindu. Yet by some strange perversion of ideas, the popular mind has come to associate the study of the human races with infidelity or, at least, skepticism. Every one admits the truth of the familiar line into which Pope condensed the advice of philosophers and sages.[22] Under every aspect except one, man has been studied assiduously, and not unsuccessfully. As an individual, in his material relations to the material world, science knows him with an accuracy which leaves comparatively little that is attainable to desire. Even in that most difficult and dangerous path, the metaphysical study of man, there are not lacking brave and earnest laborers who are willing to hew the massive quarries of thought. But so soon as science attempts to consider man as a gregarious being, classed by the Creator into certain great and distinct groups, she is stopped at the threshold of the investigation by suspicions of the lawfulness of her proceedings. To a certain extent, the students of the science of races have doubtless themselves to blame for this prejudice against them. They have, in many instances, unnecessarily brought themselves into at least apparent contradiction to Holy Writ by inquiries into the origin of man.[23] We say unnecessarily, because even if it were permitted for human shortsightedness to fathom the mysteries of the creation, it could have no personal bearing on the legitimate subjects of inquiry, whether all mankind was descended from a single pair, or whether there had been—to borrow from Mr. Agassiz's phrase—several distinct centers of creation.[24] Whether the Great Architect primarily ordained the existing differences between distinct varieties of man, or whether He subsequently effected the same object by such means as he saw proper, science has to deal only with the facts as she finds them, and her duty is confined to the solution of two problems—first, what are these differences, physical, moral, and intellectual; and secondly, are there any ascertainable means by which they can be modified or removed? If science does not transgress these bounds, it is difficult to see how she can step upon forbidden or even dangerous ground.

The second of these questions must always remain an open one, since science is compelled to prove a negative. All that can be said with any degree of absolute certainty is, that since the beginning of profane history no race of men is known to have changed its physical characteristics from any other cause than admixture; but that the moral and intellectual characteristics of all races are susceptible of development, the degree and nature of which are yet a matter of doubt. The first question, that is, what the differences actually are, is, although not easy, certainly less difficult, because the answer depends on positive facts which research is daily increasing in number. There are those who profess apprehensions in the interests of religion, as to what the answer may be. Let them not be disquieted. The plan of salvation, as it comprises all colors, comprises also all grades of intellect. As we do not measure a man's claims to Divine mercy by the weight or texture of his brains, so neither need we those of races; and there is no reason why we may not admit the same relative difference to exist among races that we know and feel to exist among men of the same race. To say that this or that race is distinguished by some peculiar aptitude or inaptitude cannot be more unjust or improper than to say that one man is superior in some respects while another is deficient. The shortest road to infidelity in morals, politics, and religion, is taken by him who sets out with the idea that all men are born equal in all respects, and that the apparent differences of later life are the results of external circumstances and accident.[25]

If then, science shall inform us that certain races of men are distinguishable by certain moral and intellectual, as well as physical attributes, it will only have done, in a wider field and with greater accuracy, what is habitually done in assigning to different nations of the same race certain peculiarities, terming one slow, another vivacious—one prone to abstract speculations, another to practical conclusions. It will have afforded no pretext for treating any race with injustice or contempt; but it will have enabled us to facilitate and further the progress of each in the career for which the Creator of all designed it. It will have shed a light over much that is now dark and mysterious in the history of the past, and in the history we ourselves are writing by our acts in our day. Fanaticism is always the child of ignorance or imperfect knowledge; or it is, at best, the contortion of a part of the truth from its true proportion to the whole truth. Individual man is but an insignificant atom in the society of which he forms a part; it was appointed that his onward march should not be singly, but in troops; and the more we know of the natural relations of the different societies, each of which has its appointed task, the more benevolent, because the more enlightened our judgment will become.

"ARMING THE NEGROES"

The *Index,* 10 September 1863

Without placing absolute credence in the startling intelligence brought by the *Hibernian,* it is safe to speculate upon it, if not as an actual fact, at least as an event which has recently entered into the range of immediate probabilities. We have, in the various rumors that preceded this last direct announcement, so many indications that the question of arming the slave population has been under careful and serious consideration in the Confederate counsels. It is also certain that the same subject has been frequently discussed by the Confederates and their friends in Europe within the last few months. The Southern mind, therefore, on both sides of the ocean, has been ripening for this step, and, if not already taken, is prepared to take it.[26]

Intelligent observers of the struggle have long been aware that as a last resort the South possessed an element of latent strength which, whenever called forth, would at once shift the numerical superiority to the side which has heretofore been the weaker, and thus end the conflict. Those who know the temper of the Southern people know that, if the alternative were fairly presented between independence and the maintenance of negro slavery, it would not hesitate an instant to sacrifice the latter to the former.[27] The choice made, it is not in the Southern character to resort to halfway measures. If the measure became expedient, it would be carried out thoroughly and without delay. If negroes were to be armed, the arming would be *en masse.* The chief obstacle lay not in any fear of the use the negroes might make of their arms; on that subject, except in the few localities where the negro has been corrupted by long contact with the Yankees, no Southern man ever entertained a doubt. The difficulty was in the repugnance which a proud nation, regarding the bearing of arms as a privilege and an honor, must necessarily feel in extending that privilege and that honor to a servile race. But at the call of patriotism, the Southerners would sacrifice this repugnance, as they have sacrificed property and life, without hesitation and without vain regrets. Our only reason for doubt, then is that we do not believe the stress of military necessity so great as to warrant the use of this last, though infallible reserve. At the same time it must be remembered that the South is led by men who will not wait until driven by necessity to resort to a measure which they foresee that the public safety may require.

The force which the South can thus suddenly throw into the scale, ensuring prompt success, is easily available. Five hundred thousand would indeed comprise nearly the whole number of able-bodied negroes within the jurisdiction of the Confederacy, but these could be spared with less detriment to agricultural pursuits than any equal proportion of any other laboring population. The South has abandoned all its usual staples. Nothing now is asked from the soil but food. For the production of this, black female labor will suffice, and in health, hardiness, and strength, the females of the African race far exceed the peasant women of Continental Europe. The rich lands of the cotton region are easily tilled, and then young and the aged who cannot fight can grow corn and tend cattle. Nor is there any serious difficulty in organizing this force. In the South, unlike the North, the relations between the white man and the black are well defined, and are accepted by both without question; they rest upon a reciprocal confidence and a perfect understanding of each other's character. The white man therefore, will not feel degraded or in an anomalous position in commanding negro troops. If the discipline of the plantation is less rigorous than that of the camp, it is nevertheless an admirable preparation for the latter, and has moreover the merit of furnishing, ready to hand, a class of efficient noncommissioned officers, accustomed to the exercise of delegated authority over those of their own color, and to the responsibility for their good behavior. Even the scarcity of arms is no insuperable obstacle. There are, probably, enough of firearms for a select corps of negroes, already familiar with their use; and as for the others, it may be doubted whether they would not be more effective in the field with some more primitive weapons which the blacksmith's shop on every plantation could readily forge out of the instruments of husbandry. A hundred thousand negro pikemen or scythemen would probably be a more formidable body for immediate service than the same number of new recruits entrusted with unwonted weapons. There is no doubt also, that the greater portion of the negro levies would be quickly thrown across the Northern border, where at worst they would have to meet foes no better armed or drilled than themselves. As for the negro's courage, when supported and led by his master, not against him, we have never entertained a doubt. The Confederate negro troops will be as much superior in steadiness and effectiveness to the black levies of the North, as the Sepoys under European officers were to the mutinous hordes of Nan Sahib.[28] Besides, what the negro lacks in that intelligence which characterizes the white American volunteer, he more than supplies by implicit obedience and insensibility to danger, and he thus possesses the very qualities which professional officers are prone to consider the highest of the soldier.

If the military importance of such an enormous accession to the numerical strength of the Confederacy is almost beyond adequate comprehension, the political and social aspects of the measure assume even more gigantic proportions. It is the most complete scheme of emancipation that visionary ever dreamed of, and, though we cannot disguise the terrible danger of this subverting at one blow the whole social fabric of a great country, it is undeniable that the experiment, if it has to be tried, is tried in this form with immensely superior practical prospects, and under fewer disadvantages. The liberated slave is spared the demoralization of a violent change of authority and a disruption of natural ties; he does not learn the duties of freedom by those lessons of domestic treachery, or murder and arson, which the North undertook to teach him; he graduates, so to speak, into liberty, under the same guidance and protection around which the best feelings of his nature have wound themselves from his childhood. What the Yankees promised him as the reward of treason, he receives as the guerdon of honorable service; where they would have implanted corroding hatred, there grow the wholesome fruits of genuine gratitude; where they would have made him the irreconcilable enemy of the Southern white man, under whose care he has advanced from African barbarism to civilization and Christianity, he continues, what he has always been, an humble but confiding friend, yet with titles to respect from the superior race which he never before or by any other means, could have enjoyed.

The general belief which the mere rumor that such a step was meditated by the South has received, and the dread which it has inspired in the North, are in themselves the most conclusive refutations of the slanders which have been so industriously propagated in regard to the treatment of the slaves by their masters. Surely, if there were a tithe of that repressed antagonism which

Abolitionist fictions describe as the relation between a cruelly oppressed race and their oppressors, this act of the South would be the maddest of suicides. If the inventors of these fictions really were so self-deluded as to believe them, they must scout the simple mention of such an act with ridicule. That they accept it as possible and even probable is a confession that they know the South's trust in the negro, and its reasons for that trust. If the South makes this great sacrifice we shall not be without fears for the future consequence upon its industry, but we shall have the consolation that at last this brave and self-devoted nation stands before a prejudiced world in its true light. The most bigoted partisan of the North will then no longer be able to shut his eyes to the only issues involved in this American struggle—a nation occupying half of a continent, rising as one man, old and young, male and female, master and serf, in self-defense against a foreign yoke. Whether or not the gift of freedom be a boon to the negro, time and experience alone can show; but only the flag under which he can earn that dangerous boon will then be the cross on the white field, the emblem of hope and faith, and not the polluted and dishonored stars and stripes, the symbol of dominion and tyranny. It will then be seen whether the professed sympathy for the slave is a genuine feeling, or only a cloak to conceal envy of the master. The hypocrisy of the North which makes the freeing of the slaves a pretext for enslaving the free man, will no longer find any so lost to shame on this side of the Atlantic as to defend it. Among the nations of the earth, the Confederate States will stand distinguished for the most courageous experiment of emancipation on record, an experiment on so unprecedented a scale that the boasted self-sacrifices of other nations in distant colonial possessions sink beside it into utter insignificance. And if ever a nation gave proofs of earnestness of purpose and of a character of heroic mould, it will have been that nation which battled for years against a vastly superior foe, and which did not account wealth, dominion, cherished prejudices, both present and future prosperity—nay, its entire social fabric—too dear a price to pay for independence.

"THE NEGRO'S PLACE IN NATURE"

The *Index,* 10 December 1863

The very able, learned, and truly philosophic paper lately read by Dr. Hunt before the Anthropological Society, and which was published in the last two numbers of the *Index,* cannot fail to command the critical attention of the scientific world, and the consequent discussion thereon will, it is to be hoped, do much towards solving the problem on which it treats.[29] But it will be unfortunate if only those who are professed anthropologists should give heed to this valuable contribution to a hitherto greatly neglected, but highly important, subject. In the investigation of the negro's place in nature the statesman, the philanthropist, and the Christian are not less interested than the philosopher. The truism that nothing has been created in vain is especially applicable to man, the noblest work of the Creator. In the same country and among the same race, there are diversities of gifts, and the greater welfare of the community is best advanced, not by vainly striving to bring about equality, but by each class occupying itself in the sphere of usefulness for which it is especially adapted. And this principle appertains to all the different races that inhabit the earth. The golden rule for the individual, for the nation, for all the peoples of the globe, is that happiness and progress depend upon the right man being in the right place. Dr. Hunt justly deplores the misery that has arisen from ignorance and neglect of this law, and from this cause the negro has suffered more than any other race. Instead, then, of using the negro as a political shuttlecock, it is the bounden duty of all those who desire to promote his welfare to first find out his proper place in nature, and then to employ all legitimate means to see that it is where he should be.

But this inquiry cannot be prosecuted with any measure of success unless we are actuated by the motive that evidently prompted Dr. Hunt—an earnest, single desire to discover the truth. So long as the beam of prejudice is in the eye we cannot discern the truth, be it ever so palpable and manifest to the unclouded vision. We are never tired of reciting the marvelous progress of physical science since the days of Bacon. To what do we owe the mighty revelation? To what do we owe the wonders of modern chemistry, and the steam engine, and the electric telegraph? To men of science becoming teachable instead of continuing dogmatic, and instead of seeking for facts to support pet theories, that they discarded all theories that were not based upon ascertained facts. If we adopt the like course with respect to moral and social science, the results will be equally satisfactory. In proof of this we may adduce the essay we are considering. Dr. Hunt's facts, taken separately, are sometimes antagonistic to favorable theories, but yet the impartial conclusions derived from the whole of them are evidently true and useful, and so far from distressing are eminently calculated to comfort and reassure the philanthropist.

The leading facts about the negro are few in number, but they are sufficient to enable us to discern clearly his place in nature. The anatomist points out the difference between the conformation of the negro and the white races, and tells us that the brain of the negro is of smaller capacity. This class of evidence, though very important, is principally useful as an explanation of other phenomena. If anatomists had been silent we should still have known that the negro is inferior to the white man, though we should not have been aware of the immediate organic cause. If the negro race had been equal or nearly equal to other races, it would, like them, have had an independent history; but the negro has no history. When we trace his existence out of Africa in all ages we find him occupying a servile position, and at home his existence has been a blank. The negroes have never done anything in literature or science, not even to the extent of inventing a grammar. How is this? The negro has increased and multiplied as fast as other races and has had the same extraneous advantages. There is no other explanation than that the negro is indubitably inferior in intellect.

The next fact which we have to look at is the condition of the race in Africa. It is utterly impossible to exaggerate the savage barbarity and the utter degradation of the negro at home. Upon this point we have ample and concurrent testimony. Slavery of the most hideous kind prevails; human sacrifices are the rule, not the exception, and there is an almost inconceivable depth of immorality. All the accounts we have from numerous and intelligent travelers are truly horrible. And moreover, the numerous efforts that have been made to civilize and Christianize the negro in Africa have proved disastrous failures. It is, of course, not to be inferred from this that we should cease our endeavors, but the fact assists us in arriving at a conclusion as to the negro's place in nature.

What in modern times has been the negro abroad? In the West Indies the experiment has been tried of giving the negro full independence, and the result has been that a garden has become a wilderness, because the negro, except under compulsion, will not labor. In the Confederate States the negro race has been in subordination to the white race, and the result is, that it has made wonderful progress—that the savage has become a docile laborer, and that the heathen has become a Christian.

What then, is the conclusion from these facts? Not, perhaps, that the negro should remain in perpetual slavery, but surely that the guidance and the intellect and the will of the white man are indispensable to him.

The negro is far from being devoid of good qualities. In the Confederates States we see that the domestic virtues may be instilled into him, and that he, like the rest of mankind, is capable of receiving and profiting by the

Christian religion. If any better kind of subordination can be devised than *de facto,* not the theoretical, system of slavery which exists in the South, by all means let that system be propounded. But it must be apparent to the philanthropist and the Christian that the best condition of life in which the negro has until now been placed is that in which he is found in the Confederate States. Let it be distinctly understood that we are not engaged in defending or even in treating of slavery in the abstract. It would be illogical for us to assert from the above premises that the peculiar institution of the South is the only system that meets the requirements of the negro. What we do say is, that for the negro to be happy and useful, he must be in immediate subordination to a superior race. And it is right that we should remark that we do not pretend to speculate as to the future of the negro. We take him as he is. So wonderful has been the progress of the colored race under the mild, humane, and Christian rule of the Southerners, it has so greatly improved physically and morally, it has become so Christianized, and all in the space of half a century, that, supposing that the negro does not become the victim of New England cupidity, there is a fair prospect, not of the colored race becoming the equal of the white race, but of so improving as to make the very mildest form of subordination sufficient. One of the prejudices that makes the reception of the truth about the negro very difficult is that intellectual and social equality are indispensable to happiness and, therefore, to admit that the negro must always be in subordination to the white race is to condemn him to perpetual unhappiness. There never was a prejudice more unfounded. Is the child under proper control less happy than the urchin of the streets of London who is free from all control? Or to take a more general illustration. It will be conceded that women are less intellectual than men, and that physically, politically, and even socially, they are subordinate to the sex which is physically and intellectually stronger. But are women, therefore, unhappy? Would women be happier if the Yankee notion of the equality of the sexes was carried out? On the contrary, society would suffer from women being taken from their proper sphere of subordination, and women would be less happy. We are not, of course, insinuating any comparison between women and negroes, but only showing that intellectual inferiority, and consequent physical, political, and social subordination, are not incompatible with happiness, which does not consist in equality, but in each one performing the part adapted to his or her capacity.

Illustrations are however hardly necessary, because we have the negro in the Confederate States in subordination to the white race, and we see how he fares under such circumstances. In Africa, as we have already observed, the negro is a savage and a heathen, and is in a state of inconceivable degradation. In the West Indies he is idle and dissolute. In the Southern States he is, so every traveler avers, industrious, thriving and Christianized; there is not on the face of the earth a class of laborers so happy. All his wants are supplied, and he enjoys the comforts of religion. What more can the Christian or the philanthropist desire for him? Do we want the negro to continue as he is in Africa, a savage and a heathen? Do we want him to be as he is in the West Indies, a curse and an encumbrance? The philanthropist and the Christian must reply that it is better that he should be as he is in the Southern States, blest and a blessing. We may admit then, whether we are or are not emancipationists, fully and without hesitation, the conclusions that are suggested by Dr. Hunt's painstaking and clever essay. The negro's place in nature is in subordination to the white race; but let us be glad, that subordination, the result of intellectual inferiority, does not preclude happiness in this world, and thank God that no intellectual qualification is necessary for eternal Salvation.

"ABOLITIONISM AND THE NEGRO"

The *Index,* 20 October 1864

The record of the negro is a sad and inscrutable enigma. If ever it were justifiable to say "Behold the curse of the eternal," it would be so in respect to the history of the negro. History! Bitter mockery! The negro has no history. From the days when the sable sons of Africa were the slaves of the Kings of Egypt until this hour, when clad in Lincoln's livery they are driven into the very jaws of death, their existence has been a blank—a perfect blank. They have no trophies. They have left no tracings on the sand of time. When not savages they have been slaves. The monuments of antiquity raised by their labor were designed and directed by others. When they have appeared in history, it has been as tools to be cast aside and forgotten when the work was accomplished. So far as the historian can discern, literature and art, government and all other science owe no more to the negro race than to the generations of African cattle. Yet negroes are not cattle, and hence it is that their career is a riddle. Not only have they their place in nature, but they are members of the human family. Intellectually inferior to the white people, as children compared to Caucasian tribes, they are nevertheless men—men who, as the institution of negro slavery in the South shows, may be a blessing to their generation, in whose hearts kindly treatment begets grateful affection, who are capable of social progress, who under favorable circumstances are happy, and who above all else have aspirations for immortality, and like the white man are supported by the faith and rejoice in the promise of Christianity. The Abolitionists may tell us in his frenzy that the negro is intellectually equal to the white man. But what avails mere assertion in the face of the facts that we have cited? We are not afraid of the truth. We assert the negro's intellectual inferiority while we stoutly maintain his human brotherhood. And because of his humanity and of his mental childhood, we are incensed and appalled at the brutal—nay, the expression is inadequate—at the fiendish malignity with which he is persecuted by the Abolitionists of New England. What should we say of those who would corrupt children, incite them to commit infamous and bloody deeds. Meanwhile robbing their victims and subjecting them to the vilest uses; and who, to paraphrase Mr. Lincoln, would drive them into the slaughter pens as a butcher does sheep? No language is powerful enough to properly denounce such crimes, and neither can anyone fairly express the detestation by the consideration of the horrible sufferings that New England Abolitionism has inflicted on the negroes who, by the cruel fortunes of war, have fallen under its merciless and abominable yoke.

It was inevitable that the invasion of the South should do harm to the negroes, because they are a component part of the nation, and therefore enjoy the prosperity and suffer from the adversity that lights upon their home and country. It was not, however, to be supposed that they would have been, as they have been, the victims of the most ruthless passions of the invaders. What has the negro done unto the North that he should be persecuted with bloody and unparalleled ferocity? What raised New York to the rank of an Empire city, and lined her streets with marble palaces? The profits raised from dealing in the products of negro labor. And what laid the foundations of the greatness of Boston? Not Emancipation, not any theory of rights, not righteousness or philanthropy. The middle passage was revolting, but it was profitable; and the self-dubbed saints of New England waxed rich by the zealous pursuit of a highly remunerative slave trade. Why should New England hate the race that has given her riches? Because, forsooth, the negro is the cause of the dissolution of the Union? The North knows full well that negro slavery was not the cause of secession, and is not in the way of reunion. The South would have left the North even if the Government of England had not forced her to receive the negro slaves brought to her ports in English and Yankee ships; and if the South would return to the Union, slavery would be no obstacle, and Abolitionism would be no more heard of.

We understand why Mr. Lincoln desired to deport the negroes to a remote place where they might die out. Mr. Lincoln is from the West, and Western men, thanks to the insidious teaching of New England, have always been intolerant of the presence of the negro, and, from a fear that free negro labor might compete with white labor, have made it penal for the negroes to reside in their States.[30] We understand why the Irish settlers have an antipathy to the negroes, for the unscrupulous Abolitionists have told them that the negro will interfere with their labor. But we do not understand why New England should so hate the negro. Is it a mere savage instinct that makes her prone to oppress the helpless? We cannot tell. The motive is problematical, but the fact is hideously glaring.

This hate is not of recent growth, though the war has amazingly developed it. From first to last, the North has behaved inhumanly to the negro. We have seen how the Yankees for the sake of gain were active participators in the slave trade. While the Southerners were petitioning the home Government to send them no more negroes, the merchants of Boston were importing living cargoes and selling them by auction. Nor were they without an excuse. They declared that they were engaged in a holy mission. They were rescuing the "blacks" from savage life and heathenism, and bringing them into a Christian land. So long as slave labor was profitable in the Northern States, so long did the Northerners keep slaves. When the influx of immigrants and a change in the cultivation of the soil rendered slave labor unprofitable, slavery was abolished. What did the New Englanders do with their slaves? Emancipate them? What! The saints of New England sacrifice property for the sake of a professed principle? That phenomenon has not yet happened. No, the New Englanders *sold* their slaves to the South—sold the fathers and mothers of the slaves they are now seeking to destroy in the name of philanthropy. Thenceforth the negro had no rest in the North. He was free, but he was a leper. Happy for the Northern slaves that the South could purchase them, for otherwise they would have perished from sheer neglect and misery. The free negro has not prospered in the North. From 1840 to 1850 the Census of the United States informs us that in the South the free negroes increased from 170,335 to 210,955 and in the North from 215,968 to 223,248—that is, in the South about 25 per cent, and in the North about 3 per cent. And this difference cannot be mainly ascribed to the Southerners freeing their slaves, for we find that in the same period the slave population advanced from 2,519,087 to 3,112,806—or at a rate of nearly 20 per cent. So the negroes in the South were more than six times as prolific as the negroes in the North. We suppose that few persons will deny that prolificacy is an unerring test of comparative happiness, prosperity, and virtue.

"THE NEGRO IN THE SOUTHERN ARMIES"

The *Index,* 10 November 1864

There is no doubt that the people of the South have fully made up their minds, in the event of the War being continued beyond the present unfinished campaigns, to throw into the scale the enormous latent strength so long held in reserve, but which when brought into action, must give them at once and forever a decisive numerical superiority over their assailants. This momentous resolve has been with that prompt and unhesitating unanimity which always characterizes Confederate patriotism. Almost simultaneously the leading organs of the press, the President, and the Governors of the several states, gave their support to a suggestion which, if for no other reason than its stupendous dimensions and its running so radically counter to the prevailing convictions and habits of thought, might have been expected to excite opposition, or at least conflict of opinion. Yet the reception of this suggestion is not due to a hasty impulse, nor is it the eager grasping of a desperate expedient. For some time public opinion in the Confederate States has become familiarized with the idea of making the negro population available for military service, so far as might be necessary or advisable. To a limited extent this has already been done, and the employment of negroes, both free and slave, for teamsters, hospital nurses, and military laborers, is formally sanctioned by an Act of the Congress. It may be assumed that the success of the partial experiment has proved satisfactory, and warrants the adoption of the policy upon a larger scale. But the proximate cause of the present determination in reference to the negro we believe to be a recent speech of Mr. Abraham Lincoln, in which he boasts—probably with no greater regard for the truth or accuracy of figures than we are accustomed to find in Yankee statements—that 200,000 black men are employed in the federal armies, and more than intimates but for these auxiliaries the attempt to subjugate the South must ere this have been abandoned. These words have evidently sunk deep into the hearts of the Southern people. Whatever may be the actual number of negro soldiers under the Union flag, it is notorious that the Washington Government relies chiefly upon such recruits for maintaining the numerical strengths of its armies. White volunteering has ceased; the conscription has repeatedly and so utterly failed that the States can only fill their respective quotas among the defenseless slaves of occupied hostile districts; the supply derived through "emigration" from Ireland and Germany has been seriously checked, and threatens to become still more precarious. The negro, then, is the last prop of the invaders only superiority, that of numbers, and yet the negro, at least the Southern-born negro, is rarely a willing recruit for the Union. The mere weight of heretofore apparently inexhaustible numbers has protracted the struggle despite the appalling havoc Southern generalship and valor has made in the ranks of the foe. If, therefore, the South like the North places the negro in the field, it is not to prolong the war—for the annual accession to the arms-bearing white population is demonstrably adequate to this end—but by one sudden blow to end the war.

When more than a year ago, it was rumored that the South contemplated the policy of arming its slaves, we placed our views frankly on record in these columns. . . . It should be observed that the scarcity of arms, which we then contemplated as a practical difficulty in the carrying out of the policy, need no longer induce apprehension, the South being, if the supply from Europe were to cease, better provided in this respect, thanks to the development of native industry, than at any former period.

There are those, friends of the South, who will view this grave step with the liveliest apprehensions as to its future consequences. There are others, a class of Yankee partisans professing emancipation in the same manner that Satan preaches religion, and hating the negro's master only a little more than the negro, who will effect to treat it as an act of suicide, and raise a yell of exultation over their supposed victim. A few of the latter may be bold enough to drop the mask which can serve no longer, and openly avow, as on the same subject a year ago one of their principal organs did, that their philanthropy is devotion to the Union, and their love of freedom a yearning for the blessings of Abraham Lincoln's paternal rule (Vide *Morning Star,* September 14, 1863). We trust that the apprehensions of friends will rest on no sounder foundation than the exultation of foes. We do not wish to disguise the serious nature of so great a change in the social fabric of any country as this implies in the South. Were that fabric purely artificial or essentially vicious in its constitution, we should tremble for the result of so severe a test. But we have never hesitated to express our firm conviction that the relation of the inferior to the dominant race in the Confederate States has not its origin or reason in municipal laws, but is a decree of nature. If we are right in this—and our convictions spring from no mere theory—then no change which does not violently invert the habitual and natural positions of the protector and the protected, can be attended by such dangers as to be beyond the control of humane and judicious legislation. In other words, the emancipated slave who earns his freedom by loyal service to the country and the master who trusted him is a very different being, and occupies a very different place in the scale of civilization, from the mere tool of a foreign enemy employed in crimes against common humanity. The danger, if danger there is, is the negro's, not the white man's. Negro slavery in the South—and we mean no other form of the system—odious as the very name of slavery is to European ears, vilified and slandered as it has been by both honest and dishonest fanaticism, is in solemn truth an institution in which the black man has a nearer interest than the white man. The white man everywhere can prosper without it; it is yet an unsolved problem whether the black man can. Our anxiety is the same as that with which we would see children and the physically or mentally feeble adult thrown upon their own unaided recourses. It is never remembered by European theorizers that, though it may be agreeable to have no human master, it may be better to have one, almost inevitably from the nature of circumstances belonging to a cultivated class, as the negro has in the South, than to have a whole community for a master and be everybody's slave, as the negro is in the North. It is painful to us, moreover, to think of the negro, with so much that is good and amiable in his weakness, made the innocent victim of the sanguinary quarrels of a stronger race. We know that this consideration has been the main cause of Southern hesitation; but as the North has forced the necessity upon the South, and as the philanthropy of the civilized world so wills it, the African blood already shed and to be shed in this war will not be on the heads of the Southern people. And while we would not lightly or wantonly advise such an experiment as this to which the South in self-defense may resort, we rest our hopes of the future upon the large strides which the Southern negro, in fifty years of Southern tutelage, has made upon the African savage or even his enfranchised brother of Federal and British America. These hopes are confirmed by the consistency with which as a race he has during the last four years withstood temptations which might have shaken the fidelity of a colder heart coupled with a hotter brain than his. If any population of negroes can make good use of freedom, it must assuredly be that of the Confederate States, affording by the unanimous verdict of the world the best physical, moral, and intellectual types of their race.

No unprejudiced man of intelligence will doubt that the Southern slave will fight for and with his master or that on those conditions he will fight well. For the rest, the solutions of the new problems which the new contingencies will propound, we have an abiding confidence in the wisdom of a Christian community of Southern men and women, familiarly acquainted with the character and capacity of the negro, and kindly disposed to him. Above all, we trust to the merciful designs of that All-wise Providence which: "shapes our ends rough-hew them as we may."

"THE IMPENDING REVOLUTION"

The *Index,* 27 April 1865

Although we are not one of those who think that the cause of Confederate independence is irrevocably lost, it seems appropriate, in view of recent events, to reflect upon the political condition and prospects of the Union, should the war end by even the temporary overthrow of organized resistance in the Southern States.[31] Hitherto the contest between the dissevered sections has practically had all the characteristics of a foreign war. To the North, moreover, it has been distant war, removed, except at short intervals, from its territory proper, and few of the miseries and sufferings of which came directly home to its population. It is the invariable tendency of such wars, for a time at least, to concentrate all the thoughts and efforts of a nation upon this one object. All other questions were postponed; political opposition is hushed by the news of a victory or a reverse; the elements of discord are in abeyance; the first duty of every patriot is to beat the enemy. Such a war acts, in fact, as an unresistible centripetal force, and for this reason is not infrequently resorted to by unscrupulous statesmen who despise of otherwise controlling intestine discontents. Now if four years' war which Federal America has waged, had buried these discontents, removed the causes of sectional antagonisms, or settled any of the questions at stake in the quarrel, the national bankruptcy and exhaustion would not perhaps have been too heavy a price. But such is not the case. Assuming the United States to be victorious, they will have achieved a victory over their own institutions, their own liberties, their own tranquility, their own bases of credit, their own stability as a nation. They will have waged a foreign war as the preliminary of a suicidal civil revolution. Imagine the last army of the South dispersed, and the Confederate Government dissolved: there will then be constitutional problems far more difficult than those which led to secession, and the slavery question will assume a far more practical and more threatening aspect than it did before the war. The Southern wealth which, whether the cotton States owned Federal or Confederate rule, would still have enriched none more than the great Northern cities, will be irreplaceable in the present generation. The Northern debt, whether recognized or repudiated, must be paid in ruin and demoralization.

What is to be done with the conquered States? What is to be done with the negroes? Will a forcible retention of the former obviate the differences of character, of climate, of historic traditions, and of interests? If the North could colonize them with its own population, the same causes which led to secession would before many years break out in the same sectional antagonism, and so true is this that among the fiercest of the present secessionists were the men of Northern birth. If half New England could transport itself to Alabama or Georgia and Mississippi, that expatriated half would not long brook to be ruled by the other half at home. Again, if the South is to be held by main force, will the North consent to submit to similar rule? There cannot be one system of government for one half of an empire and a radically different one for the other and contiguous half. If the South is admitted to equal political rights, will it not seek and find alliances in a conservative reaction at the North—once the passions of the war have subsided—sufficiently strong for its ultimate revenge? Nay, if you enfranchised the negroes, whose votes would assuredly go with their former masters, the South would acquire a greater voting power by two-thirds of its negro population, than it had in the federal councils before the war.[32]

But the social problem is even more insoluble than the political. Emancipation settles no question; it simply opens that which slavery had practically, or least temporarily solved. How is the negro to be fed, to be clothed, to be kept from idleness, pauperism, and crime? If he is to enjoy political equality, it will be necessary to discover the average amount of liberty which can, consistently with social order, attach to the common citizenship of enfranchised Africans and Anglo-American freemen. Intentionally brought into rivalry, which it was the chief object of Southern institutions to avoid between the two races, what power or what law will protect the weaker against the stronger? Or will the North, where the negro has ceased to be a pretext, suddenly reverse its instincts and its social practice, and honestly embrace its black antipathy as a brother? It is easy for nations of a homogeneous race to decree a theoretical equality which has its only effects in remote dependencies. But fancy four millions of negroes or Hindus suddenly incorporated into the population of any European country! Fancy one sixth of the Parliament, of the bar, of the magistrature, of the learned professions, to be composed of "fellow subjects," whose not remote ancestors "came over" from the delightful regions of Dahomey and Timbuctoo. Fancy, moreover, that it was deliberately proposed to fuse these elements into one homogeneous bastard mass with a view of giving a richer tint to our English blood. This is not altogether a fancy sketch; the Central and South American Republics, as well as Mexico, show with what results such an experiment can be tried. With sounder instincts than the whites of those countries, the negroes of Haiti, when establishing a government of their own, killed or banished every person with a certain degree of white blood in his veins.

This is a faint description of the breakers against which a reconstructed federal Union must inevitably wreck. Another foreign war, but this time really foreign in its ends, may for a time avert or it may hasten the catastrophe. What the final solution may be rests with God, but we have such faith in the destinies of our race, and so little do we deem that Union necessary to the interests of civilization, that we believe the sound and fruitful seeds which the perishing husk contains, will be preserved intact.

"WHAT CAN BE DONE FOR THE NEGRO?"

The *Index,* 1 July 1865

The condition of the Southern States is truly appalling. The South is not only defeated, but crushed and ruined. Blackened ruins mark the sites where homes once stood. The fields are unsown. Who shall cultivate the ground? To whom does the ground belong? Over the whole face of the country stalk famine and destitution. Ladies who were rich four years ago, and who are still young and fair, are seen in rags and tatters. The grand dame who, four years ago, was at the head of a princely establishment, now trudges basket on arm, and humbly sees a Federal officer for rations. Men who have been prominent or rich are lurking in woods and swamps, because they are proscribed. Murder, theft, and rapine abound. Bands of negroes, led by white officers, rob and do more than rob. The *Macon* [Georgia] *Telegraph* describes one of these atrocities, and says the leader of a band "and four negroes were shot, the three who committed the rape *burnt,* and one hung." No wonder there is no mourning for the dead. Happy are those who died, and so escaped the bitterness of beholding the utter prostration of their country. Weep not for the dead, but for the living.

The condition of the negroes is so bad that its badness cannot be exaggerated. They are in many parts fast rotting away. If they were willing to work, they would not all of them be able to find employment. Those who can get employment too often refuse to work. Sudden emancipation has destroyed one system of labor, and it will be long before another system of labor can be brought into practice. We are not surprised that the anti-negro sentiment of the North is revived. Negroes are beaten in the streets of Philadelphia; they are turned out of railway cars, and are despitefully used. So little are they trusted, that negro troops are no longer furnished with weapons. Yet they need weapons. Lately, at Washington, at the seat of the Federal Government, a negro quarter was destroyed by some white soldiers; the houses were razed to the ground, the furniture was burnt, and the negroes were beaten. Well may the negroes complain that they were worse off now than when they were slaves.

Is there no remedy for this pitiable state of affairs? Must the negro race be destroyed by idleness and famine, by filth and corruption? It is agreed that something must be done. But what? Giving the negroes the suffrage will be of non-effect. The only remedy is that the negroes must be forced to work. On that point there is no difference of opinion. Whoever goes South, whether in a military or a civil capacity, sees clearly that the negro must *nolens volens,*[33] be compelled to labor. It may be said that to force the negro to labor will practically be remitting him to slavery, and that whether the negro is compelled to labor for wages, or for food, clothing, and shelter, it is the same thing; it is a compulsory system of labor, and that is slavery. We do not think it worth our while to enter any such discussion. We may remark, however, that European laborers are free, and yet compelled to work. We do not allow men to starve rather than work, and we have a severe law against vagabondism. To say then, that the negroes shall be obliged to work, does not imply any lack of ardor in the cause of emancipation. The Abolitionists never contemplated that emancipation was to free the negro from the bounden duty of earning his daily bread by the sweat of his brow. This, indeed, is an affair that nearly concerns the Abolitionists. Thanks to their zeal, the institution of negro slavery in the South has been swept away. It behooves them to do all in their power to prevent freedom from being the ruin of the negro, and the only preventative is the enforcement of labor.[34]

No doubt, stringent laws and severe penalties will be necessary. The negro must be taught that it is more painful to break a contract than to perform his allotted task. The punishment for vagabondism must be of such a nature that the negro will dread it and avoid it. The crops of the South require nearly continuous labor, and at certain seasons, the loss of labor would involve the ruin of the crops. Nor will the negro have any right to complain of the severity of the punishment that attaches to idleness. It will be his own fault if he incurs it; and it will be administered, not by his employer, but by the public executive officers. It will be found that mere imprisonment will be no terror for the negro, but on the contrary, confinement with something to eat and nothing to do would be rather enjoyable to him. Imprisonment with really hard labor would probably be effectual.

And what is to be done should be done quickly. Every day of idleness and vagabondism demoralizes the negro terribly. Every day's delay renders it more and more difficult to reorganize the industry of the South. What can be done to forthwith ameliorate the conditions of the vast country and employ the negroes? We are convinced that if the emancipation is to be happily consummated by the negroes becoming free laborers, the cordial cooperation of the Southerners is indispensable. They understand the characters and requirements of the negro, and the negroes will from instinct be more disposed to be led by their old masters than strangers. Besides, if the South is to be repeopled, many years of anarchy must ensue. It will be a hard task to altogether drive out the present inhabitants, and an equally hard task to resettle the forsaken plantations. There is, too, this further impediment. The business of planting needs skill that can only be gained by experience. The new settlers will be at the mercy of their negroes. Let there be a real amnesty proclamation, let there be an end to the proscription, and we hope and believe that the South would soon be in a vastly improved condition, and the negroes would be rescued from their present miserable plight. These views are entertained by the leading Abolitionists in the United States, who regard Southern cooperation as indispensable to perfect the work of emancipation. If political persecution ceases, that cooperation will not be withheld, and the negro race will be saved from the utter ruin that is now rapidly engulfing it.

"THE NEGRO RACE IN AMERICA"

The *Index,* 5 August 1865[35]

Of all the great crimes that have been committed in the name of Liberty, there is none so deliberately wicked in its heartlessness or the consequences of which are of such hideous dimensions as that of which the four millions of negroes in the United States are the victims. Grant all that the most reckless and fanatical philanthropy could claim, grant that slavery was "the sum of all villainies," that its overthrow was so holy an end as to justify all the means employed, that the attaining of this end fully compensates the terrible cost; and if all this were granted, there would still not have been alleged one single extenuating circumstance for the satanic mockery which to the innocent slave makes the unsought boon the instrument of his own destruction. Had the negro risen against his master and achieved his deliverance by his own act, a philanthropic world might have washed its hands of the consequences and consoled itself with the pharisaical reflection that whites and blacks suffered the penalty for their respective guilt. But in the Southern States of America the slaves remained blissfully ignorant of the cruelty perpetrated against them; they increased and prospered in spite of the oppression which melted to tears so many sympathizing bosoms thousands of miles away; they withstood temptations such as probably the laboring class of no other country was subjected to; and even to this hour the great mass of them are content and obedient, whenever allowed to be so, to the duties which are the only ones they know and understand. Without will, act, or consent of theirs, a conqueror proclaims them free. There is no preparation, no transition from a state of sheltered dependence to that of the rude and unaided struggle for existence. Let us put the case in the most favorable light for the Abolitionist. Let us, for argument's sake, admit that slavery was everything that they pretend it to have been. Then, by their own showing, it was the worst imaginable school for freedom. A child is not born into the world without some garments being got ready for its coming and here are four millions at a single birth without one shred of the necessary covering being provided. Let us suppose that slavery was to the negro a moral and mental blindness up to this hour; what would be thought of the physician who ended his cure by flooding the untried eyes with a deadly flood of light? Let us suppose that the slave has been hungering and thirsting for liberty; what shall we say of the rescuer who killed the starving man with a surfeit? But let us put the case also most favorably to the North. Let us submit, for argument sake, that the fact of emancipation was a military or political necessity. Can the same be pleaded for the form and manner of that emancipation?

In the British West Indies emancipation was a solemn act. It had been long in preparation, and notwithstanding, many fatal blunders were carried out upon the whole with deliberations and precautions. A qualified system of servitude under the name of apprenticeship—of four years for house servants and artificers, of six for field laborers—formed the transition from bondage to freedom. The freedmen were taught to look upon their former masters as their benefactors, and encouraged in retaining the habits of respect and obedience. The latter remained in possession of their estates, and the liberal compensation allotted to them seemed to afford the required guarantee for their tiding over the immediate crisis. A time of profound peace and general prosperity was the auspicious moment selected. It was a national holiday; the utmost good feeling between the two races prevailed, and no excess, unless it be of enthusiasm, marked the great change. If the experiment failed, it was assuredly not because of these wise precautions, but in spite of them. In any future repetition of it, they would not only be adopted but improved upon. It was clear that grave errors had been committed, which might be avoided, but these errors were not an excess of precautions. Let us see in what way the Government of the United States, with the disastrous experience of the British West Indies before it, has undertaken the work in which the conscientious men who led the emancipation movement in England failed.

It was in itself an aggravation of difficulties that the work should be undertaken as a military measure, and by a conqueror. Scenes of war and bloodshed, plunder and rapine, social disorder and martial law, were scarcely the best school in which the negro might learn the peaceful and laborious habits of freedom. The wholesale devastation and utter prostration of the country in which they lived scarcely presented a fair opportunity for so tremendous an experiment. Against these disadvantages, however, was to be set the fortunate circumstance that the negro in the Southern States had morally and intellectually attained a far higher level than his slave-brother in the British West Indies thirty years before. All the best feelings of our common nature, fidelity, devotion, trustfulness, affection, were in the negro centered upon his master and his master's family. During the war he had been left much to himself, and proved himself worthy of the confidence rested in him. In innumerable instances he had been the sole protector and support of defenseless women and children. A philanthropy that was sincere and conscientious would have recognized in these facts a divine warrant for its work, and rejoiced in the light thus shed upon its path. The philanthropy of the Northern people was wrath that any one, even the negro slave, should love and respect the Southern white man. The latter's humiliation would not be complete unless he was humiliated in the eyes of his former slave. There was the idea of a devilish revenge, and to this idea the negro has been criminally sacrificed. In no other manner can it be explained, why white children are forced to the same school with the blacks. Some thoughtless bigots, we are aware, even in this country hail this as a magnificent triumph of human equality. But what would be thought in England, where yet broad differences of race are unknown, of an edict compelling the children of the wealthy and cultivated classes to frequent the ragged schools? Is this, indeed, elevating the blacks, or is it not rather degrading the whites, and insulting them in the most sacred instincts of manhood and womanhood? What is to be thought of the systematic guarding of white prisoners by liberated slaves? What of the ostentatious parading of negro regiments through the streets of Southern cities? What excuse can be offered for the Chief Justice of the United States, whose office is one of higher dignity than even the President's making an electioneering tour through the Southern States, haranguing the negroes and exhorting them to assert their political rights against the whites?[36] What philanthropic mission those minor apostles of freedom and equality, who in the presence of federal officers preach to the negroes in churches and schools that they are the superior race, that God created man black, but that Cain, his face blanched by fear and his hair straightened by his rapid flight from the wrath of the Almighty, is the father of the white man? Such things would sound ludicrous to our ears, were they not uttered with so horrible a purpose, and were they not devised with such malignant ingenuity for the level of the negro's intelligence. If ever prudence, charity, gentle firmness, patience, and forbearance were needed to solve a great social problem, they were so in the adjustment of the relations in which the whites and blacks are henceforth to live in juxtaposition on the same Continent. But the spirit which presides over the Northern work of emancipation finds its only illustration in the parable of the Evil One sowing tares.

It cannot be alleged that it is folly rather than wickedness which is preparing this bloody harvest. It is not the mistaken zeal of the new convert that carries him too far. There is now among the ruling party at the North scarcely a pretence made of the negro's welfare. Whether he shall be restrained in subordination or whether he shall be trained to vagrancy, whether he shall vote or not, are simply questions of expediency, not of principle. Where abandoned plantations are leased from the Government by loyal speculators, and in a few places where the black population is largely preponderant in numbers, the discipline which the freedmen experiences at the hands of his new masters is sharp and stinging enough to make him bitterly regret the change. It is only against the Southern white man that he is taught to assume an offensive and insulting superiority. Thus far the infection, so industriously propagated, has not had time to spread far beyond the cities and garrisoned places. The negroes as a mass, to their credit be it said, are slow in catching it. But the final result is inevitable. No class, so persistently practiced upon by the arts of demagoguism, can long withstand corruption. Moreover, the negro is perforce driven to idleness and vagabondage. The $20,000 clause of Mr. Johnson's "amnesty," persisted in, must arrest all reviving industry. There cannot be enough field labor for the negro, seek he for it never so earnestly, and the only kind of work in which as a freeman he can expect to compete with the white man is field labor. The catastrophes which blight the wealth of a country always fall most heavily upon the laboring classes, and here we have a laboring class, accustomed to ease and dependence, told for the first time to shift for themselves at the very moment when with labor their means of subsistence are withdrawn.

It is not difficult to foresee what fruits the perfidious teachings of Northern abolitionism are about to bear. Recently in the streets of Mobile, a negro brutally kicked a white man out of his way. The cowardly act was too much even for the patience of a Federal soldier who witnessed it, and who administered a devastating castigation. A riot ensued, in which several white men and a greater number of negroes were killed. The occurrence is a prototype of what we may expect to see on a larger scale throughout the unhappy country which lies at the mercy of such rulers as now control the destinies of the United States. The servile war which never was dreaded, and which all the efforts of the North failed to incite, so long as the South was its own master, was reserved for the evil day when Yankees became philanthropists. That the negro race, numerically as one against two, and weaker in every other respect, will perish in such a war, is our sad conviction, and is, we are forced to conclude, the deliberate intention of the present Northern policy.

"OUR FAREWELL"

The *Index,* 12 August 1865

This is the last number of the *Index*. Many we doubt not will sympathize with the regret we feel in making the announcement. We deem it our duty to set forth why the publication of the *Index* is stopped, and also to say a few words of farewell.

This journal was established on May 1, 1862. Its promoters thought that a paper representing in an especial manner the common interests of England and the Southern States would be useful and prosperous. In May, 1862, the prospects of the Confederacy seemed gloomy. New Orleans had fallen, and

General McClellan with a vast and splendidly equipped army was marching on to Richmond. The South fought campaign after campaign, and gained brilliant victories. The names of Lee, Jackson, and Stuart became household words in Europe. Later the names of Grant and Sherman also became famous. For more than three years the war in America nearly engrossed the attention of the civilized world. No wonder that the *Index* became more and more absorbed in the great struggle. The blockade of the South rendered it necessary, for then representatives of the Confederate Government, to have some avowed channel of publication; and naturally, that position devolved upon this journal. Under such circumstances, though we regretted, we had no right to complain, that in Europe we were looked upon as the mere organ of the Confederate Government, and that we were described in the United States as "the rebel organ."

Richmond fell, General Lee surrendered, Texas gave up the contest, and the Confederacy was a thing of the past. It did not, and indeed does not, occur to us that the downfall of the Confederacy deprived us of a field of usefulness. On the contrary, we thought, and still think, that there are many problems in course of solution in America in which such a journal as the *Index* would be of some advantage as a medium for commercial intercourse between England and the States. We, therefore, continued our labors. Unfortunately we find our usefulness marred by the general impression that this journal has been nothing more than the Confederate organ. We might have battled against this impression and removed it, but the circumstances have come to our knowledge which forbids the attempt. It is impossible not to see that the public on both sides of the Atlantic regards the *Index* as a kind of protest against the decision of Providence and as the organ of a new Secession party. It is needless for us to declare that such assumptions are entirely false, but we are unable to add that they are manifestly unreasonable. To suppose that the continued publication of the *Index* has a political significance and that it must needs be hostile to the United States is natural, and almost inevitable. We have then no choice. We have sought to do the South good, and we cannot harm her to further our own view. We therefore suspend publication. The *Index* shall not be the excuse, for perpetuating a contest which can only aggravate the miseries of the conquered and disarmed.

We desire informally but sincerely to thank the many friends, widely scattered over both hemispheres, whose sympathy and confidence have never failed us. We gratefully remember the courteous attention of our contemporaries, who have been good enough to publish upon our authority such documents as were of public and general importance. We received this courtesy not only from friendly and neutral papers, but also from those vehemently opposed to us. It is the glory and strength of the English press that opinions and even partisanship do in no way hinder the publication of adverse facts. If in the heat of the most bitter controversy of the age we have sometimes employed unduly harsh terms, we trust that such faults were deemed venial and are forgotten. We may, however, without boasting, claim to have merited the confidence reposed in us by our truthfulness. To errors of judgment we plead guilty. But we believe that even those who stood against us as enemies will not assert that we have ever prostituted our columns to falsehood or exaggeration. To our candor is, we think, due what journalistic success we may claim to have achieved.

We are strongly tempted to address a few last words to our Southern readers. But alas, what words of ours can express the regret we feel at their disappointment and suffering? We may, however, finally declare that in our opinion the long agony of the South will not be without a reward. Though defeated, the South is not dishonored. The history of her independent existence does not exceed four years, but it is a complete and brilliant record that will endure so long as virtue and heroism are venerated. The South is not a separate nationality, but she is a part of a vast and powerful federation. The South has been conquered and is afflicted, but as long as she preserves the tradition of her glory she cannot be enslaved. The Southern Confederacy has fallen, but her gallant sons have not died in vain. Whatever flag waves over her capitals the South will be free. Under whatever Government her people live, their influence will be felt. As yet the land is desolate. As yet the women mourn for those who have died for their country. But time will obliterate the ravages of the fierce conflict, and the South, chastened by the will of God, and exalted by her chastening, will yet be happy and prosperous as in bygone days. To nations, as to individuals, tribulation is often the herald of blessings. We are confident it will be so with the South, and therefore it is with a good heart, though with personal pain, we bid our Southern friends farewell.

Appendix: Original Descriptive Roll of the Mobile Cadets, Co. A, Third Alabama Regiment Infantry

Mustered into the Confederate States Service as volunteers for twelve months unless sooner discharged. May 3, 1861 at Lynchburg, Virginia.[1]

Sands, Robert M.	Captain
Higley, John H.	1st Lieut.
Charles M. Forsyth	Sen. 2nd Lieut.
Brown, Thomas P.	Jr. 2nd Lieut.

1. Huger, Daniel A.	1st Sgt
2. Vass, Douglas	2nd Sgt
3. Witherspoon, Thomas Casey	3rd Sgt
4. Yniestra, Branaugh F.	4th Sgt
5. Broun, James H.	5th Sgt
6. Gazzam, George	1st Cpl
7. LaBaron, Richard D.C.	2nd Cpl
8. McNeill, William S.	3rd Cpl
9. Murray, Alfred R.	4th Cpl
10. Hartman, William	Drummer

PRIVATES:

11. Armistead, E. H.
12. Allen, T. B.
13. Averell, William H.
14. Austill, W. H.
15. Bacon, John P.

16. Berry, D. P.
17. Briegleb, J.
18. Burns, John
19. Burke, J. A.
20. Carter, Cecil
21. Cavallero, G. J. S.
22. Caulfield, William M.
23. Cleveland, Joel A.
24. Clark, Joseph G., Jr.
25. Chighizola, John
26. Colson, Edward P.
27. Cohen, J. H.
28. Conning, W. A.
29. Chidsey, Strong M.
30. Ambrose, Culman
31. Davis, Edward
32. Dickinson, W. B.
33. Dunn, Columbus
34. Drummond, W. L.
35. Easton, E. M.
36. Emmanuel, Thomas K.
37. Evans, Vivian R.
38. Foy, H. H.
39. Foy, F. B.
40. Fowler, W. R.
41. Fry, Thomas S.
42. George, Ed. V.
43. Goldthwaite, Henry
44. Gunnison, V. B.
45. Harrison, James M.
46. Hamilton, W. P.
47. Hastings, J. S.
48. Hall, W. E.
49. Herpin, J. Theodore
50. Hern, Robert W.
51. Holt, William B.
52. Hotz, Henry
53. Holcombe, G. C.

54. Hurxthal, John
55. Ingraham, C. L. B.
56. Jones, Oscar
57. Johnston, A.
58. Kelly, William H., Jr.
59. Keeler, Oliver
60. Krebs, R. L. P.
61. Ledyard, William N.
62. Ledyard, Erwin
63. Lockwood, Paul S. L.
64. Mathews, F. F.
65. Mathews, R. W.
66. Macartney, Thomas N.
67. Maguire, H. A.
68. Mordecai, Jacob
69. Moreland, William S.
70. Moffatt, Robert M.
71. Muldon, James H., Jr.
72. Neville, John W.
73. Nott, J. Deas
74. Nichol, Thomas A.
75. Oliver, Stark H.
76. Preston, S. Franklin
77. Pippen, John H.
78. Price, J. E.
79. Prichard, Cleveland
80. Quinn, R. M.
81. Redwood, John M.
82. Reynolds, J. L.
83. Reynolds, John B.
84. Roberts, J. A.
85. Richardson, W.
86. Roudet, Pierre C.
87. Roman, William B.
88. Stewart, Thomas
89. Stuart, Charles C.
90. Stewart, Fred
91. Stockley, W. H.

92. Steadman, J. L.
93. Sengstat, H. H.
94. St. John, A. Pope
95. Soto, John A.
96. Scott, Thomas
97. Spotts, S. W. B.
98. Smith, J. Morgan
99. Toulmin, Harry T.
100. Turner, Wylis G.
101. Waterhouse, E. K.
102. Warring, S. Bart
103. Welch, G. W.
104. Week, Nick, Jr.
105. Wetherby, Thomas
106. Wheeler, Daniel, Jr.
107. Woodcock, Andrew B.
108. Willis, W. B.
109. Wylis, John
110. Yniestra, Moses G.

VOLUNTEERS WITHOUT PAY-EXCESS OF MEN

111. Leslie, Frank
112. Deas, Harry A.
113. Armistead, R.B.

Notes

PREFACE

1. As complete citations of all mentioned sources are included in textual notes that follow, I will not list them here.

INTRODUCTION

1. Reginald Horsman, *Josiah Nott of Mobile: Southerner, Physician, and Racial Theorist* (Baton Rouge: Louisiana State University Press, 1987), 207. Note: The English translation of Gobineau's title is "The Inequality of Human Races."

2. John Bigelow, *Retrospection of an Active Life*, vol. 2 (New York: Baker and Taylor Co., 1909), 123. For an evaluation of Hotze's effectiveness, see Frank L. Owsley, *King Cotton Diplomacy: Foreign Relations of the Confederate States of America* (Chicago: University of Chicago Press, 1931), 155.

3. Unless otherwise stated, biographical information is taken from Hotze's obituary, which appeared in the *Mobile Register*, May 11, 1887.

4. Hotze to Gobineau, July 11, 1856, in Ludwig Schemann, *Gobineau's Rassenwerk: Aktenstucke und Betrachtungen zur Geschichte und Kritik des Essai sur L'inégalité des Races Humaines* (Stuttgart: F. Frommanns, 1910), 200. For a history of the rise of the study of racial theory, see Michael O'Brien, *Conjectures of Order: Intellectual Life in the American South, 1810–1860* (Chapel Hill: University of North Carolina Press, 2004), 215–52; *Naturalization Record Books from City Criminal Court. 12/9/1852–10/29/1856.* Mobile County Probate Court, Mobile, Alabama.

5. Hotze to Gobineau, July 11, 1856, in Schemann, *Gobineau's Rassenwerk,* 200; *Mobile Register,* April 3, 1860. See Stephen B. Oates, "Henry Hotze: Confederate Agent Abroad," *Historian* 27, no. 2 (February 1965): 134. See Charles P. Cullop, *Confederate Propaganda in Europe, 1861–1865* (Coral Gables: University of Miami Press,

1969), 19; and James M. McPherson, *Battle Cry of Freedom: The Civil War Era* (New York: Oxford University Press, 1988), 548.

6. Horsman, *Josiah Nott,* 171–76, 204–5; For additional biographical information, see Josiah Nott Papers, Mobile Public Library, Local History and Genealogy Division, Mobile, Alabama; Robert E. Bonner, "Slavery, Confederate Diplomacy, and the Racialist Mission of Henry Hotze," *Civil War History* 51, no. 3 (2005): 288–316; Nott to Gobineau, March 7, 1855, in Schemann, *Gobineau's Rassenwerk,* 192. Note that Hotze only translated volume 1 of Gobineau's three-volume work.

7. Hotze to Gobineau, January 1 and July 11, 1856, in Schemann, *Gobineau's Rassenwerk,* 199–200.

8. The lengthy, yet revealing, complete title of Hotze's translation of Gobineau's work was: *The Moral and Intellectual Diversity of Races, with Particular Reference to their Respective Influence in the Civil and Political History of Mankind from the French of Count A. De Gobineau: With an Analytical Introduction and Copious Historical Notes by H. Hotz. To Which is Added an Appendix Containing a Summary of the Latest Scientific Facts Bearing Upon the Question of Unity or Plurality of Species by J. C. Nott, M.D. of Mobile.* (Philadelphia: Lippincott, 1856). It should be noted that Gobineau's *Essai* likewise had a political purpose. After the upheavals of the Revolutions of 1848, Gobineau hoped his work would help to bring order to the chaotic situation of French society.

9. Robert J. C. Young, *Colonial Desires: Hybridity in Theory, Culture, and Race* (London: Routledge Press, 1995), 130; Hotze, ed., *Moral and Intellectual Diversity,* 27 and 16; For a good summary of the evolution of racist ideology in the eighteenth and nineteenth centuries, see George M. Frederickson, *The Black Image in the White Mind: The Debate on African American Character and Destiny, 1817–1914* (Hanover, N.H.: Wesleyan University Press, 1971), 71–90.

10. *Mobile Register,* December 19, 1855; Hotze to Gobineau, July 11, 1856, in Schemann, *Gobineau's Rassenwerk,* 202; *DeBow's Review* 21, no. 1 (July 1856): 65; Michael D. Biddiss, *Father of Racist Ideology: The Social and Political Thought of Count Gobineau* (New York: Weybright and Talley, 1970), 146–47.

11. Hotze to Gobineau, January 1 and July 11, 1856, in Schemann, *Gobineau's Rassenwerk,* 197–205.

12. Hotze to Gobineau, July 11, 1856, in ibid., 205.

13. Cullop, *Confederate Propaganda in Europe,* 19; *Mobile Register,* May 9, 14 and 16, 1858.

14. Joseph V. Trahan III, "Indefatigable Young Journalist Henry Hotze Directed the Confederacy's Propaganda Efforts Abroad," *America's Civil War* 11, no. 5 (November 1998): 18; see E. Y. Fair to Lewis Cass, November 14, 1858, in Despatches from U.S. Ministers to Belgium, RG 59, roll 5, National Archives, Washington, D.C.

15. Hotze to Gobineau, January 1, 1856, in Schemann, *Gobineau's Rassenwerk,* 197; For a biography of John Forsyth, see Lonnie A. Burnett, *The Pen Makes a Good Sword: John Forsyth of the* Mobile Register (Tuscaloosa: University of Alabama Press, 2006). For an account of Forsyth's role in the election of 1860, see Lonnie A. Burnett, "The 'Disturber' of the Democracy: John Forsyth and the Election of 1860," *Gulf South Historical Review* 17 (fall 2001): 6–35; and *Mobile Register,* April 3, 1860.

16. See James L. Huston, *Stephen A. Douglas and the Dilemma of Democratic Equality* (New York: Rowman and Littlefield, 2007), 32.

17. *Mobile Register*, May 8, 1860.

18. Hotze to L. P. Walker, April 11, 1861, Walker to Hotze, April 12, 1861, in *The War of the Rebellion: A Compilation of the Official Records of the Union and Confederate Armies,* series I, vol. 52 (Washington, D.C.: Government Printing Office, 1880–1901), 42–43 (hereafter cited as *ORA*).

19. William S. Coker, *The Mobile Cadets, 1845–1945, A Century of Honor and Fidelity* (Bagdad, Fl.: Patagonia Press, 1993), 19.

20. Mobile Cadet Papers, Mobile Public Library Local History Division, Mobile, Alabama; Henry Hotze, "Three Months in the Confederate Army," *Index,* May 1, 1862. (hereafter cited as TMCA); For a complete roster of the Cadets that includes height, weight, place of birth, hair and eye color, complexion, and occupation, see "Copy of Original Descriptive Roll of the Mobile Cadets, Co. A, Third Alabama Regiment Infantry, Robert M. Sands, Captain," Alabama Department of Archives and History, Confederate Muster Rolls Collection, SG 25009, Box 2, Folder 2 (hereafter cited as Confederate Muster Rolls Collection).

21. TMCA, *Index,* May 1, 1862; William Stanley Hoole, ed., *History of the Third Alabama Regiment, CSA by Charles Forsyth* (Tuscaloosa: University of Alabama Press, 1982), 32; *Times* (London), July 30, 1861.

22. TMCA, *Index,* May 1, 1862.

23. Coker, *Mobile Cadets,* 20–21; TMCA, *Index,* May 8, 1862.

24. TMCA, *Index,* May 29, 1862; C. A. Ryder, Mobile Rifles Diary, SPR 340, Alabama Department of Archives and History; Confederate Muster Rolls Collection.

25. TMCA, *Index,* October 16, 1862; and William Stanley Hoole, ed., *Confederate Norfolk: The Letters of a Virginia Lady to the* Mobile Register, *1861–1862* (Tuscaloosa: Confederate Publishing Company, 1984), 23.

26. Nott to *Mobile Register,* July 7, 1861 (published July 16, 1861); CADET to *Mobile Register,* May 30, 1861 (published June 7, 1861); TMCA, *Index,* May 29, 1862.

27. TMCA, *Index,* October 16, 1862; CADET to *Mobile Register,* August 27, 1861 (published September 3, 1861); and Nott to *Mobile Register,* July 7, 1861 (published July 16, 1861).

28. TMCA, *Index,* October 23, 1862; and Hoole, ed., *Confederate Norfolk,* 17.

Note: The identity of this "Virginia Lady" is unknown. Hoole speculated that she might be Miss Virginia Gordon, a member of one of Norfolk's oldest and wealthiest families.

29. Colin John McRae (1813–1877) was a prominent Mobile businessman, a member of the Confederate Provisional Congress, and eventually the Confederacy's chief financial agent in Europe. For a short biography, see Charles S. Davis, *Colin J. McRae: Confederate Financial Agent* (Tuscaloosa: Confederate Publishing Company, 1961).

30. McRae to L. P. Walker, July 21, 1861, Hotze to McRae, August 16, 1861, and Hotze to McRae, August 16, 1861, RG 109, Compiled Service Records of Confederate Soldiers who Served in Organizations from Alabama, reel 107, National Archives, Washington, D.C. (hereafter cited as Compiled Service Records).

31. Hotze to McRae, August 16, 1861, McRae to Walker, August 25, 1861, Compiled Service Records.

32. Walker to Hotze, August 31, 1861, in *ORA,* series IV, vol. 1, 596; and Hotze to Joel White, September 14, 1861, in ibid., 611. Hotze's discharge was dated November 6, 1861, by Special Order of the Adjutant and Inspector General's Office, see Compiled Service Records.

33. Hotze to Joel White, September 14, 1861, in *ORA,* series IV, vol. 1, 611–12.

34. Charles M. Hubbard, *The Burden of Confederate Diplomacy* (Knoxville: University of Tennessee Press, 1998), 21; Henry Blumenthal, "Confederate Diplomacy: Popular Notions and International Realities," *Journal of Southern History* 32, no. 2 (May 1966): 152; The most recent biographer of Yancey is more charitable in his evaluation of his diplomatic tenure. See Eric H. Walther, *William Lowndes Yancey and the Coming of the Civil War* (Chapel Hill: University of North Carolina Press, 2006), 321; Mason to William H. Gregory, December 18, 1862, Gregory Family Papers, Series 4.1b, Box 24, Woodruff Library, Emory University, Atlanta, Georgia; Cullop, *Confederate Propaganda in Europe,* 23.

35. See Hubbard, "Burden of Confederate Diplomacy," xv.

36. R. M. T. Hunter to Hotze, November 14, 1861, in *The War of the Rebellion: A Compilation of the Official Records of the Union and Confederate Navies,* series II, vol. 3 (Washington, D.C.: Government Printing Office, 1894–1927), 293–94 (hereafter cited as *ORN*); Owsley, *King Cotton Diplomacy,* 156.

37. *ORN,* series II, vol. 3, 314–15; Owsley, *King Cotton Diplomacy,* 157.

38. E. D. Adams, *Great Britain and the American Civil War* (London: Longmans, Green and Company, 1925); Donaldson Jordan and Edwin J. Pratt, *Europe and the American Civil War* (New York: Houghton Mifflin Company, 1931); Owsley, *King Cotton Diplomacy; D. P.* Crook, *American Democracy in English Politics, 1815–1850* (London: Oxford University Press, 1965) and *The North, the South and the Pow-*

ers, 1861–1865 (New York: Wiley, 1974); Mary Ellison, *Support for Secession: Lancashire and the American Civil War* (Chicago: University of Chicago Press, 1972), ix; See also Donald Bellows, "A Study of British Conservative Reaction to the American Civil War," *Journal of Southern History* 51, no. 4 (November 1985): 507; Brian Jenkins, *Britain and the War for the Union*, 2 vols. (Montreal: McGill-Queen's University Press, 1974); R. J. M. Blackett, *Divided Hearts: Britain and the American Civil War* (Baton Rouge: Louisiana State University Press, 2001) and "Pressure from Without: African Americans, British Public Opinion, and Civil War Diplomacy," in Robert E. May, ed., *The Union, the Confederacy, and the Atlantic Rim* (West Lafayette, Ind.: Purdue University Press, 1995); and Duncan Campbell, *English Public Opinion and the American Civil War* (Woodbridge, Suffolk: Royal Historical Society, 2003).

39. Hotze to Benjamin, September 26, 1862, in *ORN*, series II, vol. 3, 535.

40. Special agent (signed "X") to John Bigelow, November 23, 1861, John Bigelow Papers, New York Public Library Manuscript Collection.

41. Russell vacillated on his position regarding intervention. Bright, a leading radical, saw a Union victory as beneficial to his goal of extending the franchise in Britain.

42. Hotze to Hunter, February 28, 1862, in *ORN*, series II, vol. 3, 352–53; see also Douglas A. Lorimer, "The Role of Anti-Slavery Sentiment in English Reaction to the American Civil War," *The Historical Journal* 19, no. 2 (June 1976): 405–20; and Wilbur Devereux Jones, "The British Conservatives and the American Civil War," *The American Historical Review* 58, no. 3 (April 1953): 529.

43. Bellows, "Study of British Conservative Reaction," 505; Henry Brooks Adams to Henry J. Raymond, January 24, 1862, in Henry J. Raymond Papers, New York Public Library Manuscript and Archives Division; Howard Jones, *Union in Peril: The Crisis over British Intervention in the Civil War* (Chapel Hill: University of North Carolina Press, 1992), 8, 50.

44. *ORN*, series II, vol. 3, 346–47; See the *Morning Post* (London), February 22 and March 17, 20, 24, 31, 1862.

45. Hotze to Hunter, February 28, 1862, in *ORN*, series II, vol. 3, 352–53; W. Stanley Hoole, ed., "William L. Yancey's European Diary, March–June 1861, *Alabama Review* 25, no. 2 (April 1972): 137; Stanley Lebergott, "Why the South Lost: Commercial Purpose in the Confederacy, 1861–1865," *Journal of American History* 70, no. 1 (June 1983): 61; Russell to Lyons, March 2, 1862, in Wilbur Devereux Jones, "The British Conservatives and the American Civil War," 531; *New Orleans Delta*, July 11, 1861; C. Vann Woodward, ed., *Mary Chesnut's Civil War* (New Haven, Conn.: Yale University Press, 1993), 112.

46. Hotze to Confederate Secretary of State, April 25, 1862, in *ORN*, series II, vol. 3, 400.

47. Owsley, *King Cotton Diplomacy*, 158–59; Oates, "Henry Hotze," 100; Hotze to Benjamin, January 17, 1863, in *ORN*, series II, vol. 3, 661; Hotze to Benjamin, April 25, 1862, in *ORN*, series II, vol. 3, 401.

48. *Index*, May 1, 1862.

49. Owsley, *King Cotton Diplomacy*, 160; Oates, "Henry Hotze," 142; Norman Rich, *Great Power Diplomacy, 1814–1914* (Boston: McGraw-Hill, 1992), 150.

50. Hotze to Benjamin, August 4, 1862; Hotze to Gregory, August 1, 1861, in Gregory Family Papers; Hotze to Benjamin, May 9, 1863, September 26, 1862, October 24, 1862, June 6, 1863, in *ORN*, series II, vol. 3, 505–7, 760, 535–36, 565–67, 784–85; Jones, "British Conservatives," 535; *Times* (London), October 7, 1862; *Saturday Review*, October 11, 1862. For a detailed examination of the effects of both the Emancipation Proclamation and Antietam on the prospects for British recognition, see Howard Jones, "History and Mythology: The Crisis over British Intervention in the Civil War," in May, ed., *The Union, the Confederacy, and the Atlantic Rim*, 29–53, and Kinley J. Brauer, "British Mediation and the American Civil War: A Reconsideration," *Journal of Southern History* 38 (1972): 50–51.

51. Jones, "History and Mythology," 31–33, 49–52; See also Hubbard, *Burden of Confederate Diplomacy*, 120-24; Hotze to Benjamin, November 22, 1862, in *ORN*, series II, vol. 3, 611.

52. Hotze to Benjamin, July 6 and July 23, 1863, Benjamin to Hotze, September 19, 1863, and January 9, 1864, in *ORN*, series II, vol. 3, 840, 849, 903, 995.

53. Hotze to Benjamin, March 12, 1864, in *ORN*, series II, vol. 3, 1066, and Hotze to Benjamin, September 17, 1863, in ibid., 1209–10.

54. Ibid., 1209; Hotze to Benjamin, July 29, 1864, Benjamin to Hotze, September 15, 1864, in *ORN*, series II, vol. 3, 1177, 1205–6; Hotze to S. Ricker, July 8, 1864, in Hotze Papers, Letterbook, Library of Congress Manuscript Division, Washington, D.C. (hereafter cited as Letterbook).

55. "The South and Slavery," *Index*, November 6, 1862; "A Word for the Negro," *Index*, February 12, 1863.

56. For an excellent article on this transformation, see Bonner, "Slavery, Confederate Diplomacy, and the Racialist Mission of Henry Hotze," 288–316. For a discussion of the history of the ASL, see Conrad C. Reining, "A Lost Period of Applied Anthropology," *American Anthropology* 64 (1962): 593–600.

57. Hotze to Benjamin, August 27, 1863, in *ORN*, series II, vol. 3, 878.

58. *Index*, December 3 and November 26, 1863; "The Negro's Place in Nature," *Index*, December 10, 1863.

59. "The Natural History of Man," *Index*, July 23, 1863; "Arming the Negros," *Index*, September 10, 1863; C. J. McRae to Hotze, September 17, 1863, Hotze Papers, Misc. Letters, Library of Congress Manuscript Division.

60. "The Negro in the Southern Armies," *Index*, November 10, 1864; "The Im-

pending Revolution," *Index,* April 27, 1865; "What can be Done for the Negro," *Index,* July 1, 1865; and "The Negro Race in America," *Index,* August 5, 1865.

61. Hotze to Percy Gregg, August 18, 1864, Hotze Papers, Letterbook. He did go on to state that the eye condition was "now happily removed." Hotze to Nichols, May 28, 1864, Hotze to S. Ricker, June 18, 1864, Hotze to Benjamin, September 2, 1864, Hotze to W. A. Eickhoff, Hotze to S. F. Wilson, Hotze to Y. A. Haslebaum, March 8, 1865, and Hotze to L. Q. Washington, March 14, 1865, Hotze Papers, Letterbook.

62. Hotze to Joel Cook, April 21, 1865, and Hotze to E. C. Hancock, June 1, 1865, Hotze Papers, Letterbook. Joel Cook was a Philadelphia journalist who contributed periodic military reviews to the *Index.*

63. Hotze to W. A. Hall, May 14, 1865, and Hotze to E. C. Hancock, June 1, 1865, Hotze Papers, Letterbook.

64. "Our Farewell," *Index,* August 12, 1865.

65. Ibid.

66. *Mobile Register,* May 11, 1887; see also Coker, *Mobile Cadets,* xii.

67. Bonner, "Slavery, Confederate Diplomacy, and the Racialist Mission of Henry Hotze," 316.

68. Hotze to John George Witt, August 11, 1864, Hotze Papers, Letterbook.

69. William Stanley Hoole, ed., *The Diplomacy of the Confederate Cabinet of Richmond and its Agents Abroad. By Paul Pecquet Du Bellet* (Tuscaloosa: Confederate Publishing Co., 1963), 40–42.

70. Hotze to Benjamin, January 17, 1863, in *ORN,* series 3, vol. 2, 661; Hotze to Hunter, February 23, 1863, in *ORN,* series II, vol. 3, 347; and Hoole, ed. *Diplomacy of the Confederate Cabinet,* 43.

71. Hotze to John George Witt, August 11, 1864, Hotze Papers, Letterbook.

72. Burton J. Hendrick, *Statesmen of the Lost Cause: Jefferson Davis and His Cabinet* (New York: Literary Guild of America, 1939), 392; Cullop, *Confederate Propaganda in Europe,* 131; Owsley, *King Cotton Diplomacy,* 155.

73. Hotze to Witt, August 11, 1864, Hotze Papers, Letterbook; Hotze to Edward Lucas, September 3, 1864, Hotze Papers, Letterbook; Douglas Southall Freeman, *The South to Posterity: An Introduction to the Writing of Confederate History* (Wendell, N.C.: Broadfoot Bookmark, 1983), 24.

74. Bonner, "Slavery, Confederate Diplomacy, and the Racialist Mission of Henry Hotze," 314–15.

75. Laura Rice, "African Conscripts/European Conflicts: Race, Memory, and Lessons of War," *Cultural Critique* 45 (spring 2000): 118; Paul L. Fortier, "Gobineau and German Racism," *Comparative Literature* 19, no. 4 (autumn 1967): 344; see chapter 1 of Fritz Bennecke, *Vom deutschen Volk and seimem Lebensraum. Handbuch fur die Schulung in der HJ* (Munich: Franz Eher, 1937).

PART ONE

1. Hotze's journal appeared in nine installments in the *Index* at various intervals from May 1 to October 23, 1862. This selection appeared on May 1, 1862. Note: Although the "Three Months in the Confederate Army" series appeared in print a year after the publication of the CADET letters, I have placed it first in my text because it covers earlier events.

2. The governor of Alabama at this time was Andrew Barry Moore (1801–1873). The other volunteer company was the Mobile Rifles.

3. The Mobile Cadets were organized in 1844. The state of Alabama commissioned its officers in October 1845. The Cadets were exempted from service in the Mexican War because of their young age. See William S. Coker, *The Mobile Cadets, 1845–1945: A Century of Honor and Fidelity* (Bagdad, Fl.: Patagonia Press, 1993); and "Company Histories: The Mobile Cadets," Mobile Cadet File, Mobile Public Library, Mobile, Alabama.

4. Appeared in the *Index* on May 1, 1862.

5. Appeared in the *Index* on May 8, 1862.

6. A broom made of twigs tied together on a long handle.

7. The First and Second Alabama Regiments were organized in March and early April 1861, respectively. They remained as home organizations serving on garrison duty at Pensacola and Fort Morgan.

8. In addition to Withers, the elected officers included Tennent Lomax of Montgomery, lieutenant colonel; and Cullen A. Battle, of Tuskegee, major. See Brandon H. Beck, *Third Alabama! The Civil War Memoir of Brigadier General Cullen Andrews Battle, CSA* (Tuscaloosa: University of Alabama Press, 2000), 7.

9. Note that Hotze, in mentioning the "ultra-democratic vices" of the North, is appealing to the traditional British distrust of popular democracy.

10. This is an expression taken from *Aesop's Fables*. King Log symbolizes an overly passive ruler, while King Stork represents an overly aggressive one.

11. Appeared in the *Index* on May 22, 1862.

12. William Gannaway Brownlow was an east Tennessee minister/editor with pro-unionist views. He was imprisoned in December 1861 and eventually physically expelled from the Confederacy. He continued to write in the North during the war and returned to Tennessee to succeed Andrew Johnson as governor in 1865. He eventually served in the United States Senate. See E. Merton Coulter, *William G. Brownlow, Fighting Parson of the Southern Highlands* (Chapel Hill: University of North Carolina Press, 1937).

13. Translated: "save which can."

14. Appeared in the *Index* on May 29, 1862.

15. While writing this journal, Hotze was simultaneously sending his CADET reports to the *Mobile Register*.

16. The three men who were "ordered to the rear" were R. B. Armistead, H. A. Deas, and F. A. Leslie. See Coker, ed., *Mobile Cadets*, 21.

17. In the fresh air or out of doors.

18. Garrett Jesse Pendergrast (1802–1862) was the flag officer of the Union navy squadron that patrolled the Hampton Roads area.

19. Appeared in the *Index* on June 26, 1862.

20. The *Merrimac* would be refitted with iron plates and renamed the CSS *Virginia*. On March 9, 1862, she did battle with the Union *Monitor* in one of the most famous naval engagements in history.

21. Appeared in the *Index* on September 25, 1862. This is the only installment in which Hotze admittedly reflects on events in light of the past year.

22. The manual referred to here is General William Joseph, Hardee's *Rifle and Light Infantry Tactics* (Philadelphia: Lippincott, 1855). Volume 1 of this work was entitled "Schools of the Soldier and Company; Instructions for Skirmishes." Volume 2 was "Schools for the Battalion."

23. Treacle is a type of cane syrup.

24. Appeared in the *Index* on October 2, 1862. Note: In the original text, this account is dated May 1862. This is an obvious type-set error so I have placed the correct date in this transcription.

25. The "murderer" was identified as "Hunt" in Hotze's CADET letter of June 5, 1861 (published in the *Mobile Register* on June 13, 1861).

26. Henry R. Storrs of Wetumpka.

27. Withers's successor as mayor of Mobile was Hotze's boss at the *Mobile Register*, John Forsyth.

28. The "bride of our second lieutenant" was Laura Sprague Forsyth, wife of Charles Forsyth. The couple had exchanged vows on April 10, 1861. The "daughter of the colonel himself" was Jones M. Withers's oldest daughter Harriet, married to Sergeant Daniel Huger.

29. Appeared in the *Index* on October 16, 1862.

30. One should note that Hotze often pointed out what he claimed to be the inaccuracy of the Union war reports. When this journal was published in Britain, he was trying to convince the British government that the war was going much better for the South than was being reported in the Northern newspapers.

31. This "young lady" is identified in Hotze's CADET letter of June 25, 1861 (published in the *Mobile Register* on July 2, 1861) as Augusta Jane Evans, a well-known "authoress" from Mobile. Miss Evans, who had two brothers serving with the Third Alabama, was one of the most popular writers in the nation. By this time, her second

novel, *Beulah,* was a best seller. Her fourth novel, *St. Elmo,* sold more copies than any other nineteenth-century fiction work except *Uncle Tom's Cabin.* See Rebecca Grant Sexton, *A Southern Woman of Letters: The Correspondence of Augusta Jane Evans Wilson* (Columbia: University of South Carolina Press, 2002), xxi–xxxv.

32. Appeared in the *Index,* October 23, 1862.

33. General John Bankhead Magruder (1807–1871) of Virginia was the commander of the Confederate Department of the Peninsula from May 21, 1861, to April 12, 1862. General Benjamin F. Butler (1818–1893) of New Hampshire was the Union commander of the Department of Virginia, from May 22 to August 17, 1861.

34. For the official accounts of the Battle of Great Bethel, see *ORA*, series I, vol. 2, 77–104.

35. Major Theodore Winthrop (1828–1861), a descendent of John Winthrop, was a lawyer and aspiring novelist. The official report of this battle notes: "His conduct, his courage, his efficiency in the field, were spoken of in terms of praise by all who saw him." See *ORA,* series I, vol. 2, 81.

36. Hotze is referring to himself. See his explanation in his CADET letter of May 29, 1861 (published in the *Mobile Register* on June 7, 1861).

37. The wounded soldier was identified as Private Drisch of the Washington Light Infantry in the CADET letter of June 17, 1861 (published in the *Mobile Register,* June 28, 1861).

38. A fascine is a bundle of sticks bound together used in the construction of earthworks.

39. Hotze himself took advantage of this policy to make a brief visit to Mobile in the early summer.

40. A legal motion to end a prosecution.

41. Hotze would soon be on his way to his diplomatic mission (see Part 2).

42. The CADET letters appeared in the *Mobile Register* periodically from June 7 to August 27, 1861.

43. This is a quote from Oliver Goldsmith (1730[?]–1774). In *The Hermit,* Goldsmith wrote, "Man wants but little from below, nor wants that very long" (chapter viii, stanza 8).

44. From this reference to another letter, we can assume that CADET had already started his correspondence. This issue of the *Register* did not survive.

45. Love of self or conceit.

46. Appeared in the *Mobile Register* on June 7, 1861.

47. Refers to the strategy of Roman general Fabius Maximus, who, by avoiding decisive engagements, defeated Hannibal.

48. Theodore Guesnard was the proprietor of a cigar store at 18 South Royal Street.

49. Appeared in the *Mobile Register* on June 13, 1861.

50. Hotze had recently been appointed to the adjutant general's staff.

51. Appeared in the *Mobile Register* on June 28, 1861.

52. A veteran of the War of 1812 as well as the Mexican War, General Winfield Scott retired from active service on November 1, 1861.

53. A "faggot" is another name for a fascine (see note 38).

54. General Benjamin Huger (1805–1877) commanded the Department of Norfolk from May 26, 1861, to April 12, 1862.

55. Hotze uses several (derisive) names for General Benjamin F. Butler. In addition to the one here noted, he is referred to later as Bethel Failure Butler.

56. In this paragraph, Hotze refers to Augusta Evans (see note 31); Howell Cobb (1815–1868), former Speaker of the U.S. House of Representatives and presiding officer of the provisional Confederate congress, and Johnson J. Hooper (1815–1863), an author and editor in addition to his duties with the Confederate government.

57. Appeared in the *Mobile Register* on July 2, 1861.

58. Miss Evans described this incident to a friend in a personal letter. See Augusta Evans to Rachel Lyons, June 26, 1861, in Sexton, *Southern Woman of Letters,* 33.

59. Bagur and Co. Cigars was a popular Mobile establishment on the corner of Royal and Dauphin Streets.

60. Appeared in the *Mobile Register* on July 7, 1861.

61. Hotze preferred the term "revolution" to "rebellion." *See* "Are the Confederates Rebels?" in the *Index,* June 26, 1862.

62. Appeared in the *Mobile Register* on July 21, 1861.

63. Cullen A. Battle (1829–1905) eventually became the commanding officer of the Third Alabama.

64. Josiah C. Nott (1804–1873) was a Mobile physician and good friend of Hotze. It was Nott who enlisted Hotze to Translate Gobineau's *Inequality of the Human Races.* Nott's son, James Deas, was a member of the Mobile Cadets.

65. Appeared in the *Mobile Register* on August 27, 1861.

66. Appeared in the *Mobile Register* on September 3, 1861.

67. Heightened alert.

68. John Ellis Wool (1784–1869) commanded the Department of Virginia from August 17, 1861, to June 2, 1862.

PART TWO

1. The *Mobile Tribune* was a Southern Rights newspaper edited by H. Ballentyne. The editors were often at odds with the *Register* for its pro-Douglas position.

2. For a description of the rise of "Know-Nothingism" in Mobile, see Burnett, *The Pen Makes a Good Sword*, 65–69.

3. Albert Gallatin (1761–1849) was born in Geneva. He became U.S. secretary of treasury under Presidents Jefferson and Madison. Louis Agassiz (1807–1873) was born in Fribourg. He was a noted Harvard professor who produced writings on topics ranging from the Ice Age to race.

4. Robert Mercer Taliaferro Hunter (1809–1887), former Speaker of the U.S. House of Representatives, U.S. senator from 1847 to 1861, was Confederate secretary of state from July 1861 to February 1862.

5. James Mason (1798–1871), a grandson of notable Virginian patriot George Mason, had been the chairman of the Senate Committee on Foreign Affairs for ten years. He was appointed the Confederate commissioner to Great Britain.

6. John Slidell (1793–1871), a Louisianan, had served in both houses of the national legislature before being appointed as the Confederate commissioner to France.

7. Lord Palmerston (Henry John Temple, Viscount, 1784–1865) of the Liberal Party, was a three-time British prime minister, including the period covering the entire American Civil War.

8. Hotze had probably gotten his fill of "newspaper controversies" while on the staff of John Forsyth at the *Mobile Register*. Hotze worked at the *Register* from 1859 to 1861, during Forsyth's controversial campaign on behalf of Stephen A. Douglas.

9. In February 1861 representatives from South Carolina, Mississippi, Alabama, Florida, Georgia, Louisiana, and Texas met in Montgomery, Alabama, to form the Confederate States of America. The provisional government called for elections in November 1861, with the winners to take office on February 22, 1862. This leader appeared on that date.

10. Hotze is here referring to the sixteenth-century struggle between Spain and her Dutch provinces.

11. Hotze is appealing to the British distaste for popular democracy. According to Henry Pelling, as the war dragged on, "The Civil War problems of blockade rights, or British maritime interests, of free trade, and of the supplies of cotton for the Lancashire mills, had largely lost their relevance, or had become subordinate to the main debate on the merits and defects of a democratic system." See Henry Pelling, *America and the British Left: From Bright to Bevan* (New York: New York University Press, 1957), 10.

12. On March 10, 1862, British foreign minister Lord John Russell delivered a speech in the House of Lords in which he suggested that the American war would soon be settled peacefully with the formation of separate nations.

13. Union forces occupied Nashville, Tennessee, on February 23, 1862. A few weeks after this letter, Baton Rouge, Louisiana, would become the second southern capital to fall.

14. Refusing to recognize the legitimacy of the Confederacy, President Lincoln treated captured privateers as pirates. Some crew members from the *Jefferson Davis* were tried and sentenced to death. Before the sentences could be imposed, Lincoln bowed to international pressure and Southern threats of retaliation and, on February 3, 1862, announced that privateers would be treated as prisoners of war.

15. Article 1 of the Treaty of Paris (1783) states: "His Brittanic Majesty acknowledges the said United States, viz., New Hampshire, Massachusetts Bay, Rhode Island and Providence Plantations, Connecticut, New York, New Jersey, Pennsylvania, Maryland, Virginia, North Carolina, South Carolina and Georgia, to be free sovereign and independent states, that he treats with them as such, and for himself, his heirs, and successors, relinquishes all claims to the government, propriety, and territorial rights of the same and every part thereof."

16. The Morrill Tariff raised rates from a pre-war level of 18 percent to nearly 48 percent in 1861.

17. On May 13, 1861, the Government of Great Britain issued a formal proclamation recognizing the belligerent status of the Confederate States of America.

18. "*Possee comitatus*" (Latin) means "force of the country." This refers to the common law practice of a local official such as a sheriff forcing people to assist law enforcement in extreme circumstances.

19. This explanatory leader appeared in the first issue of the *Index*.

20. Hotze's strong stand for journalistic freedom must come under question when one considers that he suggested to the Confederate authorities that tighter controls should be placed over Southern editors who reported discouraging news. See Hotze to Confederate Secretary of State, March 24, 1862, in *ORN,* series II, vol. 3, 371.

21. Hotze is again referring here to the sixteenth-century Dutch Revolt against Spain. See note 10.

22. In this paragraph, Hotze mentions several notable Union personalities. Colonel William Wilson led the Sixth New York Infantry Regiment. A story in *Harper's Weekly* referred to his men as a "corps of roughs." Franz Sigel (1824–1902) was born in Baden, Germany. He took part in the German Revolution of 1848 and was forced to flee to Switzerland. He later became a general in the Union army. Carl Schurz (1829–1906) was born in Cologne. He came to America and became a leader in the Republican Party. During the war, he rose to the rank of major general. He was elected to the U.S. Senate and, in 1877, was appointed by President Hayes as secretary of the interior. Silas Casey (1807–1882) was a career army officer who also rose to the rank of major general. He is best known as the author of the three-volume *System of Infantry Tactics*—a manual used by both sides.

23. Bright was an English radical and a staunch supporter of the Federal Union.

24. Fort Donelson surrendered to Union Forces on February 16, 1862. Coupled

with the fall of Fort Henry, this loss gave the Union effective control of major portions of the Tennessee River.

25. Three important characters are mentioned in this paragraph. William H. Gregory was one of the most enthusiastic supporters of the Confederacy in the House of Commons. Lord George H. Campbell was the leading Southern advocate in the House of Lords. Lord John Russell was the British foreign minister. He would become prime minister upon the death of Palmerston in 1865.

26. Lord Edward Smith Stanley, Earl of Derby, led the Conservative Party for twenty-two years. He would become prime minister (for the third time) in 1866.

27. To terminate a session of Parliament.

28. The *Index* made its first appearance on May 1, 1862.

29. James Spence was the author of *The American Union,* a work that was highly supportive of Southern recognition.

30. In late August 1862, Confederate forces under Lee and Jackson had won a major victory at the Second Battle of Bull Run. Hotze had not yet received word about Antietam.

31. Hotze refers here to a letter President Lincoln sent to Horace Greeley on August 22, 1862 in which he stated, "If I could save the Union without freeing any slave I would do it."

32. This retreat occurred after the ill-fated invasion of Maryland, culminating in the Confederate loss at Antietam in September 1862.

33. In January 1863 a revolt had broken out in Poland by citizens trying to overthrow Russian rule. The revolt threatened to turn into a general European war.

34. For the complete text of this "address," see the *Index,* June 18, 1863.

35. Literally meaning "after me, the flood," this phrase was uttered by Madam de Pompadour during the days of French King Louis XV. It became a prophecy of the French Revolution.

36. Hotze refers here to the Erlanger loan of 1863.

37. In making the case that slaveholders or those impacted by slavery made up a substantial proportion of Southern society, Hotze anticipated the thesis of Otto Olsen's classic essay "Historians and the Extent of Slave Ownership in the Southern United States," *Civil War History* 18 (1972): 112–13.

38. Taken from a letter from Hotze to John George Witt, August 11, 1864, Hotze Papers, Letterbook, Library of Congress. I have omitted the first few paragraphs dealing with personal matters. This letter was published in its entirety by Richard Barksdale Harwell under the title "The Creed of a Propagandist: Letter from a Confederate Editor," in *Journalism Quarterly* (spring 1951).

39. Literally art to conceal art.

40. I have omitted the opening paragraph dealing with business details.

PART THREE

1. Hotze cited *Researches into the Physical History of Mankind,* by James C. Prichard (1786–1848). Prichard was a proponent of the theory of the unity of species.

2. Adam Smith (1723–1790). His *Inquiry into the Nature and Causes of the Wealth of Nations* was published in 1776.

3. In his *Essay Concerning Human Understanding* (1690), John Locke (1632–1704) wrote about the influence of education and environment on a person.

4. Gobineau, in his first seven chapters of the *Essai,* refuted claims that religion, government, geography have any lasting effect on moral or intellectual development.

5. Matthew 11:25.

6. See Genesis 11:1–9.

7. The Parable of the Talents is found in Matthew 25:14–29.

8. In addition to the aforementioned "Copious Notes," Hotze wrote lengthy footnotes and chapter explanations in his translation of Gobineau's work. This selection is one such example.

9. Gobineau classified the races into "white" (Caucasian, Shemitic, Japhetic), "black" (Hamitic, African, etc.), and "yellow" (Altaic, Mongolian, Finnic, and Tartar).

10. Hotze is quoting from the work of William Frederick van Amringe (b. 1791), a New York lawyer and amateur racial theorist. For a full account of van Amringe's philosophy, including the words Hotze is using here, see "The Natural History of Man," *United States Democratic Review* 26, no. 142 (April 1850): 327–45.

11. Translated: "The friends of our friends are our friends." These two "friends" were Josiah C. Nott and George R. Gliddon. Nott and Gliddon had collaborated on *Types of Mankind,* a leading American text on human racial differences.

12. Gobineau was actually born in France in 1816.

13. A reference to the practice of attempting to contact the souls of the deceased.

14. Chapter XV of the *Essai* was entitled "The Different Languages are Unequal, and Correspond Perfectly in Relative Merit to the Races that Use Them."

15. Francois Guizot (1787–1874) was a French historian; Wilhelm von Humboldt (1767–1835) was a German philosopher. His primary area of investigation was languages; Edward Gibbon (1737–1794), a historian, wrote *The History of the Decline and Fall of the Roman Empire* (1776, 1781). Gibbon documented the various external causes of the fall. This was diametrically opposed to Gobineau's belief that "degeneracy" was in no way related to external factors. George Bancroft (1800–1891) was an American historian and statesman who was known for his pro-education and anti-slavery views.

16. Translated "The utility is to show that it is useless."

17. The "Unitarian" believed in the unity of a single creation while the "Polygenist" believed in multiple creations.

18. David Hume (1711–1776) was a Scottish philosopher and historian.

19. The Brothers August Wilhelm von Schlegel (1767–1845) and Karl Wilhelm Friedrich von Schlegel (1772–1829) were leaders of the German movement of literary romanticism; Elihu Burritt (1810–1879) was an American philanthropist and social activist who promoted universal brotherhood; Ralph Waldo Emerson (1803–1882), in addition to being a transcendentalist writer, was a devout abolitionist. A phalanstery was a utopian communal society modeled after the teachings of Charles Fourier.

20. Hotze's "Analytical Introduction and Copious Historical Notes" was over one hundred pages in length.

21. Hotze is referring to a letter Abraham Lincoln sent to Horace Greeley on August 22, 1862.

22. Alexander Pope (1688–1744), in *An Essay on Criticism* (1709), wrote this line: "A little learning is a dangerous thing."

23. This is apparently a reference to the work of Gliddon and Nott, both of whom championed the notion of separate creations as the explanation for racial inequalities.

24. Louis Agassiz (1807–1873) was a Harvard zoologist and geologist. He was one of America's first world renowned scientists.

25. Note that, nearly a decade later, Hotze returns to the major theme of his introduction to the *Essai*.

26. Hotze is somewhat premature in this pronouncement. In January 1864, Confederate general Patrick R. Cleburne presented a memorandum to his superiors in which he advocated enlisting slaves to the Confederate cause. His proposal was soundly rejected by his superiors. Hotze himself was chastised for offering this view. For complete treatments of this debate, see Bruce Levine, *Confederate Emancipation: Southern Plans to Free and Arm Slaves during the Civil War* (New York: Oxford University Press, 2006), and Robert Franklin Durden, *The Gray and the Black: The Confederate Debate on Emancipation* (Baton Rouge: Louisiana State University Press, 1972).

27. John Forsyth would later express the same sentiment when he wrote, "If we are conquered, slavery is ended, and to secure our freedom and independence, we ought and must, whenever it becomes necessary, to lay the institution itself on the alter of sacrifice." *Mobile Register*, December 31, 1861.

28. Nana Sahib (born Dhondu Pant) was a leader in the Sepoy Rebellion of 1857.

A sepoy was an Indian native employed as a soldier by the British during colonial rule.

29. Dr. James Hunt was a leading nineteenth-century anthropologist. He was one of the founders of the Anthropological Society of London (founded in 1863). The paper to which Hotze refers here was delivered before the society on November 17, 1863. For a complete transcript of the address, see *Index,* November 26 and December 3, 1863.

30. See James M. McPherson, *Battle Cry of Freedom* (New York: Oxford University Press, 1988), 508–9.

31. After the news of Lee's surrender reached him, Hotze began to focus his attention on the postwar situation of the South.

32. This was certainly Hotze's biggest miscalculation as the freedmen voted overwhelmingly for the Republicans. See Eric Foner, *Reconstruction: America's Unfinished Revolution, 1863–1877* (New York: Harper and Row, 1988), 62, 267, and 311–13.

33. Translated "Willing or unwilling."

34. Here Hotze was speaking prophetically of the future labor system under which many freedmen found themselves during Reconstruction. For a good discussion of Reconstruction labor issues, see chapter 4 of Foner's *Reconstruction,* 124–75.

35. This was Hotze's final public pronouncement on the racial situation as the *Index* suspended publication the following week.

36. Salmon P. Chase (1808–1873) served as chief justice from 1864 until his death. He went on a tour of several Southern states in May 1865 to promote black suffrage.

APPENDIX

1. Source: Alabama Department of Archives and History. Confederate Muster Rolls Collection. Third Alabama Infantry Regiment, SG25009, Box 2, Folder 1. Note: I have followed the same numbering as the original. Some entries are not in alphabetical order.

Index